Dealing with Confidence

Staffan Furusten and Andreas Werr (eds.)

Dealing with Confidence

The Construction of Need and Trust in Management
Advisory Services

Copenhagen Business School Press

Dealing with Confidence

The Construction of Need and Trust in Management Advisory Services

© Copenhagen Business School Press
Printed in Denmark by Holbæk Amts Bogtrykkeri
Cover design by Morten Højmark
1. edition 2005

ISBN 87-630-0146-2

Distribution:

Scandinavia
DJØF/DBK, Mimersvej 4
DK-4600 Køge, Denmark
Phone: +45 3269 7788, fax: +45 3269 7789

North America
Copenhagen Business School Press
Books International Inc.
P.O. Box 605
Herndon, VA 20172-0605, USA
Phone: +1 703 661 1500, fax: +1 703 661 1501

Rest of the World
Marston Book Services, P.O. Box 269
Abingdon, Oxfordshire, OX14 4YN, UK
Phone: +44 (0) 1235 465500, fax: +44 (0) 1235 4656555
E-mail Direct Customers: direct.order@marston.co.uk
E-mail Booksellers: trade.order@marston.co.uk

Table of Contents

Table of Contents

Preface

This book is the result of a casual encounter between the two of us in early 2002. Both of us had done research on management consulting for some time, although from rather different perspectives, and realized at that time that our interests had driven us towards the same empirical phenomenon – how to purchase management consulting and other Management Advice Services. In late 2002, we gathered a group of colleagues from various disciplines including management, marketing, accounting, sociology, and social anthropology, from the Stockholm School of Economics, Score, Uppsala University, the School of Economics and Commercial Law at Göteborg University and the National Institute of Working Life. In one way or another, all of those invited had dealt with the dilemmas organizations face when forced to bring in experts on management matters from external providers. For some, this focus on purchasing expertise was an opportunity to re-interpret data they already had, for others it meant entering new ground. The initial purpose was to find out whether there was anything worth investigating further about this phenomenon, which we collectively discovered that there was. As discussions progressed, ambitions gradually rose from "compiling a number of empirical illustrations" to "writing an integrated book on the issue." We soon found ourselves on a joint journey manifested in a number of workshops at Score (Stockholm Center for Organizational Research) and the Stockholm School of Economics, where all participated actively in lively discussions and contributed with comments on each other's chapters. For us as editors, we have seen as our most important task that of holding the process and book together, and we have struggled to create a platform upon which the chapters could rest. It is thus our hope that the book will be read not only as a collection of chapters by different authors, but as an integrated contribution to our understanding of the phenomenon that had caught our interest – the purchasing of management advice services.

When working with this book, we had a number of different readers in mind. We hope that the subject matter presented here will be of interest to both providers of management advice services and the buyers of these services as well as those – students and researchers – who seek a better understanding about what is going on between these actors. With its cross-disciplinary authorship, the book can be relevant to a number of different disciplines in the social sciences, such as general management, service management, organization, marketing, purchasing of expert services, consultation, professionalization, expertise and working life issues.

The success of our ambition to hold the book together and make it interesting for different categories of readers, however, we leave to be judged by the reader.

Acknowledgements
This book would never have been completed without a grant from VINNOVA (Swedish Agency for Innovation Systems) and a guarantee from Score for language and layout editing (many thanks to Kelly Vegh Olsson and Peter Hyllman for helping us with this). Without research grants from VINNOVA, FAS (the Swedish Council for Working Life and Social Research), and The Bank of Sweden Tercentenary Foundation, which have provided the funding for the research behind most of our contributions in the book, the processes resulting – and hopefully not ending – in this book would never have started.

Stockholm, May 2005

Staffan Furusten and Andreas Werr

CHAPTER 1

Bringing in Managerial Expertise from External Markets

STAFFAN FURUSTEN AND ANDREAS WERR

A growing advice business and increasing uncertainty in organizations

This book deals with one of the most ubiquitous phenomena of management practice in the past two decades namely, organizations' increasing use of external providers of various forms of managerial expertise. Instead of having people employed with certain expertise or specialized competence, it has become increasingly common for organizations to temporarily contract experts from external markets whenever their expertise is needed. In the past few decades in particular, the management advice industry has exploded and today occupies a large and increasing number of people. Although organizations have long relied on advice from lawyers and auditors, during the past two decades we have witnessed an exceptional growth of services such as investment banking, IT consulting, temporary staffing and management consulting. New organizations have emerged to deliver these services, and older types of organizations, such as auditing firms, have added new advisory services to their traditional service portfolio.

It is often argued that this development is driven by organizations' strive for efficiency, flexibility and access to the latest expertise. Temporarily contracting external experts rather than hiring permanent staff means that organizations pay for a particular competence only when they need it and are thus able to operate more efficiently. Furthermore, it is argued that the hiring of temporary experts makes organizations more flexible to adapt to changing conditions in their environment since they have less people employed in the organization that they have to either let go or retrain. Finally, it is argued, that only dedicated expert organizations have the resources needed to stay ahead in increasingly specialized, globalized and fast developing fields of knowledge (Badaracco, 1991).

There are thus many good arguments for why organizations should buy expert services from external markets when they need them rather than maintaining a permanent staff of experts. However, this does not mean that relying on external expertise in filling the (sometimes daily) need for specialized competence and knowledge in organizations is unproblematic. For instance, by relying on external expertise, organizations leave the control of the content and quality of the expert services to mechanisms of external markets. This leads to situations where people in organizations are forced to purchase expert services, a task that entails a number of uncertainties. To begin with, they need to correctly identify their need for experts, and decide whether to employ permanent experts or hire them temporarily from the market. They also need to make choices between different suppliers, in an attempt to find the one best suited for supporting their organization and they need to establish the value of the service as well as a reasonable price for it, and to be prepared to justify these choices to both superiors and colleagues.

Together, the characteristics of management advisory services (MAS) and their knowledge base create a situation in which both the "make or buy" decision and the choice of individual supplier, once a buy decision has been made, are highly complex. The lack of professional systems to define the knowledge base of most MAS, as well as their interactive character, make their value uncertain and debatable and, at the same time, make it hard to evaluate alternative suppliers.

These characteristics of MAS leave buyers of these services feeling extremely uncertain. This uncertainty revolves around two basic issues that need to be dealt with when bringing in external expertise into organizations, and which provide the basic issues dealt with in this book:

1. *A legitimate need for external experts has to be established, thus motivating the question: How is the need for particular management advisory services in organizations constructed?*
2. *A "good" provider of the service has to be identified, motivating the question: How is trust for suppliers of management advisory services constructed?*

In formulating these two questions, the term "construction" figures prominently. By focusing on construction, attention is directed towards the debatable nature of both the need for MAS and the quality of the suppliers of these services. Given the problems of defining and evaluating the service and its contribution, buyers must engage in a process of *constructing* the service and its supplier in the local situation. The service has to be made a necessity accepted by the buyer and his or her environment. Similarly, the individual supplier needs to be established as a professional one, well-suited to delivering the needed service. Our interest lies in the interacting forces that influence evolving situations in which organizations decide that they should buy a service instead of producing it themselves, and in the covarying mechanisms that lead to a supplier being perceived as "good" enough for a buyer to choose that particular service provider from among all the possible suppliers on the market. In sum, our interest is in the forces that create confident buyers – both in terms of feeling a legitimate need for the service and in terms of feeling confident in the chosen supplier. We believe that such confidence cannot be defined in objective terms, but rather represents a state that is socially constructed both in a primary order, in relations between particular individuals, and in a secondary order, in the institutionalized norms of wider collectives (cf. Berger and Luckmann, 1966).

While professionals and professional services on the one hand (e.g. Løwendahl et al. 2001; Newell et al. 2002; Reed, 1996) and the purchasing of services on the other (e.g. Axelsson and Wynstra, 2002) have gained increasing interest in the literature in recent years, the question of how organizations deal with the kinds of semi-professional services (lacking a formal professional knowledge base) represented by MAS remains largely unstudied. The (limited) existing literature provides a very inconclusive picture. Empirical studies of purchasing practices indicate a very local and trust-based handling of professional services (e.g. Dawes et al. 1992; Glückler and Armbrüster, 2003) while the normatively oriented literature is picturing a rationalistic, transaction-based management of these services (e.g. Kubr, 1993; McGonagle and Vella, 2001).

The different chapters of this volume aim to fill this void of empirical studies on how organizations deal with what here are called "new-professional" experts.[1] The studies illustrate how needs and expertise are constructed in areas such as general management, IT/media, business law, investment banking, and auditing. It will be

---

[1] The meaning of this concept will be developed in more detail later in this chapter and in Chapter 2.

argued that earlier studies of expertise, consulting, service management, service marketing and professional purchasing do not give us satisfying explanations of the mechanisms involved in dealing with the uncertainties in defining a need for a particular service and trust for a particular supplier of MAS. By drawing upon theories of both collectivism (professionalization) and individualism (interaction), the aim of this book is therefore to increase our understanding of, and develop theory for, the mechanisms by which confident deals between buyers and suppliers of MAS come about.

In the remainder of this chapter, we will first elaborate on the trends creating an increasing need for organizations to purchase external experts in a number of competence areas. This is followed by a discussion of the research questions addressed in the book, why they are important, and why there is a need for empirical studies to answer them. Finally, we discuss how the different chapters in the book contribute to answering the two research questions (relating to the construction of needs for MAS and the establishment of trust for particular MAS suppliers).

From organizations to markets and back again

One way to understand the recent growth and influence of the management advice industry is to see it as the result of a relocation of organizational boundaries driven by trends of specialization and globalization (Ackroyd and Lawrenson, 1996; Badaracco, 1991). One of the most frequently used concepts to represent this phenomenon in recent years has been that of "outsourcing", though concepts such as "alliance" and "partnership" are also used in reflecting this development. The popularity of these concepts is an indicator of traditional advisors having increasingly moved towards running their businesses with new forms of relations instead of the more traditional, distanced advisory role. The American management consultancy Accenture, for example, is moving more and more towards "transformative outsourcing", a service in which they take over entire functions from their clients, increase their efficiency and then sell back the service or entire operation. Many consultancies are also involved in initiatives to create formal partnerships and alliances with their clients, implying long-term relations and different forms of risk- and revenue sharing. One such example is Value-Based Pricing, in which buyers and suppliers are supposed to share the risks as well as the benefits of the advisor's work (see Chapter 12 for a more thorough discussion).

This relocation of organizational boundaries and the associated growth of markets for managerial expertise create a situation in which management is increasingly dependent on services provided by more or less well-defined external experts. Managers, who earlier relied to a large extent on internal resources for analysis and improvement work, are increasingly becoming buyers of these resources from external markets. In these markets, various forms of management expertise is increasingly commodified and standardized to make it fit many organizations and make it easier to sell. Many organizations today therefore see a steady flow of ever-changing advisors passing through, with whom employees must collaborate in developing strategies for the future, developing administrative, technical, legal and operating processes, or just running the day-to-day business.

This shift of expertise from local hierarchies to markets unearths a number of potential conflicts of interest between buyers and suppliers of MAS, creating considerable uncertainties for managers and their organizations. The buyer wants to rely on his/her local, existing knowledge, while the expert wants to establish his/her expertise as esoteric and essential; the buyer wants to pay as little as possible, while the expert wants to charge as much as possible; the buyer wants to assimilate as much competence as possible to become independent from the expert, while the expert wants to keep as much competence as possible, without dissatisfying the client, in order to make him/herself indispensable.

At the heart of the uncertainties facing the buyer of MAS are the difficulties of assessing and evaluating management advisory services. Unlike "traditional" resources, MAS are immaterial, i.e. intangible and invisible. This makes it difficult to tell what the service needed really is, what the characteristics of a "good" service are, or whether the "right" service has been delivered. Consequently, it has been argued that MAS are likely to be created in interaction between buyers and sellers during the delivery process (Clark, 1995). This also makes the service heterogeneous (ibid.), implying that the exact same service may not be delivered twice. Immateriality in combination with heterogeneity makes it hard for the buyer to evaluate different service offerings before their delivery.

The above argumentation suggests that the relation between a buyer and a seller of management advisory services is a reciprocal one. Ideas flow back and forth between advisor and buyer, and any potential value is created in the interaction between the two. Consequently, it is not only difficult to evaluate and compare different offers from different suppliers beforehand, it is also complicated to evaluate them afterwards. What was really delivered? What was the consultant's part in the delivery? What effect did it have on the organization? Cause and effect are relations that are problematic when it comes to MAS.

Consequently, on several dimensions, the conditions for dealing with MAS on external markets fall short of what we traditionally expect from markets in terms of standardized, comparable products, rational buyers, etc. (see e.g. Williamson, 1975). The increasing tendency for organizations to relocate expertise from hierarchies to markets does not seem to have resulted in clear-cut market situations where the roles of supplier and buyer are well-defined. Still, an abundance of deals are made. This means that, somehow, organizations experience some kind of need for MAS, and then somehow put their trust in certain MAS suppliers to deliver them. To better understand how this takes place is what this book is all about.

The construction of needs for management advisory services

It is often claimed, that we live in a "modern" era, which may be characterized by the prevalence of three rationalized global myths, i.e. sets of ideas that are to a large extent taken for granted – the rationality myth, the globalization myth and the universality myth (Meyer, 1994). The *rationality myth* represents the ongoing rationalization of society at large, which includes creating and seeing organizations in terms of means-ends relationships and standardized systems of control over activities and actors (Scott and Meyer, 1994). It also entails the increasingly dominating norm of scientific rationality as a universal guiding principle for all action, commonly manifested in specialization and the forming of formal expertise (Meyer and Jepperson, 2000). The *globalization myth* incorporates the assumption that organizations in different settings are more similar than they may have been in the past (Strang and Meyer, 1994). However, globalization is not seen primarily as a new form of substantive locality in which actors must function, but rather as a development that increases competitive pressures for efficiency and rationality. Globalization as a myth brings new uncertainty (of a highly rationalized sort) that responsible organizations must confront (Meyer and Jepperson, 2000). Finally, the *universality myth* involves more generalized claims of authority, reflecting the assumption that rationalized models of management and other areas of expertise can be decontextualized and successfully implemented in organizations regardless of their national- and culture specifics (Meyer, 1994). Based on these three myths representing central aspects of "being modern", in the following, we argue that the observed trend towards an increasing reliance on external MAS represents a rather natural development.

Being modern – Buying experts

Modern organizations are expected to base their operations on the latest "expert" knowledge in different areas, including management. Given the increasingly global development of knowledge in all areas, keeping abreast of this development becomes an extensive task, best carried out by specialized "expert" organizations. Instead of housing all forms of expertise in the internal hierarchy, it may be argued that it is much more rational to purchase this expertise from specialized markets when it is needed, for the period of time it is needed. This enables the buying organization to concentrate on its "core competencies" and their development, while leaving more peripheral tasks to other organizations, that have them as their "core competency" and thus demonstrate "world-class" expertise in carrying them out. The specialization of organizations in systems of delivery is thus an important credo of modernity making increasing reliance on external experts a natural consequence.

This trend of specialization and expertization may be observed in many areas of expertise today (Burrell, 1996; Scarbrough, 1996), and we see it both in unsophisticated services such as cleaning, and more sophisticated and complex services such as business law, IT consulting and management consulting. To some extent, this evolution can be described as a consequence of the rationality myth driving the expertization of society where more and more tasks are expertized, professionalized, commodified, and commercialized.

In the wake of this development, we see the rise of markets for expertise as a means of coordinating the specialized resources housed by specialized firms. Giddens (1990) describes this development as a consequence of modernity. Instead of having everyone learn how to build airplanes, how to fly, and how to pump up oil from deserts or oceans and transform it into fuel, and instead of having everyone negotiate what altitude, what speed, etc, to fly at to fly safely, systems of expertise that divide these tasks into areas of expertise and guarantee their professional performance have evolved. For practical reasons, we leave certain tasks that we cannot do ourselves in the hands of others to do for us. We trust them and the systems they represent to take responsibility for their special tasks. We trust the travel agency to put us on safe airlines that do not cost us a fortune. The travel agencies in turn trust the airlines to provide safe planes and well-educated pilots, and the airlines trust airports and national- and international air traffic authorities to organize safe flights and landings, etc.

Development of this kind of rational order of society requires the assumption that different processes have clear borders, and thereby clear interfaces to other processes. From a modernist perspective, the mission is to make it obvious where a process starts, where it ends, and where it interfaces with other processes. This is the logic behind both technical and organizational standardization. The International Standardization Organization (ISO) has developed many such standards over the years. ISO standards are to be found for numerous ordinary technical things such as how nuts and bolts fit together, electrical safety, and the trailer hitch on the back of your car. In the past two decades, however, we have witnessed even greater expansion of the areas in which ISO standards are launched, including organizational structures and processes. The most well-known of these new standards is probably the quality standard in organization, ISO 9000. This standard represents the idea that all organizations should be understood as networks of processes, with an owner to each process (Furusten, 2000). This is supposed to make it easier to define clear interfaces between different processes and organizations. The ultimate goal is to create systems of organizations in which all actors have clear roles, all processes have clear objectives, and all managers and employees have clear strategies on how to reach these objectives. This can be described as an organizational "Legoland" where all organizations and processes within them have standardized interfaces so that other processes can easily hook on where one process ends. This creates the potential of numerous combinations of processes to be realized.

The idea of specialization and the consequential standardization of organizational processes rest on a modernistic belief that knowledge can be objectively proven and transformed into generally applicable and practically relevant models. In terms of the MAS in focus in this book, this means that it should be clear what knowledge and competence it takes to perform certain managerial tasks and act in certain management roles. From a modernistic viewpoint, it is obvious what competence managers at certain levels need in certain situations, what knowledge can be brought in from external experts, and what characterizes a "good" provider of this knowledge. In other words, the belief in a modern knowledge society implies a view of knowledge and expertise as highly generalized and universal and, thus, a strong belief in science as the outpost of this kind of knowledge (Strang and Meyer, 1994). From a modernist perspective, the buying of expertise is a natural and unproblematic aspect of organizational life.

Going collective – Getting pure professionals

The notion of the modern organization buying specialized competence from external experts goes hand in hand with a belief in the universal knowledge of organizations, and how organizations function, work and should be managed. In a modern world, what expert knowledge is and who owns it (experts) is viewed as obvious. This implies restricted access to expert knowledge to actors other than legitimate experts. These restrictions may be either competence-based (experts with extensive and specialized education/training) or based on specialization (managers lacking the time to stay updated on the most recent developments in management knowledge).

In this context, managers' need for expertise is easily identified and, once identified, filled by legitimate experts. If there are authorized experts in the area, these are the ones that are assumed to have the best capacity to deliver the best knowledge there is. Law and auditing can be seen as established professional systems with clear rules for licensing and authorization. In cases where expertise in these areas is demanded, it is therefore not too complex to judge whether someone can be expected to be a trustworthy and competent expert. Either you have an authorization as an auditor from the professional auditors association, giving you the "license" to act as auditor, or you do not. If you do not have it, you are not allowed to practice auditing. It is as simple as that. In a developed professional system, like auditing or law, all experts are supposed to be true representatives of the system. The system of professionals thus guarantees the buyer that services delivered by anyone belonging to the core will live up to its standards and be based on the expertise developed by the core as a collective (Larson, 1977; Abbott, 1988; Burrage and Torstendahl, 1990). The profession thus ensures that the buyer can expect to get the same expertise delivered from anyone authorized by the core.

Under such conditions of specialization and clearly defined experts, the market seems a suitable way to organize organizations' access to expertise in most situations. What should determine the "make or buy" choice is ultimately a question of transaction costs. Entities with the lowest transaction costs should concentrate on tasks where they have comparative advantage (Coase, 1937; Williamsson, 1975). If it is cheaper to buy it than to produce it with internal resources, it should be bought rather than produced internally. The hierarchy as a method of coordinating work should only be chosen if entities within a particular organization can perform these processes cheaper than external entities.

The emergence of new professionalism

In many cases, however, the above situation with clear-cut expertise and experts is an ideal that is far from fulfilled. Along with the belief in the modern society Giddens (1990) claims that abstract expert systems are currently emerging outside the traditional professions (cf. Ackroyd and Lawrenson, 1996). Lately, we have seen a rise of expert systems in areas of a much less technical character than the traditional professions like medicine or law, such as management, organization and administration (Burrell, 1996; Scarbrough, 1996). In such areas of competence, the situation for the buyer of expertise becomes more ambiguous. The expert systems in these areas are more blurred, and there is no professional body accredited by the professionals or the state (as is the case in the traditional professions) to regulate the profession. In such fields of competence, several forms of certification and legitimization often exist. However, in the case of management consulting, no certification or legitimization form is widely accepted by all who claim to be management consultants.

A central characteristic of these "new" professions is the uncertainty concerning their knowledge base. Unlike traditional professions, the knowledge base of the new professions is less clear and therefore debatable. Consequently, a main concern of the literature on management consulting and other MAS has been the nature and content of knowledge that underlies "good" consulting, and the consequential value delivered by management advisors based on this knowledge. In this respect, the literature may be divided into two main groups, which take quite different perspectives on MAS (see Fincham and Clark, 2002; Kipping and Armbrüster, 1998 for more detailed categorization of the literature). The first group takes a *functionalist perspective* and is concerned mainly with improving or securing the effectiveness of management consulting (see e.g. Block, 2000; Greiner and Metzger, 1983; Kubr, 1996; Schein, 1988). In this literature, the consultants' expertise is taken for granted. Consultants are assumed to possess superior expertise and the literature to a large extent addresses how to apply this expertise in order to create value for the client.

The second group – the *critical consulting* literature – takes a more pessimistic view of consultants' knowledge. Based on a lack of universal standards of knowledge and expertise in areas such as management consulting, there is instead a focus on the ways in which consultants create the impression of having superior knowledge and delivering value. From a critical perspective, the question of whether consultants' have any functional expertise at all is raised, and whether their work in organizations is of any value in improving organizational performance. Instead, alternative "values" of consulting are highlighted, such as the reduction of managerial anguish (Huczynski, 1993) or the enforcement of managerial identity (Clark and Salaman, 1996b; Kieser, 1998).

Consequently, it is (still?) very rare for advisory services to management to be standardized to such a degree that the choice to make or buy can be reduced to a comparison of costs. For instance, it is quite problematic to evaluate the quality and value of delivered management advice. The relation between a delivered service and results is highly ambiguous and may be characterized by long time lags. Has the organization become more effective than before? Is money being saved, is the organization more successful and does it have stronger market positions? And is this the result of the consulting advice (cf. Clark, 1995)? Different MAS may here pose different difficulties. The more "technified" and standardized a service is, the more its effects may be possible to isolate. For instance, it is not too hard to determine whether an information system of computers, network cables, etc, works or not. Either you can make backups on the server, connect to the Internet and use e-mail, or you cannot. Nevertheless, although it is easy to evaluate if it works or not, there may still be uncertainties when it comes to judging the value of the service and the system to the organization.

The other extreme is a service that scores low in both the degree of technification and standardization. A typical service of this kind is strategy consulting. The technology used here can be reduced to analysis methods and standardized management tools. These seldom work as strict guides for the consultant's problem-solving, however, but rather represent facilitators of a communication process between consultant and client, making them a starting point for improvisation (Werr, 1999; Furusten, 2003). Such services are therefore difficult to evaluate since it is hard to know what really was delivered, whether it had anything to do with the initial formulation of the assignment, whether it was based on the best available knowledge and, last but not least, what it really resulted in. This creates a whole set of uncertainties to be dealt with by the buyer, including questions about the actual need of the organization to be satisfied by the service provider, the content of the delivered service, and its effects. Furthermore, the lack of a clear knowledge base and professional standards makes it hard to distinguish the "professional" supplier from the "non-professional" This issue will be dealt with in the next section.

The construction of trust for suppliers of management advisory services

When collective, professional systems fail to reduce uncertainty as to who is a trustworthy supplier of a certain service, another mechanism for reducing the buyer's uncertainty often comes in play – namely, the close interaction between buyer and seller. From the purchaser's point of view, this mechanism involves getting to know a service provider through his/her actions in order to be able to judge for oneself whether that service provider is trustworthy or not. Research on management consulting, for example, has shown that this is a common mechanism for reducing uncertainty regarding the professionalism of management consultants. Their own personal experiences of a certain consultant as well as the experience of trusted colleagues are repeatedly mentioned as criteria for choosing management consultants (see e.g. Clark, 1995; Dawes et al. 1992; Furusten, 2003). Interaction based trust has also been shown to be important for the judgment of suppliers in other professional services. Grey's (1998) analysis of auditors, for example, shows that it is not enough for buyers that the auditor is authorized by the professional system (although auditors have a rather strong professional system). Buyers still make an effort to establish close relations to the auditor they want to hire in order to trust him or her (Glückler and Armbrüster, 2003).

Individualism

Referring to the literature on business relations between buyers and sellers of management consulting services, it is obvious that social accomplishments play a central role in the establishment of the working relationship between buyer and supplier. Still, these relationships have been discussed in a rather inconclusive way, providing images of the buyer of consulting services ranging from a "customer" in complete control of the advisory process, via a "client" dependant on professional experts or a "victim" in the hands of manipulative charlatans.

The image of the buyer as *a customer* assumes that a system of professionalism that guarantees that all suppliers are pure experts is in place, enabling the buyer to make professional purchases, i.e. by thoroughly evaluating and comparing alternative suppliers. This perspective empowers the buyer since he/she is assumed to have the ability to make rational choices of whom to hire, supported by a system of professionalism that ensures that those who act in the role of a consultant are authorized representatives of the profession.

The *client* image of the buyer is an intermediate form between the two extremes "customer" and "victim". The "client" is a much more vulnerable buyer than the consulting "customer" putting great faith in management consultants and their expertise. The client is characterized by knowledge deficiencies in relation to the consultant and therefore temporarily puts him/herself into a dependent position. This dependent position might be perceived as uncomfortable by the client and illegitimate by his or her environment (Maister, 1993; Schein, 1988). The client, however, is assumed to be protected from exploitation by the consultant expert by the consultant's professional ethics and norms. In this respect, the consultant is often equated with an organizational therapist (e.g. Rhenman, 1973; Schein, 1988).

The third image of the buyer of management consulting services is at the other end of the continuum from the customer. The *victim* of consulting services is a naïve buyer who is completely in the hands of opportunistic, self-serving consultants. Caught in the pressures of the managerial role (reinforced in part by the consultants) victim buyers seek help in controlling both their organizations and their careers (Watson, 1994). Consultants offer help in both areas by constructing the organization and its problems in a way that makes it possible to solve the problems (Czarniawska-Joerges, 1988), and renders the consultant the natural solver of the problem (Bloomfield and Best, 1992; Bloomfield and Vurdubakis, 1994). Consultants also reproduce an image of management as powerful, important and in control (Clark and Salaman, 1996).

While these three images of the buyer were derived from the literature on management consulting, the categories are generally applicable to buyers of most forms of management advisory services. Depending on the degree of collective professionalism in the area of expertise, the external service supplier will gain varying "expert power" over the buyer. A strong professional system provides the consultant with strong expert power, but also puts into place mechanisms aimed at counteracting undue exploitation of the buyer based on that power. Depending on the kind of professional system, the providers' use of this system, and how the buyer perceives him/herself, different buyer images will be enacted.

Rather than being a characteristic of a certain service, we thus see the respective roles of the service provider and the buyer of the service as local and social accomplishments based on the interaction between buyer and supplier. While the literature has argued for different depictions of the buyer's positions *vis a vis* the supplier of MAS, the images of the customer, client and victim are presented in rather different streams of the literature. In this book, these images are viewed as complementary outcomes of local negotiations.

The buyer-supplier relationship:
In-between individualism and collectivism

Some attention to the formation of the buyer-supplier relationship in the purchasing of services has been given by the literature on purchasing business services.[2] Although this literature provides a thorough treatment of the specific issues and choices involved in the purchasing of business services, it provides more limited insights into the formation of the buyer-supplier relationship and especially the interplay between the individual buyer-supplier relation, service characteristics, and the context in which the purchase is carried out. The focus of this literature is often the relation between actors in networks. Building relations between actors is the major process in the uncertainty reduction strategy we called "individualism" above. By focusing on interactions between actors, however, this literature does not attend to the institutional setting in which the relations are embedded. Sure, trust is established in individual relations, but how and why these relations take certain forms cannot be understood without relating them to existing factors such as institutionalized norms on the buying as well as the selling side (see Bryntse, 2000 and Planander, 2002 for more basic discussions about trust-building).

The focus on interpersonal relations and networks in much of the literature on purchasing business services as well as the existing empirical studies on managers' purchasing behavior when it comes to MAS (Clark, 1995; Dawes et al. 1992) indicates that buyers tend not to fully trust guarantees made by a collective of experts. Instead, buyers tend to want to meet their service providers face to face and develop a personal relation with them before daring to trust them enough to sign a contract with them. Thus, for the service provider, the construction of trust tends to occur in two parallel dimensions, *the collective* and *the individual*. In the collective dimension, trust-building has to do with the construction of general experts and general expertise. In the individual dimension, it is about interpersonal relations.

While the collective building of trust through the establishment of general experts is well studied in the context of traditional professions, in the context of MAS we can see its application also in less well established "professions" such as management consulting and

---

[2]   See Chapter 3 for a more detailed discussion.

investment banking. The collective building of trust in these kinds of services is less well understood, however, and seems to follow somewhat different patterns than for the traditional professions. This means that questions need to be asked concerning the construction and character of expert power and its possessors, what role it plays in trust-building for the closing of deals, how it interacts with local circumstances, interpersonal mechanisms and institutional structures, etc. These are issues that are currently not answered in the literature about professions, professional purchasing of services or the functionalist and critical literature on business relations between buyers and sellers of management advisory services.

Dealing with confidence in arenas for expertise construction

This book focuses on the local construction of management advisory services within the field of tension between collective rules and norms and individual trust-based relations. Based on the empirical observations to be presented in the book, the modernistic idea of "professionalism" emerges as a concept that offers only limited understanding of the purchase of the kind of expertise the book focuses on. However, rather than abandoning the concept, our aim is to reinterpret it in light of the emergence of "new" professions, or rather what can be called "new professionalism". Thus, our interest lies in the institutionalization of norms for professional behavior in areas where there is no central actor that can be held accountable for the conduct of the professionals. Although there are ongoing activities also in the new professions, to establish communities of practice in order to regulate the expertise in different fields, their impact is generally rather limited.

In order to capture the construction of expertise as interplay between various forms of collective professionalization on the one hand, and individual interaction on the other, we view this as taking place in "arenas for expertise construction". These metaphoric arenas provide the context in which individual buyers and suppliers meet to negotiate the service, as well as their need for it, and who may be regarded a legitimate supplier. While the negotiations take place between individuals, like battles took place between individual gladiators, they are conditioned by the prerequisites provided by the arena and the rules for the specific type of battle to be fought. It may be argued that the kind of MAS in focus here, mainly representing new- rather than established professions, provide a different kind of arena than the more established professions. Rules concerning the new professions are more ambiguous and informal, leaving the individual combatants larger freedom of action, as compared to the established professions. Still, the encounters concerning new-professional services are limited in numerous dimensions, which we will come back to in the final chapters of this book.

Understanding the nature and structure of these arenas for expertise construction in new-professional fields is a central aim of this book. Since dealing with these kinds of new professionals has become a part of the daily routines of modern organizations, understanding the characteristics of new professionalism is important, and earlier literature about business relations between service suppliers and buyers as well as on professions offers only fragmentary explanations. Although our ambition is not to develop a full theory for the dealing with the kind of new-professional services represented by most MAS, we set out to at least develop an outline for a more comprehensive theoretical understanding of the dilemmas involved than what has been made thus far. In doing this, the chapters of this book cover a wide range of different kinds of MAS, such as management consulting, IT consulting, finance consulting, consulting by auditors, business lawyers and temporary staffing agencies. This range of services represents differences in a number of central dimensions, including the degree of commodification, technification, individualism and collectivism. Such variety enables us to engage in a concluding, more general discussion of the meaning of new professionalism in the area of management advice (see chapter 14).

A central aspect of how arenas for expertise construction work is how they deal with different kinds of uncertainties for both users and providers of management advisory services. Uncertainties concerning both the need for the service (is it really needed?) as well as the quality of the provider (who is a good provider?) are important facets of the relationship between buyer and supplier of MAS. They make the process of dealing with MAS a complex and open-ended one, ultimately aimed at the establishment of confidence in its double meaning – confidence in the decision to hire an advisor and confidence in the specific supplier hired.

Outline of the Book

The book is made up of three main parts. The first provides an elaboration of both the practical and theoretical issues sketched out in this introductory chapter, Chapter 1. Chapter 2, by Staffan Furusten and Christina Garsten, elaborates on the issue of "new professionalism" by studying the characteristics of expertise in management consulting and temporary work respectively. In Chapter 3, Björn Axelsson provides an introduction to the purchasing and supply-chain management literature and how this views professional buying of expert services, and Chapter 4, by Antti Ainamo, explores what may be learned about the purchasing of services from the service marketing literature by discussing this in relation to law services.

The second part of the book deals with the first key element of uncertainty for buyers of MAS argued for above, namely, their need for the service. How is this need constructed? Organizations differ in their use of external expert services. They have a choice of buying external services or applying internal resources, and they need to be able to justify this choice to their environment. This part of the book explores this "make or buy" choice when it comes to MAS and discusses its dimensions and formative forces. In Chapter 5, Karin Svedberg Nilsson and Karin Winroth explore a management service that has emerged rather recently as an "expert service" – corporate finance – and discuss how this area has become established as an unquestionable domain for the use of external experts. In Chapter 6, Andreas Werr discusses the forces that drive different kinds of uses of management consulting services in different organizations. In Chapter 7, Fredrik Augustsson discusses organizations' use of external vs. internal resources in the field of interactive media solutions, and Chapter 8 by Niclas Hellman deals with organizations' choices to purchase additional advisory services from their auditing firms.

The *third part* of the book deals with the construction of the professional supplier of MAS. In Chapter 9, Lars Engwall and Carin Ericsson focus on CEO's dealings with management consultants and ask how we can understand why they are used in spite of a considerable distrust of them. Nina Lindberg and Staffan Furusten, (Chapter 10) study how managers and buyers handle the formal law on public procurement and point out a strong tension between the prescribed procedures and what the parties perceive as efficient in a deal. Moving from the public to the private sector, Jonas Bäcklund and Andreas Werr (Chapter 11) explore how the same ideas as in the law of public procurement are realized (although in a somewhat more flexible way) in the efforts of large companies to become more professional buyers of MAS. Finally, Chapter 12, by Susanna Alexius and Staffan Furusten, focuses on the formal contract as a more objective way than individualism or collectivism of reducing uncertainty in the relationship between buyers and suppliers of management consulting services. Attempts by a consultancy to use a value-based pricing method are studied and it is argued that it carries little impact in the construction of confidence for a consultancy. The final two chapters (chapters 13 and 14), by the editors, conclude by drawing together some of what was learned from the other chapters included in the book. Chapter 13 discusses the handling of two central uncertainties in the purchase of MAS – the need for MAS and the choice of MAS supplier – and explores how these processes are embedded in the local, the organizational and the institutional context. Finally, Chapter 14 elaborates on the idea of arenas for need and trust construction and how what happens in these arenas can be understood in relation to concepts such as markets and organization.

CHAPTER 2

"New" Professionalism

Conditions for expertise in management consulting and temporary administrative staffing

STAFFAN FURUSTEN AND
CHRISTINA GARSTEN

In Chapter 1 it was argued that today many organizational, managerial and administrative services are produced outside the organizations that consume them. This is seen by Burrel (1996) and Scarbrough (1996) as a general trend of our modern times. Burrel also argues that old professions, such as physicians, are challenged by new types of experts whose expertise is related more to political ideologies than to abstract expert systems. Burrel's argument draws attention to how we might look upon the role of external suppliers of MAS and how the expertise they carry along from organization to organization is constructed. If upcoming new types of experts are being given more power to set the agenda, forcing older traditional professions into the background, this means that the meaning of expert power is changing or at least being contested.

In this chapter, it will be argued that the expert power of suppliers of MAS is not only a function of some people having passed certain passage rites, which is one of the most crucial prerequisites for the meaning of a "full profession" (e.g. Abbott, 1988; Larson, 1977). As we will see in empirical examples in several chapters of this book, the formalization of expertise is, for most MAS suppliers, not the most important issue on their agenda. First of all, they struggle hard to sell their services. If formalization of their expertise is able to comfort them in this, they are likely to emphasize collectivism and rules for professionalism. If on the other hand they see nothing positive in this, they might also struggle against formalization of professionalism for the kind of services they provide. Still, as long as they manage to sell their services that is, to create trust in their relations to their clients, they also manage to keep up their image as experts in particular business relations. We use the concept "new" professionalism to label the form of expert system represented by MAS and its suppliers.

This chapter raises the question of how the expertise of MAS suppliers, that modern organizations must bring in from external markets, is constructed. We do this by focusing on the suppliers, and the construction of their professionalism, and by discussing how new professionalism deviates from the traditional meaning of professionalism.

New types of experts and new forms of expertise

In the literature on professions, it is made clear that a professional is someone who fulfills the prerequisites for professionalism produced by the professional system they belong to (e.g. Larson, 1977; Abbott, 1988). There is, for example, only one way to become a lawyer. One is only allowed to practice civil law in the courtroom if one has become a member of the national association for lawyers or followed the career path to become a judge, starting as an assistant and advancing step by step to the local prosecutor. The rules for physicians are even more rigid. What these, which many call "traditional professions" (e.g. Ackroyd, 1996) have in common, is that the prerequisites of today have emerged over a long period of time, where it can now take five years of undergraduate studies and two years of practical medical training to become legitimized as a physician.[1] Once this has been done, one is a formal professional as long as one manages to follow the rules of professionalism and thereby uphold legitimacy. Similar systems can be found in law and auditing, where there are clear rules for who is the expert (i.e. the professional) and who is not (i.e. the layman). The passage rites are definite and work as a barrier to stop laymen from interfering in decision-making involving the expertise and criteria for actors in the expert role. Such systems also give expert power to experts since they are the only ones who formally uphold true expert knowledge. Thus, the expertise of traditional professionals consists of the expert knowledge they have earned through their undergraduate studies, the required well-documented experience, and their status in the society as individual representatives of a specified

---

[1]   This time frame refers to the Swedish system.

field of expert knowledge. Those who represent all this are also automatically accorded expert power in relations to clients (Reed, 1996).

The kind of situation just described is an ideal one. It suggests that knowledge can- and should be disembedded from its local context, standardized, produced and packaged by the expert community. However, the conditions for expertise and professionalism in the new emerging forms of expert services today are of a different kind. Moreover, as shown by Grey (1998) in his study of the big auditing firms, professionals like auditors need to be knowledgeable in at least two dimensions in order to gain the trust of their clients. First, they need to pass the formal passage rites necessary to become a full member of the expert community. Second, they need to know how to commercialize their expertise. Fulfilling formal prerequisites for professionalism is thus not enough today (if it has ever been).

As will be argued more thoroughly below, and in several other chapters, professionals today also need to create trust for themselves and their firms in business relations with their clients. This means that their formalized expert power can be questioned, as can their formalized expert knowledge, as can the very notion that professionalism can be represented in disembedded generalized standards in globalized systems of professionalism.

This means that the notion of the disembedded expert knowledge can be questioned as a prerequisite for experienced professionalism in local business relations. It appears that individualism rather than collectivism, interaction rather than expert power, and temporality rather than stability characterize the expertise of MAS suppliers (cf. Chapter 1).

In the following, we will discuss the meaning of expertise for the kind of "new" professionals this book focuses on with respect to two core aspects of the traditional understanding of professionalism: the standardization of work tasks and the collectivization of expert knowledge.

Standardization of work tasks

The phenomenon discussed above has been observed by many others. Giddens (1990), for instance, talks in a generalized sense about the disembedding of social systems. He suggests that, although this is a feature of modern times, it has not forced us into a state of full modernity. In management consultancy work, the disembedding may be evinced in efforts towards professionalization of expert work which is one side of the coin, whereas close interaction and local, individualized trust-building is the other. In order to understand how both sides of the coin can work together, we are going to compare the two extremes of external expert services to management, namely, management consulting and temporary administrative staffing. In their ideal forms, the latter entails the hiring of individuals to perform routine administrative tasks, while the former represents the outsourcing of more qualified tasks devoted to organizational change rather than stability in particular organizational processes, which is the idea in the former. These ideals mark two end points on a continuum of standardization of work tasks, where the ideal management consultant scores low, and the ideal temporal administrative staff scores high (Figure 2:1). However, it is important to bear in mind that these are ideal types and that there are several examples of less idealized forms of both types of services in practice (illustrated by the dotted arrows in the figure below).

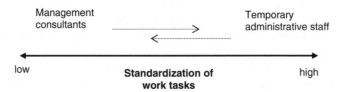

Figure 2:1 Standardization of work tasks

In their ideal forms, management consulting and temporary administrative staffing are different. Management consultants can appear in many varied forms, ranging from specialized experts on certain methods or management techniques (Greiner and Metzger, 1983), "organizational therapists" (Schein, 1988) and "merchants of meanings" (Czarniawska-Joerges, 1988), to "organizational witchdoctors" (Clark and Salaman, 1996b). Temporary employees may likewise either be professionals, such as physicists or engineers, or clerical staff with little professional training, such as switchboard operators, receptionists and secretaries. Another difference is that a "temp" is generally not supposed to change the work practices of the client organization. This is, on the other hand, what a consultant is often expected to do.

Seen from this angle, it is consultants that remind us most of traditional professional work. They move in a dimension where they have the upper hand in controlling what is relevant knowledge and reasonable practice. Temporary administrative staff, on the other hand, rarely represent unique professional knowledge. Their expertise is more often based on their experience of doing routine work in a number of different settings.

Still, many of the services that "consultants" provide resemble those offered by temps. Services such as "management for hire" may be provided by a temp agency as well as by a management consultancy. Whereas there used to be a relatively strict line between providing temporary personnel and recruiting, the large temp agencies of today claim to offer a variety of solutions to the problem of staffing in general. Still, comparing the ideal forms of consultancy work and the work represented by temporary administrative staffing will provide us with a base to discuss the conditions for MAS as a form of expert work offered to many external markets.

Management consultants represent more traditional expert work, while agencies for temporary administrative services represent specialized work tasks. The motive for comparing them is that, in their ideal forms, they represent two different sources of expertise: science and practice. This covers expertise in a very broad meaning and suggests that almost anything can be seen as expert work as long as it entails trusting others to do things that we, for different reasons, are unable or unwilling to do ourselves. This is also at the core of the expertise concept Giddens (1990) refers to when he argues that the disembeddedness of social systems is a key aspect of expert work in modern times. He argues that disembedding means "the lifting out of social relations from local contexts of interaction and the restructuring across indefinite spans of time-space" (ibid., p. 21). However, following Giddens, the idea of disembeddedness becomes complicated when one considers the need for re-embedding, hence the "re-appropriation or recasting of disembedded social relations so as to pin them down (however partially or transitorily) to local conditions of time and place" (ibid., p. 79-80). We will begin below by discussing the complexity of disembedding expertise, i.e. expert knowledge, expert experience, and expert education. We will then discuss the complexity of the disembedding of experts. Finally, we will argue that many of the new types of experts on the rise in modern society can be viewed in terms of "new" professionalism.

Collectivization of expert knowledge

The extent to which we have moved beyond tradition and a sense of relative security has been discussed intensively for some time (cf. Adam, 1995). In social science and among practitioners alike, images of an uncertain and fragmented future society are evoked. Many of these images stem from post-modern or post-traditional perspectives, which, despite being increasingly subject to criticism and qualification, have not lost momentum. Much current theorizing in social science is concerned with the decline of the belief in a predetermined or natural order of things, the development of fragile social structures and contingent communities (see e.g. Bauman, 1995; Beck, 1992; Heelas et al, 1996), and the prevalence of risks with global reach (Beck, 1992). The vocabularies and techniques of risk, as noted by Rose (1996, p. 320), open up new roles for MAS suppliers, educators, and managers of risk. New languages and techniques become available for organizations, which makes their future appear more controllable.

These languages and techniques are not always constructed within organizational hierarchies. More often, they are cultivated in communities of expertise and offered on markets. According to Pfeffer and Baron (1988, p. 263), "taking the workers back out" of their organizations represents perhaps the most visible and pronounced trend in the structuring of work arrangements. This trend also includes, we may add, a preference for reduction of formal levels of hierarchy, an emphasis on flexibility rather than rule-following, and images of a more permeable boundary between the inside and the outside of organizations – as denoted by an increased use of sub-contracting, temporary workers and consultants rather than a permanent and/or in-house expertise (Garsten and Grey, 2001; Garsten, 2003). The "post-bureaucratic trend", as Heckscher and Donnellon (1994) call it, invites market dynamics into what used to be intra-organizational matters and seeks to rid the organization of activities that are not directly linked to its focal service or product. This development fits well with ideas of modernity and a generalized knowledge society with more or less world-wide rationalization.

These perspectives challenge existing notions of institutional and structural stability, arguing instead that many of the institutions and structures of today are relatively contingent and fragile phenomena. While the extent to which these tendencies make a break from preceding structures of modernity and relative stability may be questioned, we may agree on the fact that they interpenetrate and compete with processes of institution- and tradition maintenance and rejuvenation of boundaries and structures. Moreover, they bring in their wake a market for temporary expert services. "In times of uncertainty, the expert rises to prominence," Hochschild (1983, p. 75) argues. Although this market, along with others, has faced hard times in the early 2000s it is a fact that an increasing number of service providers feed on notions of fragmentation and contingency in order to create a market from which to distribute services that would render organizations and individuals within them more adaptive and efficient. Therefore, we see that while ideas and their diffusion is an integral aspect of globalizing processes, a concomitant disembedding and commodification of such knowledge takes place.

"New" professional expert knowledge

In expert systems, it is supposed to be very clear what kind of expert knowledge experts need to be equipped with. This is also what the idea of the disembedding of knowledge suggests. For management consultants and professional temporary employees, this would mean that the nature of the knowledge used by them should be such that it facilitates the sharing of ideas and experiences across space and time. Some consulting and temp firms act accordingly and even turn this into a world-wide strategy. For example, management consulting firms such as McKinsey or Accenture have offices almost all around the world and also have internal knowledge banks from which every single employed consultant in these firms can withdraw knowledge whenever they need to, wherever they are in the world. This means that consultants in these firms may find their way through the global network of offices relatively easily, and may also be hired to work on particular projects in different countries. Thus, the knowledge they sell is of a kind that has been lifted out of local contexts of interaction and reorganized across large time-space distances (cf. Giddens, 1990). Likewise, individuals who work for temporary employment agencies sell knowledge of a kind that may often be easily transferred from one office to the other without losing its value. Quite often, it is argued that the reason why this is possible is that organizational fields are now more global and homogenized, suggesting that the same ideas are shared and recognized by those who belong to and move in these fields (cf. DiMaggio and Powell, 1983/1991). This in turn suggests that those who provide services that build on such widely recognized knowledge also gain a certain power. They have access to a specialized field of knowledge that may be denied to the layman, or have the time to excel in competencies actors in organizations generally do not have. For the client, the contact with the consultant or administrative service supplier may be a unique experience and also their only direct line into this attractive, specialized field of knowledge. However, the expert power of service suppliers does not only lie in their access to a specialized field of knowledge, it is much more complicated than that.

In fact, the expertise of temporary administrative staff scores low in terms of collectivization of expert knowledge. This is, however, not to be understood as if they have no expertise to offer. Their expertise lies in their professional attitude to what they do, in combination with the fact that they are skilled in a specialized area of competence. Management consultants, on the other hand, score higher in the collectivization of expert knowledge. It can hardly be argued, however, that they score high here, since there is some controversy in the knowledge field regarding what the expert knowledge of management consultants really consists of. Still, there are dimensions of the knowledge management consultants provide that are collective. There are, for instance, national as well as international associations in which membership is allowed to those who fulfill certain prerequisites. There are also widely institutionalized codes of conduct, knowledge systems, and methods that a professional consultant is expected to follow, to carry around, and to use. However, these are not codified in rules, and although they are widely institutionalized, they are not followed by everyone at all times. That is why management consultants in general can be said to score about medium in terms of collectivization of expert knowledge (figure 2:2)

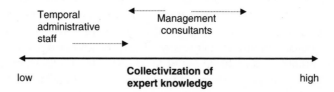

Figure 2:2 The degree of collectivism in expert knowledge

This suggests that professionalism in MAS is not all that tightly connected to a core of specified expert knowledge. In the case of administrative services, it is more a matter of a shared work-related identity connected to a membership in a collective. This can take formalized forms, like in the case of administrative services where the association for temporal employees (SPUR in Sweden) has had an important role to play for its organizational members, or, as in the case of management consultants, it may be seen in the internalization of institutionalized norms.

In this regard, the two forms of services in focus in this chapter, "management consultants" and "temporary staff", may be seen as representatives for new versions of professions in Ackroyd's view (1996), or as Reed (1996) calls them "entrepreneurial professions" (such as financial/business consultants, R&D engineers). What distinguishes them from traditional professions (physicians, lawyers) is that their legitimacy is not authorized by the state and that their prestige and status on the market is not based on monopolization by a particular occupational group of the kind of work they deliver. This means that the kind of expertise they represent is constructed, authorized and controlled in non-traditional processes of professionalism. Thus, being authorized as a professional management consultant or a temporally employed secretary has little to do with the passing of particular exams, having a particular- and documented practical experience, authorizations controlled by the state, or membership in certain highly prestigious professional associations, or with adhering to formal ethical codes and codes of conduct.

Professionalism in a traditional sense is believed to be stable both in time and space (e.g. Larson, 1977; Abbott, 1988; Burrage and Torstendahl, 1990). Once you have passed the exams, become a full member of the professional association, technically authorized by the state as a professional, and then continuously follow the professional ethics and codes of conduct, you will always be a professional, at least in a formal sense. This is, however, not the case in less traditional professional groups such as those described in this chapter and in other chapters in this book, where the service provider must continuously prove his/her expertise and earn legitimacy for it.[2]

The disembedding of experts

To talk of groups of actors in general is of course complicated and to generalize across two such groups makes it no easier since our cases, management consultants and temporary employees, differ in the kinds of expertise they offer. To complicate the picture even more, however,

---

[2] Studies in the so-called STS (Social Studies of Technology) also note that, although the formalities in traditional professions are strong, the practice is often characterized by many controversies, e.g. regarding what is to be considered expert knowledge and professional behavior (e.g. Latour, 1996 and Helgesson et al, 2004).

they also differ among themselves, in offering a great variety of types of experts representing different technical competence.

The "temps" studied here typically work in clerical or administrative positions. The temps, who are largely female although with a growing male presence, are placed via a temping agency with various client organizations who can thereby fill their labor needs "flexibly" (Garsten and Grey, 2001). In broad terms, we suggest that while management consultants claim to offer specialized knowledge of organizational dynamics, techniques and instruments for transforming organizations and behavior within organizations, temporary employees as a category offer none of these things. Instead, they have the experience, skills and personal characteristics that enable them to adapt to a variety of situations and client needs. Their expert knowledge is hardly of the kind we generally associate with expertise, but of an acquired skill to be versatile, or "flexible". This means that it is not an "expert" in the traditional sense we see here. It is an "expert" who only gains expert power through authorization by individual clients. Hence, no one form of expertise is more objectively true than another form, it is merely a matter of its social relativity (e.g. Berger and Luckmann, 1966). Still, there is something generalized for those who claim to be treated as professionals to draw upon. What this is, however, is in most cases both vaguely referred to- and defined by central actors.

The re-embedded and temporalized professional

Compared to traditional professionalism, "new" professionalism represents a vagueness and temporality in what is considered expertise. This means that there are no predetermined ways for the temporary expert to learn how to become one or for the client to judge who is the best. It is, however, quite clear that it takes certain competence in order for a consultant or a temp to be able to act like experts and to commercialize and make good business out of the service they provide.

How is it possible, then, to act in the expert role and claim that one represents professionalism? A chief executive at a consulting firm with about 25 employed consultants says that a management consultant has to have the "feel" for what actions are relevant, but also a competence in transforming this gut feeling into techniques and instruments, and knowing how they can be duplicated and taught. He suggests that consultants who have developed such a feeling that they "just know" what is relevant to know in particular situations and how this knowledge can be transformed into the service he and his colleagues in the firm offer. This he describes as bits and pieces suddenly falling together. In his words, you suddenly discover that "yes, now something has happened here, we have to revise this quickly by developing a new form of technique, or getting a new instrument, or training our consultants so that they can better handle this situation." However, this is a competence not all consultants have. It is a skill it takes a lot of experience to develop. A skill that enables you to see that the same observation has been made on several occasions, and possibly by several individual consultants in the firm.

To develop the feel for management consulting, however, is not easy. Where does this ability to feel, to see, to transform, to duplicate and to teach come from? The same respondent says that "techniques are developed from what you – in one way or another – already have, but – in one way or another – need to, upgrade." This can be understood as meaning that the expert know-how is not just something you can learn from books. It is something that comes with experience and things you have learned elsewhere, in combination with efforts to constantly remain informed about the development in different industries and sectors as well as the development in relevant fields of knowledge. The expert knowledge on which this particular firm bases its services, is rather organization-specific and very much related to what each individual consultant does with it. It is not a body of knowledge controlled by a particular occupational group and which you can upgrade. Instead, the expert has to relate what s/he already knows and everything s/he takes in from different sources to ongoing projects and the specific profile the consulting firm wants to have. This implies some set of basic qualities, although the basics are not composed of a particular set of management techniques or methods for change, that consultants have to learn.

A senior consultant at a small consultancy (about 15 consultants) explains that:

A huge amount of knowledge is accumulated in your head, body, in your bookshelves, in your fingertips, feelings, sense of smell, and hearing. My point is that it's know-how that's completely different from technical know-how. A clever chief physician – in contrast to an ordinary physician who has the same technical knowledge – has the sense, imagination intuition and experience. What is this? Well, he has no doubt seen a lot more patients and made more diagnoses than his colleagues, and therefore can put it all together – like: "Strange, he has a blue and a red ear. Hey - I saw this once 17 years ago at Uddevalla Hospital!" It's this competence, not the remembering, but the ability to put things together. It's an enormous amount of accumulated know-how.

This particular quotation summarizes what many consultants declared. It is *the skill to combine* experience with know-how, technical skills and a feeling for what knowledge is relevant in a particular situation that seems to be what is required to be able to be authorized as an expert. That is, as long as you have no strong brand name to rely on like the large more or less, globally operating, often American-based, consultancies have.[3]

Temporary administrative staff share with consultants the built-in mobility of work. In moving between client organizations, they constantly transgress organizational boundaries. The local particularities of each client organization provide the basis for the construction of knowledge of a more universal applicability. This organized mobility is an important aspect in the development of expertise in temporal administrative services and the learning of how to become one who can be authorized by his clients as a "position expert". Speaking about the open labor market in Silicon Valley, Annalee Saxenian (1994, pp. 23-24) makes the observation that:

Learning occurs in Silicon Valley as individuals move between firms and industries, acquiring new skills, experiences, and know-how. It occurs as they exchange technical and market information in both formal and informal forums, and as shifting teams of entrepreneurs regroup to experiment with new technologies and applications. Learning occurs as firms of different sizes and specializations jointly solve shared problems. Above all, learning occurs through failure, which is as common as success.

In the same manner, temps learn as they move between client organizations. They acquire skills, experience and competence across a wide range of organizations and markets; above all, they learn how to make use of different skills in different organizations. In other words, they learn to be versatile, or "flexible". Transferable skills are often thought of in terms of their capacity to be used in different contexts without losing their value (Hannerz, 1990). This transferability and flexibility refers not only to a particular skills bundle but also to attributes of the self. Empirical work on temporary workers (Garsten, 1999a; b) is illustrative of this.

The temp agencies will have hundreds, if not thousands, of temps on their books at any one time and the extent to which agency staff know

---

[3] The reference here is to firms such as Accenture (formerly Andersen Consulting), PriceWaterhouseCoopers, Cap Gemini (formerly CapGemini Ernst & Young), McKinsey & Co, Booz Allen Hamilton.

the temps personally is limited. On the other hand, the agency does know a good deal about the requirements of client organizations, at least where these are regular clients, and will seek to ensure that particularly difficult jobs or clients are dealt with by "good temps". Good temps, unlike the mass of the temping staff, will be known to agency staff who will go to some lengths to keep a good temp on the agency's books. The attributes of a good temp are not so much skill as the capacity to fit in with whatever organization they are assigned to. Flexibility is often described, by agency staff and temps in Sweden, in the UK and in the US alike, as a readiness to adapt to the needs of the client. In a popular self-help book for temps, the temp is given the advice to (Hassett, 1997, p. 100):

Be a Gumby. Temping is an imprecise art and a lot of different people, moods, and circumstances are involved in its creation. ...That's why Gumby-like flexibility is such a valued commodity. If you can bend – work sometimes when you don't really want to, stay later than you were booked, sometimes all night, or be nice about a cancellation at the last minute – suddenly you make that long-odds gamble less risky for all.

Thus what is at stake is the transferable self, rather than transferable skills. That a person can be relied upon (by the agency and the client) to perform in a predictable way (to fit in, adapt, do a professional job) is to be a good temp, which is another way of saying that trust is achieved. Symptomatically, the staff at one of the big staffing agencies in Sweden sometimes refer to the temps as "chameleons", with a capacity to adapt effortlessly to the needs of the customer (Garsten and Grey, 2001). There are also understandings of what constitutes a "good job". Although this is partly an issue of "personalities", the temps report that large companies and companies which regularly use temps (which may or may not be the same companies) are good jobs to be on. In the former case, reflecting the points made earlier, it is because such companies were relatively predictable in how they behaved and the tasks asked of the temp. They have learned what it means to be a client organization, in addition to being a manufacturer or purchaser of products and services. In the latter case, it is because the expectations of what could reasonably be asked of the temp were realistic. So, like the good temp, the good job turns out to be bound up with the trustworthiness of each actor being flexible towards the other. Interestingly, these two notions have a tendency toward self-fulfilling effects: agencies wish to keep good temps on their books for use with their most valued clients and will therefore seek to accommodate the temp's desires. The temp prefers to go to a good job, and in such jobs it is easier to be seen as a good temp because these are the large, predictable organizations that habitually use temps. And it is of course also these clients who are most valued by the agencies. The lynchpin of this set of relations, which may be considered as paradigmatic of post-bureaucracy, is the strong interdependency and trust generated between the different parties involved such that even the most impermanent types of employment are rendered at least somewhat predictable (Garsten and Grey, 2001).

Thus, what characterizes the expertise of temporally employed administrative staff in one important dimension is their ability to be flexible, to jump from organization to organization. This takes a form of professionalism that has very little to do with a particularized core of expert knowledge in an area of competence. This skill is the most important one for the new professionalism we focus on in this book.

Among entrepreneurial and "new" professionals

For some new fields of expertise, the "entrepreneurial expert", as Reed (1996) expresses it, may be an appropriate label. This goes to say that the professionalization of this particular community of practice is in an early stage and that bits and pieces of the characteristics of a full profession are installed gradually. An example of efforts made in this direction is the foundation of associations for specialized service providers such as SAMC (Swedish Association for Management Consultancies), FEACO (Fédération Européenne des Associations de Conseils en Organisation) and ICMCI (International Council for Management Consulting Institutes) for management consultants, and SPUR for temporary administrative staff. To earn membership in such associations (except SPUR), individual service providers must meet certain requirements like having certain experience, a particular education and a specific number of years in the business.

In traditional professions, these dimensions of professionalism are very rigid. For instance, it is not possible to practice medicine as a physician at a hospital in the Western world without a university degree in medicine, or to practice law without a law degree, etc. There are both state-governed legislation and association-governed rules for professionals that regulate such practice. The importance of these rules, and thus also the rigidity and robustness of the professional system, differ between different communities of practice. In terms of formalizing collective temporary staffing may be classified as being in an early entrepreneurial stage of professionalization, while the system for management consulting is much more vague. It can in fact be questioned whether the professionals really are interested in emphasizing professionalization to any higher degree (Rydmark, 2004) since a great deal of them claim that the prerequisites for membership are far too general (Furusten, 2003). "The prerequisites emphasize what everyone does anyhow," as the dilemma was expressed by one management consultant. However, this can also be interpreted as there being institutionalized structures for professionalism that everyone practicing management consulting follows, although there are no formal rules stipulating that it has to be this way. Thus, there might very well be quite clear norms for what professional management consulting means, but these norms tend to be taken for granted rather than textualized in formal rules.

So, there are differences in the expertise of the traditional-, the entrepreneurial-, and the new professional. The traditional professional is embedded in a robust abstract expert system. The entrepreneurial professional is embedded in upcoming structures and a gradually emerging robustness where the professionals themselves are heavily involved and interested in developing and strengthening the profession, i.e. to turn it into a full profession. The new professional, on the other hand, has little interest in building up the profession into formal structures where the mystique of what their expertise consists of is clearly laid out on the table. Thus, the first two types of expertise are more stable in time and space due to their emphasis on formalized collectivism, while the third is more temporary and locally authorized. We must keep in mind, however, that these three forms of professionalism are ideal types, and that the practice for most professionals is best described as various combinations of these ideal types. What has been neglected in the literature about professions thus far, however, is the ideal type – "new" professionalism.

If the two dimensions of professionalism introduced above are recalled and brought together (standardization of work tasks and collectivization of expert knowledge), the following figure (Figure 2:3) can be drawn, in which the three forms of professionalism discussed here can be placed. Their placement in the figure originates from their ideal positions. The arrow pointing "north-east", and thus towards a high score in both dimensions, marks the direction the professionalization literature describes as the only way towards pure professionalism, which is also the direction that ideal entrepreneurial professionalism is expected to take. The ideal type for a traditional profession then scores high in terms of collectivization of expert knowledge and about medium in standardization of tasks since they are expected to deal with complex situations. New professionalism, on the other hand, has a more dubious placement in the figure. Depending on the new profession's focal service, its position as an ideal type is likely to vary. In general, however, it can be argued that its position is characterized by a relatively high score in terms of standardization of tasks and a relatively low score in collectivization of expert knowledge due to the fact that the meaning of this is locally constructed (cf. Furusten, 2003). The dotted lines mark the directions in which we argue that our ideal types move in practice. As these lines show, they all end up in something of a practical professionalism where nothing is pure, where work tasks cannot really be standardized and where the existence of collective expert knowledge can be questioned. These are the conditions that characterize the new professionalism, meaning that the characteristics of new professionalism are also likely to be found in the practice of traditional professionals.

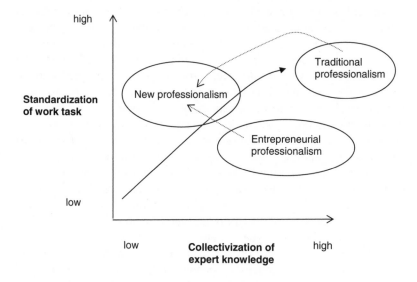

Figure 2:3 Professionalism, standardization and expert knowledge

The construction of temporally re-embedded new professionalism

There are several important dimensions of management consulting and administrative services where they can be seen as representing similar forms of expertise construction. *First*, the expertise of management consulting and temporary staffing is temporary. Unlike auditors, consultants and temps are often hired once and for a limited period of time in order to help the client organization to solve a particular problem. An auditor, on the other hand, is supposed to be hired repetitively, i.e. every year s/he is called in, and every joint-stock corporation must register their auditor with a certain public agency (PRV in Sweden). Moreover, in order to be allowed to practice auditing, the auditor must meet the requirements for membership in a national professional association for auditors. Consequently, the expertise represented by the new-professional expert also becomes temporary, specific and local, while the expertise of the auditor is stable, general and formally authorized by the state.

Second, as noted by Grey (1998), professional knowledge is one thing and professional behavior another. In his study of auditors, he draws the conclusion that "for professionals in BSF[4], the meaning of being a professional is primarily bound up with a series of ways of self-conduct rather than with issues of technical competence and accreditation" (p. 584). Still, he continues:

That does not, of course, mean that qualification and knowledge were unimportant. On the contrary, failure to qualify would mean an end to one's career in BSF. However, professional and "appropriate" forms of behavior are used so as to be "taken seriously" by colleagues and clients.

Consequently, when their relations to their clients are considered, not even the expertise of traditional professionals is built solely on technical skills and formal assets. The client wants more from the expert than excellence in technicalities. Still, there is a closing mechanism here since no one can act as a full auditing expert without the formal authorization as an expert. This means that auditing represents an expertise controlled partly by the profession and partly by the state. However, this is just one aspect. According to Grey, they must also be accepted as experts by their colleagues and clients. To achieve this, they also need social skills, i.e. to know how to handle relationships and to generate business.

For consultants and temps, the importance of relevant technical know-how is of great importance, but this need not be constituted by a particular generalized set of knowledge. Thus, they need to be competent in the areas in which they provide their services, but what authorizes them as experts, temporarily, is how their clients perceive them. There is no occupational group that has formal control over their

---

[4] Big Six firms (now Big Four), referring to the big, international auditing firms in which Grey carried out his study.

expertise and no dominant public definitions of their tasks (Reed, 1996; Grey, 1998). Their expertise is temporary and continuously re-constructed in every business situation. That is why the ways in which the temporary service providers present advice and solutions to the client is a critical point for the development of the expertise they represent and their possibilities of becoming authorized (cf. Giddens, 1990). With the increased significance of this new-professional expert knowledge, two major challenges for them are to overcome the gap between lay- and expert knowledge and to create and maintain trust. This takes relevant technical know-how and a great proportion of social skills.

Third, it is obvious that there is competition between different suppliers of the expertise. Actors on this market have to play their role as experts convincingly. Clients are likely to have to deal, not only with the uncertainty encountered in their field of business, but also with the uncertainty of not knowing which of the competitors on the market possess "the best" expertise.

Fourth, another complexity is that their expertise cannot be stored. Even if they were seen as experts once, this does not mean that their expertise can be automatically reproduced in another setting or in another organization. It is in the relation between expert and client that expertise is constructed. Hence, there is a strong social and relational component involved in the process. In Chapter 1, this dimension was called "individualism".

Fifth, following from the above argumentation management consultants and temporary employees represent a kind of expertise that is a mix of knowledge, know-how, experience, and technical and social skills that only occurs when authorized by the clients. The expert rarely controls this complexity of skills and experience him- or herself, but rather has control of the access to the bundle of knowledge and ideas needed to solve a particular problem. He knows how to get hold of, manipulate and present knowledge and ideas to the layman. Consequently, this kind of expertise is not an objective capacity that is generally applicable in all situations in all organizations all over the world. Instead, it is more likely to be described as a locally constructed temporary capacity or social accomplishment that takes on different meanings in different social networks and situations. In these networks, different interpretations of what expertise is believed to represent may very well occur – and the expert, in order to become authorized by his clients as an expert, needs to be skilled in relevant technicalities as well as socially.

Conclusions: Temporary new professionalism as a social accomplishment

In the above, we have discussed some aspects of the social construction of expertise in the fields of management consulting and temporary staffing. The tendency to "bring the workers back out", or to externalize expertise, draws our attention to the relational aspects of expertise construction, suggesting that it is a social accomplishment, at least with respect to consultants and temps, when they are brought back into organizations. We have suggested that the prevailing post-bureaucratic trends in organizing bring with them a market for expertise. This expertise is often of a kind that can easily be lifted out of one particular, local context and put to use in yet another, without losing its value. These mobile experts have the upper hand in stating the problems and providing solutions to them. The construction of this expertise rests on the capacity of the expert to fit in with, adapt to, respond to, and create and sustain a relationship with the client – in other words, it rests on a degree of social competence to be there, "just in time". Without the social component, there is little chance for the expertise to gain the authority needed to conduct this kind of business.

Social competence and authority are built in various ways depending on the type of expertise provided. *First*, the construction of expertise provided by experts who work with relatively specialized and commodified expertise tends to a greater extent to be based on relatively standardized and well-structured components. This can be experts such as large consultancies and temp agencies that offer specialized and commodified services and de-individualized and exchangeable persons. *Second*, the construction of expertise provided by small- and mid-sized management consultants, on the other hand, tends to build more on the individual capacity of the single expert. The expertise is embodied in the individual rather than in the firm he represents. Standardized components are still of importance, but not in the delivery. These experts follow established professional codes for consulting, although they tend not to use membership in professional associations as a basis for their authority (Furusten and Brunsson, 2000), and they improvise on standardized well-known management techniques (Furusten, 2003). Although "pure" management consultants and "pure" temps may represent rather different forms of expertise, in practice the boundaries between theses services are blurred. In some cases, it happens that they are exchangeable, which means that the expertise delivered has similarities even though it is framed differently.

We suggest that the new professionals depend on a strong relational component. Expertise and authority in these relations are built up, defined and legitimized in ongoing relations between experts and clients. We view the establishment of temporary services as a social accomplishment that takes on different meanings in different social networks and situations.

For some, the notion of entrepreneurial professionalism is relevant, since certain actors see themselves as a collective and struggle to develop rules for generalized professionalism. Others, on the other hand, emphasize that they are individuals while at the same time struggling not to deviate from institutionalized norms for professional behavior.

Our two cases of professionals highlight the conditions many modern professionals live under. They do not fulfill the prerequisites for pure professionalism, but the behavior of many of them resembles that of entrepreneurial and new professionals as discussed here. To conclude, individualism is an important dimension for the modern professional, as is temporality of their expertise. Collectivism is for many a hidden agenda that has to be there but has little credibility in local trust building if it is recalled. Interaction with local clients is therefore an important dimension in the construction of today's new-professional expertise. This means that the expertise of modern professionals relies very much on combinations of taken-for-granted structures and social accomplishments. This is a dimension of professionalism often neglected in the traditional literature on professionalism, but a crucial one in our understanding of what it is that gives modern professionals the authority to perform in their roles as experts hired from external markets.

CHAPTER 3

Purchasing as Supply Management

A modern view of professional purchasing and its implications for the purchase of management advisory services

BJÖRN AXELSSON

The development of purchasing

The development of the role of the purchasing function is sometimes described as a process in which the responsibility has gone from *buying*, via *procurement* to *supply management* (Anderson and Narus, 2004; Van Weele, 2001). The various steps have meant an increase in scope as well as stronger general impact on the activities of the organization.

Purchasing as in *"buying"* represents purchasing activities and responsibilities that deal with buying the goods and services needed and making sure that a basic function of the items bought is acquired at favorable conditions. This is a rather narrow scope with low degree of sophistication. The conceptual development is sometimes dated to the 1950s. The implementation of this emerging commercial content on a broad scale (initial steps to "play the market") is sometimes dated a decade later.[1]

Purchasing as in *"procurement"* deals with acquisition, optimizing the flow of materials (materials management, logistics), and implies a

---

[1] The reference here is to the development in Western countries in the EU and the US.

widened role. It means (among others) that not only price but also volume and time aspects are being taken into account. The optimization aspect deals with buying large quantities to get a low price; not too large – to avoid expensive stocks, but large enough to avoid shortages and production downtime. The conceptual development is often dated to the 1960s and 1970s and the realization of it on a broad scale a decade later.

Purchasing as in *"supply management"* increases the scope several steps further, and includes also the formation of supplier structures, the development of suppliers' capabilities (resources, knowledge), improving administrative routines, etc. – all in order to reduce total costs, not only the price of the specific products bought but also other costs like quality and administrative effects. This approach also includes efforts by purchasing officers to increase the creation of new values in terms of product development and the like. The Japanese car- and electronics industries' way of organizing their supply structures is often referred to as role model for this view of purchasing. Concepts like just-in-time and first, second and third tier suppliers are important signals of this concept. These and related concepts were carefully analyzed by, among others, Womack, Jones and Roos (1990) in the seminal book *The Machine that Changed the World*. "Purchasing as supply management" thus includes aspects such as joint product development, development of administrative routines and so forth (Axelsson and Wynstra, 2002).

There are several reasons behind this gradual increase of importance and scope for the purchasing function. Much is due to the continuous ongoing specialization, meaning that every firm specializes in a smaller range of value added activities in its production process (be it manufacturing or service related activities), which leads to an increased share of purchased goods and services. The purchasing ratio is today in the range of 50-70 percent for manufacturing industries in general, 80-95 percent for retailing firms, and 30-60 percent for service organizations (van Weele, 2001)

As noted in Chapter 1, in many organizations – manufacturing and service companies, public and private organizations – service activities previously performed internally have to a substantial extent been outsourced to external suppliers. In the past decade(s), this has led to a major increase of purchased services. Not only information and communication related (ICT) services are bought. There are a huge number of services to be sourced, e.g. in functional areas such as transport, printing/reproduction, temporary manpower, library services, maintenance and catering services. All in all, the purchasing ratios presented above have been affected due to an increased propensity to outsource services. A North American investigation of 116 companies and organizations showed that services accounted for a weighted average of 54 percent of total purchases (39 percent on average for the 59 manufacturing companies in the study, 81 percent for the 23 service companies and 62 percent for the 34 public authorities) (Fearon and Bales, 1995).

There are also other reasons behind the described pattern of change, e.g. a development of new managerial principles and concepts such as Total Quality Management (TQM), the Just-in-Time concept (JIT), Efficient Consumer Response (ECR) and so forth, often enabled by new Information and Communication Technology (ICT). These concepts naturally lead to a strong focus on the need to consider inter-organizational relations in efforts to improve quality, efficiency and effectiveness in organizations. Connected to this development has also been an ongoing process of increased sophistication of the purchasing techniques, concepts and professionals. These techniques and concepts have been applied to a varying degree in various types of firms and also in relation to the goods and services bought. This is soon to be explored.

Other general trends may also have had an impact on the process described. To begin with, it would seem that competition has intensified in many industries, partly due to the globalization of markets. This has caused firms to also trim their purchasing and supply activities. Today there is a strong focus on services bought, as well as a growing interest for purchasing activities in the business community at large. Not least public authorities are exposed to strong demands on efficiency and effectiveness, putting supply issues in focus. In this field of purchasing, the European market is strongly influenced by the Public Procurement Act. This legislation gives important direction on how the purchasing organization should act. As it has been implemented during the last decade or so, it has had a strong impact on public procurement activities in Europe. Similar regulations are in place in other markets, e.g. in the US.

Purchasing activities in small- and medium-sized firms also attract interest. Leading firms in the car industry, for example, argue that it is difficult to improve the effectiveness of their supply chains if the small- and medium-sized firms far down the supply chain are unable to apply good purchasing practices. Thus, there seem to be many good reasons behind the development of purchasing as a function in today's private firms and public authorities.

Definition of purchasing

Over the years, various definitions of purchasing have been used. In earlier literature, purchasing has often been interpreted in a narrow and operational way. This has led to a strong orientation toward the position of the buyer and a narrow understanding of the organizational issues pertaining to the solution and organization of purchasing tasks. Heinritz et al (1986, p. 9), for example, refers to purchasing as "buying materials of the right quality, in the right quantity, at the right time, at the right price, from the right source." However, following the trends of the last two decades, the definition of purchasing has broadened considerably to a more strategic understanding of the underlying processes, leading to definitions such as "managing the external resources of the firm" (Dobler and Burt, 1996; Van Weele, 2001). Gadde and Håkansson (1993, p. 13) even describe purchasing as broadly as "a company's behaviour in relation to its suppliers."

The following definition: *"managing the external resources of the firm, aimed at acquiring inputs at the most favourable conditions"* (Wynstra, 1998), is perhaps best suited to the overall intentions of this book. This definition explicitly includes the possibility that inputs may be less tangible than goods, as in the case of services (e.g. knowledge), and acknowledges that purchasing may involve activities that are only indirectly concerned with ("aimed at") obtaining inputs, such as relationship building and supplier development programs. The word "acquiring" implies that inputs may not only be bought, but could also be leased, rented, borrowed or traded (e.g. as in the case of counter trade). Another, very pragmatic but in most situations very suitable definition, which also fits well with the scope of this book is: *"purchasing involves all activities that lead to an incoming invoice."*

Many services are bought without much involvement from purchasing specialists, yet the performed acts still result in incoming invoices. This brings us to the distinction between the purchasing function (or process) and the purchasing department. Most organizations do have specialized purchasing departments even though the way they are organized and their roles can differ considerably. Sometimes the departments have a strong and strategic role that may be manifested by the purchasing manager being a member of the company's top management team and/or involved in all important supply issues. In other cases, the role of the purchasing department and the purchasing professionals is limited and many of the strategic issues are taken care of by other specialists from engineering, marketing, materials management, the management team, etc. This means that other professionals in the organization can act as "part-time purchasers". Still, the *purchasing function* or the *purchasing process* is performed. In the continuation of this chapter, the reference is to the purchasing function as a whole, thus including also the part-time purchasers.

Different approaches to purchasing and supply management

There has been an ongoing discussion in the field of purchasing over the years, of whether one should choose a transactional or a relational approach to purchasing. The two concepts could be characterized in the following key words (Table 3:1):

Transaction-oriented approach	Relationship-oriented approach
Many alternative suppliers	Select one or a few suppliers
Short-term, every deal is new business Choose the best at every single moment	Long-term, every deal and every problem is a part of the relationship
Choose from the existing suppliers in the market	Create tailor-made solutions and forge the suppliers into a perfect fit
Stimulate competition among the suppliers	Stimulate cooperation and joint competitiveness
Split the deals into small pieces Connect to functions	Connected/systems solutions, broad scope
Buy well-defined products Push standardization arguments	Buy a partner including its supply chains
Price orientation	Cost and joint value creating orientation

Table 3:1 Two approaches to purchasing

This is a simplified presentation of two archetypes of how to approach purchasing. The transactional approach (column on left) is said to be strong in reaching a low price for well-defined products available in the marketplace. The relationship-oriented approach (column on right) is said to be better geared, i.e. through combined and coordinated efforts among buyers and sellers (and other actors in the system), toward lower total cost as well as joint development of new functions.

In some contexts, the key aspect could be to establish and exploit the lowest possible price on a well-defined product. In other contexts, the total costs (including administrative costs, quality costs, adaptation to production and/or product development, etc.) are more in focus, thus fostering the relationship approach. But, as pointed out by, among others, Axelsson and Wynstra (2002), the choice of purchasing orientation is also a matter of competence and skills of the purchasing organization. When considering management advisory services, it is entirely possible to apply both approaches to purchasing them, though the transaction approach seems relevant only if it is a one-time operation. When continued business and repeated activities are at stake, it is more likely for advisory services to be bought in line with the relationship approach. This is mainly because of the complexity of the service and the need for considerable learning efforts before a service can be delivered.

The two approaches used to be considered an "either or" issue, when it comes to the basic idea on how to deal with supply issues and suppliers. Today, there seems to be a general understanding, among both academics and practitioners, on some kind of segmented view. Both approaches have their strengths and weaknesses. This suggests a growing recognition that both approaches may be preferred, but in different contexts, including actors' various aims and aspirations. A widely used model to segment purchasing needs, and also to forge a strategic view to purchasing and supply management, is Kraljic's model (1983).

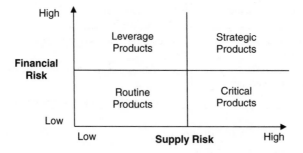

Figure 3:1 Kraljic's matrix for segmenting purchased products (Kraljic, 1983)

The matrix points to two dimensions as key indicators deciding what kind of approach to purchasing to apply. Van Weele (2001) has further elaborated the preferred approaches to purchasing in each quadrant. The degrees of financial- and supply risk indicate various contexts and have implications with respect to the preferred strategy, as well as the approach to purchasing.

Routine products are cheap (low financial risk), the supply market consists of many possible suppliers, and the consequences of supply problems are limited (low supply risk). In such situations, the suggested approach is to find ways to create a sourcing system, where a selected number of suppliers deliver a broad range of these "simple" products. This is most relevant in situations with a need for enduring supply of such products. The primary effect sought is saving time spent on purchasing matters. In the leverage product situation, there are many financial gains to be made in combination with low risk. The suggested approach is one of competitive bidding but – maybe – for somewhat longer time periods than indicated in the description of the transactional approach above. Again, this is dependent on the applied time frame in the specific situation. The strategic products are connected with both high supply risk and high financial risk, and the suggested approach, according to Van Weele, is partnering. Partnering is very much in line with the relationship approach discussed above, but again, has to do with the time frame as well. Finally, the leverage products with a high degree of supply risk and low financial risk tend also to be best suited to a partnering approach.

If we refer again to management advisory services, one would hardly find any of these services among the routine products. Instead, they are most likely to be connected with rather high supply risks. That concept is interpreted as giving rise to severe consequences if the service delivery does not meet expectations. Similarly, they are likely to be positioned quite high on the vertical scale even though they might not amount to any substantial percentage of purchasing expenditures. Management advisory services are normally intended to influence the work methods of the buyer and are likely to have an impact that will lead to substantial effects on the buying firm's finances.

From this brief overview, it would seem that the relationship-oriented approach should be applied more often than the transactional approach. In practice, however, it seems as though the transaction-oriented approach dominates. But as shown by Jonsson (1998), it also turns out that manufacturing firms often tend to apply some kind of combined approach, in an attempt to combine the strengths of the two approaches, e.g. the so-called "jigsaw method" where a small number – two or three – suppliers are selected and the amount of supply from each supplier varies from occasion to occasion based on past performance. This signals that the description has thus far been somewhat simplified.

There have been a number of attempts to discuss and define various levels of purchasing sophistication (or maturity), based on how well firms succeed in taking advantage of various techniques and synchronizing their efforts in professional purchasing.

Degrees of sophistication or purchasing maturity

In Figure 3:2 below, six levels of purchasing maturity are defined. Level 1, the lowest level of maturity, or professionalism (transactional orientation), is said to be prevalent for the clerical purchase. This is recognized in a very passive purchase operation where the purchasing professionals, in principle, merely administer the purchasing tasks. Level 2 (commercial orientation) is a somewhat more developed commercial handling with regular requests for tender, comparisons of various bids from suppliers and negotiations, as well as an operation with pre-qualified suppliers. Level 3 (purchasing orientation) emphasizes a work mode where the buying company has strong control over purchased volumes, the number of suppliers and of the products purchased. This enables the organization to exercise more powerful and coordinated actions. Common to these first three levels, is a functional approach where the purchasing department acts – more or less – on its own with the general purchasing issues, and where the higher levels (2 and 3) call for increased centralization of the purchasing operations.

Level 4 (internal integration) is where the organization also handles the assortments purchased in a more developed manner, utilizing cross-functional teams with the relevant competencies, which take responsibility for the important goods and services (functions) bought. Obvious prerequisites are well-functioning and well-communicated systems inside the organization (e.g. purchasing systems, business systems, and MPS (materials planning systems). Furthermore, such organizations also utilize not only pre-qualified but also ranked suppliers, connected in various ways to development- and improvement programs supported by performance-based contracts. Level 5 (external integration) adds one aspect to the professionalism as it introduces synchronization and optimization of supply chains. It also adds the awareness of where in the supply chain relevant business conditions are set, and introduces systematic efforts to coordinate suppliers on various levels upstream the supply chain. For this to work, there is a need for active utilization of ICT technologies, e.g. EDI systems or web-based interfaces. There is also a need for information to be coordinated across several levels in supply networks and for the organization to be able to apply various models to decide on the most appropriate way of operating the supply chain in question. Level 6 (value chain integration), which is looked upon as the most sophisticated, adds a clear connection to the buying firm's own customers, i.e. purchasing management means to do all the synchronized purchasing operations in previous steps – and – actively contribute to the creation of customer value in addition to lower costs and thereby the possibility to offer lower prices to the customers. An in-depth understanding of the customer's needs, and willingness and capability to satisfy them, is the basic purchasing concept for level 6. This presupposes that, in addition to the demands of the previous steps, purchasing also takes a global view toward finding suitable suppliers that possess the ability to initiate and run supplier development programs.

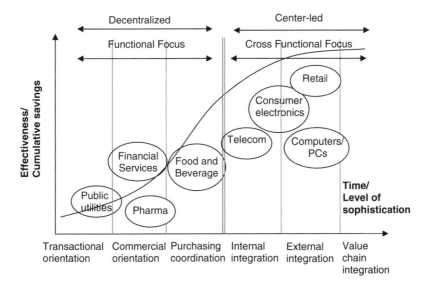

Figure 3:2 Six levels of purchasing maturity (Adapted from Van Weele, 2001, p. 94)

In terms of the organization of activities, there are a number of common ingredients for levels 4 (Internal integration) to 6 (Value chain integration). Cross-functional teams and center-led operations seem to be an important prerequisite here. A center-led function could- but need not imply the dominance of a centrally placed purchasing unit. The most important thing is that every assortment is kept together from one point and the necessary competence is tied to the purchasing activities. The tentative positions of various industries indicated in Figure 3:2 point to retailing, automotive and consumer electronics as hosting the most sophisticated purchasing operations. The variable "time" on the horizontal axis is there to simultaneously illustrate that there has been a general development from level 1 towards level 6 over time.

A critical analyst of this purchasing maturity model could also question why the one aspect should be considered more advanced and sophisticated than the other. A purchasing organization could do a very good job in terms of performance even when not operating at the highest possible level of sophistication. It could very well be the case that the more advanced ways of operating demand higher skills and thereby higher salaries among the purchasing staff. This could also demand more expensive supporting technologies (ICT hard- and software for example). In certain cases (e.g. in small firms), this could turn out to be too high a price to pay in comparison with the potential improvements. Still, these models do reflect judgments that often are expressed in today's business practice and textbooks when modern and obsolete work modes are on the agenda. In fact, they help to construct views on bad, good and excellent behavior, with this model reflecting a common understanding of good and bad purchasing practices of today.

The development of the purchasing profession

In line with the above there has been tremendous development in the purchasing profession itself. It is often stated that, in the early days, operative people from production moved into the firm's clerical units to apply their understanding of production-related issues and to learn and apply some commercial practices. These professionals were placed in a purchasing unit and did their job in isolation – at best in some cooperation with other purchasing specialists. Purchasing in manufacturing industries was for decades considered a low status job. One illustration of this is the following quote from an IBM manager:

> *In the past when you could do nothing else at IBM we made you a buyer. When you couldn't design anything, when you couldn't build anything, when you couldn't carry anything, when you couldn't deliver anything. We put you into the purchasing organization. (Gadde and Håkansson, 2001)*

Before continuing, it should be recognized that people in purchasing, e.g. in retail, have always had a strong position in their organizations. In such industries, purchasing has always been recognized as a very critical function. A typical retail firm has a purchasing ratio of close to 90 percent, as it does not normally add value to the products they buy. Their value creation rests in the assortment of products created and the service attached to it.

The early industrial development saw the emergence of a new cadre of purchasing specialists. This function has gradually developed to include an increased openness and intensified dialogue with other functional specialists. Later developments include steps where purchasing acts as an integrated function in the organization with participants from "all" relevant units, as illustrated in figure 3:3 below.

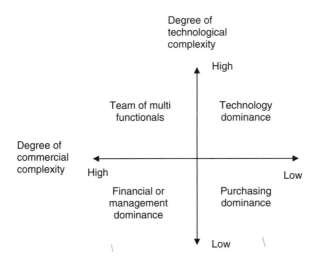

Figure 3:3 The profile and dominance of various competencies in the purchasing organization as decided by two basic dimensions (Fisher, 1970)

It seems natural that actors who represent the most relevant areas of competence should dominate the purchasing process. If there is a large amount of technological expertise needed to carry out a professional job, those technological specialists should be involved, and if there is a low financial complexity involved – they should dominate. It must be emphasized that the term "technological" should, in this context, not only refer to engineering. In addition to engineering, e.g. in a mechanical industry, we are thinking of what could be briefly characterized as "areas of knowledge". This could entail knowledge in law-related issues if the service bought has to do with juridical expertise, or logistics if the service in question has to do with such issues. In cases of low technological complexity, as well as low financial complexity, purchasing specialists are likely to dominate. In cases of a high degree of technological complexity in combination with high commercial complexity, the natural set-up of a purchasing group would be a team of experts that matches the needs and importance of the purchase in question. And finally, in situations with high financial complexity and low technological complexity, financial and/or managerial experts (CEO or other business area managers) are likely to dominate. The financial complexity involves a combination of both (possible) heavy spending on the service in question and the outcome effects of the choice. If we refer again to management advisory services, it is likely to be one of the specific services that falls into this category. Other services that may also fit include cases that involve decisions to outsource substantial previous in-house production, decisions to analyze the possibilities of buying or selling specific business areas, etc.

Although it has been emphasized that there are many actors in a firm who act as "part-time purchasers", the specialists themselves have also experienced an increase in qualifications and recognition. This is reflected in, among other things, an upgrade of purchasing in corporate hierarchies. In large firms, we more frequently find functions such as "Chief Purchasing Officer" (CPO), "Vice President of Purchasing" or "Purchasing Directors". It is becoming more common for purchasing specialists to constitute self-evident actors in an organization's product development teams. Also from job description documents and recruitment processes, it is easy to infer that the profession has advanced.

Along with the description of the professional purchasing briefly touched upon above, follow ideas of good practices. If we turn again to the model of purchasing maturity above, some of the practices that constitute part of the profession are the following:

- The basic connection between the corporate or business area strategy, the purchasing and supply strategy, and the everyday operative purchasing operations. A purchasing organization should be very well aware of the role of its function in relation to the overall corporate mission.
- Utilize ICT technologies to have immediate access to all statistics, but also to create databases, run reverse auctions when applicable, support the integration of processes and activities to optimize synchronization, etc.
- The purchasing process as such. A defined and applied purchasing process where a "case" passes through a number of toll gates. All cases, such as starting to utilize a new supplier, buying a new component or service, etc, should pass through such a process. Applying such processes is a way to make sure that no important aspects are omitted. It is also a way to structure the purchasing job.

- Organizing purchasing and supply activities internally in a way that secures smooth functioning and that involves the relevant competencies in the process.
- Segment the various purchased products (see above) and forge separate strategies for each of the products/functions purchased.
- Supplier evaluation process. One stage in the process above is choosing suppliers. This means either a search for new suppliers or staying with the ones known from before. What criteria should a new supplier meet? How should a performance measurement system be designed?
- Supplier development programs, e.g. initiatives to trigger capability development at suppliers when appropriate.
- Supply chain integration, making sure that the purchasing strategy for a product takes advantage of the best organized activity chains, either by buying from a supplier next door, or playing an active role in integrating chains of actors to create joint synergies.

Strategic purchasers/supply managers should be aware of these aspects and preferably also be skilled in implementing them. The increasing degree of professionalism in the field is thus also reflected in the skills demanded for people in purchasing. We see a much more systematic approach today to analyzing the competencies needed among purchasing staff. For example, it is common to recruit from the industry that the purchasers buy from, and it is also getting more common to provide individual career plans as well as improvement programs both for the function as such and for each individual (competence profiles, adapted capabilities in the teamed buying center). In general, there seems to be a strong awareness of the need for adequate, matching competencies on both sides of the business transaction.

The specifics of buying services

That organizations tend to buy a lot of services has already been mentioned. As this is about management advisory services, there is good reason to take a closer look at the specifics of services as compared to products (and functions) bought. There exist several classifications of services. One way to identify various services is the following (Figure 3:4):

Service oriented towards the organization as such	Services oriented towards supporting the product/business	Services that are part of, included in, the product sold
Local services: Cleaning, security, reception, restaurant, refurbishment... **Qualified assign-ments:** Law, accounting, health care, insurances, management consultancy, etc.	**Marketing and sales:** Market research, customer support, reselling, business travel, etc. **Business engineering:** Technical expertise, management consultancy, logistics, etc.	**Services as components:** Advice, education/training, instructions, diagnosis, financial services, etc. **Services as semi-manufacture:** Market research data, basic software in need for customer adaptation, etc.

Figure 3:4 An overview of various services and their utilization in a buying firm

Many of these service categories naturally fit into more than one of these broad groups. Some logistics services could, for example, be bought to support the organization/business firm as such, but also specifically to support a certain business area (or product sold). It could also be included as a component or a semi-manufacture (Axelsson and Wynstra, 2002), in the product offering delivered to the customer, and thus included in the product sold to customers. A "component" is a product that is bought by a firm, included in its market offering and in unchanged fashion transferred to the customer's customer. A "semi-manufacture" is a product that is included in the market offering and thus reaches the customer, but is further forged by the buyer.

The fact that the same service could fit into more than one category is dependent on the kind of business the specific firm is involved in. Management advisory services could of course be bought to find support for the organization as such, e.g. regarding how to best organize on a general level. Such services could also be utilized to better understand customer markets and forge business offerings. They could also be a complementary service delivered as a component or semi-manufacture to other services in a total service package. The basic idea behind the classification is to demonstrate the multitude of services bought and utilized by organizations. The general classification does, however, not tell us very much about important managerial aspects of the various services. Nor does it tell anything about the specific problems in the procurement of services in general or in procuring a specific service.

A complementary classification that tells more about important aspects of both the marketing and purchasing of the specific service (as well as its production) is the following (Figure 3:5):

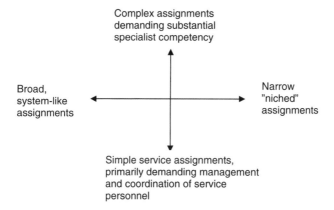

Figure 3:5 A general classification of service firms based on characteristics of the service operation

Depending on where the (management advice) service is positioned, the company will likely have to address varying key issues. The most important dimension may be is the vertical one (see Figure 3:5), which signifies the difference between simple services and complex assignments. The latter demand expert knowledge provided by cadres of specialists in their fields, like the lawyer in law, the engineer in engineering, and the doctor in medical firms. Some of the key characteristics of organizations that deliver complex, knowledge-based services as opposed to organizations that deliver simple services are listed below (Axelsson and Wynstra, 2002):

- A KNOWLEDGE-BASED business deals with complex, difficult-to-define assignments, often defined, run and produced as projects.
- It uses less strict routines and relies more on being able to solve new types of problems. It is also more dependent on specific individuals (professionals).
- Development takes place largely within customer projects, learning from- and with one another via internal or external dialogues.
- Marketing and distribution are about credibility. Who can solve the hard-to-define problem? This makes issues such as staff qualifications, references from performed projects, and documented ability to run development processes vital.

- There is a strong focus on specifying input, i.e. individuals involved in the assignment or the business relation.
- Production is a balance between creating new- and reusing knowledge and methods, as well as the disposition of project teams.
- Resource acquisition deals largely with attracting the best individuals and possessing a contact network to handle varying capacity demands.
- SERVICE companies perform simple services that are repeated many times (transport, transactions, cleaning).
- Service companies frequently have a lot of routines and are standardized.
- Development issues, i.e. construction of services using e.g. blueprinting techniques, establishing new systems and routines, trimming processes and staff.
- Marketing and distribution are to a great extent a matter of availability and communicating the service.
- Production of services is clearly defined, and capacity issues (volume) are often important. Rationalization is achieved by new technology, new routines, involvement of the customer, etc.
- Acquisition involves technology resources and personnel with adequate skills.

Common to both kinds of firms is that they handle development, marketing, production and resource acquisition issues.

Generally one would position management advisory services towards the upper end of the vertical axis in figure 3:5. The management advice firm could, in addition, be either highly specialized in a narrow scope of services or cover a broader range. However, the concept "management advice" is sometimes utilized also for firms marketing and producing rather simple services. Such advisory business is basically utilized by buyers to relieve their own staff from some tasks that others can do in their place, making it possible for their own staff to concentrate on more qualified activities. If, however, a management advice firm exhibits the characteristics listed for "knowledge-based" firms above, the firm is likely to face a number of challenges in line with the ones mentioned. But, what about buying advisory services and, thereby, dealing with such companies as suppliers? What key issues are relevant when buying services, especially management advisory services?

Key aspects in the purchasing of qualified services

It was mentioned in the beginning of the chapter that services seem to lag behind when it comes to applying the most advanced purchasing techniques. In the following, the buying of qualified services will be confronted with some of the most important purchasing activities.

The first purchasing issue is whether to buy or produce, i.e. the:

- Make – buy issue.

If a company takes the decision to buy the service (e.g. a management advisory service), the typical purchasing process includes the following steps:

- Defining the needs
- Specifying and tendering
- Supplier search, evaluation and choice
- Expediting
- Follow-up and learning

In general, there are additional purchasing considerations among which the following are significant:

- Transaction-based vs. relation-based purchasing
- Segmenting the purchasing assortment
- Organizing the buyer-supplier interface
- Getting organized for purchasing
- Driving purchasing development

Bearing in mind what has been said about various degrees of sophistication in purchasing and supply, especially of services, the specifics of services, especially of management advisory services, and the characteristics of various services suppliers, the following comments apply.

The very first aspect, the "make or buy" issue, is likely similar for most services (or goods) under consideration. When there is more uncertainty regarding the skills and capabilities (i.e. so-called "tacit knowledge"; Nonaka and Reinmoeller, 2000) that underlie production of a service, however, this decision may become more difficult.

The make or buy decision can and maybe should always be considered also when management advice is concerned. One advantage of buying such services is that it increases the possibilities of finding a supplier with the relevant knowledge, e.g. generated through working with other companies with similar problems. One advantage of in-house problem-solving is the likely deeper understanding of the specific context and the possibility to generate, from experience, a genuine learning experience and accumulate knowledge. It should also be emphasized that, even if the company reaches a decision to purchase, it needs to engage in the production of the service and to be a qualified buyer.

The steps related to the purchasing process should basically apply, even though they may be performed in a somewhat different manner when a service (especially a qualified management advisory service) is bought. It is often argued that the process, from need recognition to final purchase and post-purchase evaluation, is dependent on the degree of uncertainty experienced by the buyer. The buying party could perceive uncertainty from basically three sources: the needs, the market and the transaction (Håkansson and Wootz, 1975). When a high degree of need uncertainty is perceived, this causes the supplier to search for more information on the issues. The same goes for market uncertainty, which has to do with the buyer's knowledge and understanding of the market. Similarly, transaction uncertainty deals with the buyer's perception of whether or not a chosen (or potential) supplier will be able to carry out the business intended.

It may be that the need recognition process could be somewhat more difficult to carry out when expert services are concerned. In the case of complex and qualified services, it is not unusual that the buyer of a service is not able to identify and clarify its true needs. This could be a highly relevant aspect when it comes to buying management advice. It is often a situation of genuine uncertainty.

The request for tender could also show specific demands due to the difficulty of defining the service and the importance for the coming evaluation of the service – when (unclear) expectations from the early stages of the process will be confronted by the delivered and experienced service. It is likely also key that the request for tender gives a good overall description of the context, the organization, its aims, the problems experienced, etc, in which the service is expected to solve problems. If this is done, it forces the buyer to think through the situation and it gives the supplier a reasonable possibility to interpret the situation correctly.

Supplier search, evaluation and choice could also be expected to demonstrate specific features. The search and evaluation process is made more difficult due to the expected heterogeneity of these services. Normally this should trigger a more extensive evaluation process and/or the utilization of complementary criteria. The evaluation process would most likely be based on references: what the supplier has done before, and the image and market position of the supplier; opinions in the market when it comes to experiences from working with the supplier, etc. In terms of general evaluation criteria of the supplier, some of the critical processes mentioned above would be highly relevant. What kind of development and learning processes is the supplier exercising, what kind of partners can the supplier mobilize, is there a great danger of key individual (single person) dependency? The buying firm's previous experiences with the specific supplier (and other suppliers) is likely to have a strong impact in this part of the process. What kind of priority could the buying firm expect if and when something unexpected happens?

Expediting is a part of the purchasing process that is often taken for granted. But when there are complex, difficult-to-specify services, this part of the process is very important. How will the interplay between the supplier and buyer (and other parties involved) be organized in various stages of the process, and how can the two (or more) parties gradually calibrate their expectations of the outcome?

Follow-up and learning is also a complex issue. It has already been indirectly stated that continual follow-up during the process of service production is important. This generates learning. There is of course also a need for some kind of project evaluation after the service has been delivered. Did the project develop in line with expectations, have the initially defined goals been achieved, and what experience will be saved until the next project by the buyer and by the supplier?

The further key aspects of purchasing management mentioned have largely already been addressed above. The transaction- vs. relation-based approaches to purchasing apply also for services, not least management advisory services. The issue of segmenting the total purchases, not only based on the various groups of services as such but also in a way that gives direction for strategic choices in ways to handle every specific assortment (e.g. the Kraljic matrix), has also been found to be applicable to services – even though in practice it may not be systematically applied to management advisory services. The needs to organize the best needed and fitted competence in relation to various services purchased and/or service suppliers dealt with has also been discussed and broadly applied to services. Similarly, the "getting organized for purchasing" issue has been briefly noted in relation to services. It is more or less self-evident that various ways of designing and organizing the purchasing and supply organization will also have effects on the buying of management advisory services. In the discussion of purchasing sophistication, there were indications that firms would have less comprehensive approaches, in terms of defined purchasing processes and well thought through principles, when buying management advisory services. Still, the purchasing organization aspects are of high relevance also for buying services. Driving purchasing development is a general issue that should always be relevant – also when it comes to services.

Conclusions

This chapter has described a function, purchasing and supply management, which has undergone steady development leading to increased scope and responsibility. There seems to be an accepted understanding of the various degrees of sophistication and professionalism that could be in operation for this function. Some industries are considered more advanced than others and some products purchased seem to have been more subject to systematic purchasing efforts than others. Services are generally considered as not fully exposed to the more sophisticated concepts and techniques – a notion that is probably also relevant for management advisory services.

On average, about half of the total purchasing expenditures in private firms (manufacturing and services firms) and public authorities taken together, consist of services of various kinds. Most organizations buy a broad range of services and it would seem that all general purchasing techniques and concepts should apply. But, it is also clear that there is a great need to adapt the expedition of the service buying process to the general specifics of services. Also management advisory services fit into the general frame for purchasing and supply management and for the specifics of services. However, many aspects need to be dealt with in adapted ways, due to the complexity, difficult to specify, etc, characteristics of management advisory services in general. It is possibly to, in general, point to some such specific problems but much of it needs to be further explored. Some of this urgently needed exploration will be carried out in the following chapters.

CHAPTER 4

Selling Business Law Services

ANTTI AINAMO

The Nobel laureate Douglass C. North (1981) has argued that economies of scale and depersonalization of commerce have emerged in contexts where clearly specified rules of the game allow for relative certainty and depersonalization. Others have added that widely shared norms of professionalization (Greenwood et al., 2005) and popular models to be imitated and to be applied in particular settings similarly promote depersonalization and economies of scale (Djelic, 1998). In contrast, that which is commercially marketed in contexts of high uncertainty will typically continue to take the form of "personalized exchange", that is, person to person or in small groups (North, 1981). It was Sturdy (1997a) who established that the processes of negotiation, sale, and delivery in management consulting services represent elements of high uncertainty for both the seller and the buyer. As argued in Chapter 1 of this volume, the uncertainty surrounding management consulting suggests that the negotiation, sale and delivery of all professional business services, such as those of auditing or legal services (see also Maister, 1993), represent clear cases of personalized exchange where there can be no well-developed system for mass-marketing activities in a traditional sense.

Then again, as argued by the large literature on "services marketing" in the marketing discipline, the prevalence of "high uncertainty" purchasing situations need never mean that marketing activities become fully impossible. The services marketing literature suggests that there are differences as to the particular ways of marketing that are appropriate for contexts of high uncertainty versus those of high certainty – but, despite these differences, marketing and well-developed systems for negotiation, sale, and delivery of services can exist at both extremes, as well as in more intermediate contexts.

With this background, in an effort to better understand the distinguishing characteristics of management advisory services that are in focus in this book, the current chapter will explore the applicability of the large literature on services marketing to the specific context of management advisory services. The large literature on services marketing will be argued to represent a *grammar* for the peculiar language spoken and discourses enacted by business service professionals and their clients in general, and in law firms in particular. The discipline of marketing may be a grammar that, in large part, has been hidden from many legal practitioners and their clients. However, this discipline would nonetheless appear to represent some form of a meta-language for building an understanding about the ways that lawyers and their administrative staff jointly represent their firms and their professions. The current study will attempt to further develop this type of understanding about business services and why and how they are marketed at the micro-level by business services professionals. The chapter will build explicitly on some of the most classic findings of the services marketing research literature.

In order to avoid the pitfalls of "model-based" or overly abstract argumentation (e.g. Kieser, 1994), the chapter will frame its analysis on the sociological theory of professionalization and, more specifically, on studies of professionalization in terms of the legal profession. Furthermore, the chapter will use top law firms in Finland as an empirical anchor.

The top segment of law firms is an especially interesting one for several reasons. These law firms have clients that, for the most part, lead other local business organizations, whether these clients are local or more international in origin. At the same time, the top law firms are subject to such substantial pressures for change as globalization and the acute dislocation of legal frameworks earlier contained within the boundaries of individual nation-states (Vähänäkki, 1991). Given that law firms in this segment face changing rules of the game in relationships with their clients, they provide a sample of, and opportunities for, organizational research into the traditions, legacy and changes in marketing. These law firms are also the type of law firms that have the most complex projects or assignments, while still having their share of simple and routine jobs. The fact that they focus on corporate clients rather than on the public sector or personal legal matters makes these firms and their services readily comparable with other professional business services firms, such as management consultants (e.g. Abrahamson, 1996; Sturdy, 1997; Berglund and

Werr, 2000; Armbrüster and Barchewitz, 2004) and auditors (e.g. Greenwood et al., 2005).

The chapter proceeds as follows. After a more thorough discussion of the characteristics of the legal profession, we will turn to the challenges of marketing these services. Three central characteristics of these services will be identified and elaborated upon – intangibility, simultaneous production and consumption, and a lack of standardization – and the consequences of these characteristics for the marketing practices will then be described and discussed. In a final section, the overall findings will be recapitulated and further discussed.

Professionalization and the legal profession

In the professionalization research stream of organizational research, it has been argued that the understanding of activities in professional settings cannot be decoupled from the broader process of professionalization in which they are embedded. In other words, "understanding of any organized formalization of activities in a profession [such as the marketing of services by lawyers] is meaningless unless we can understand their context. This relates back to the power of the professions' knowledge systems, their abstracting ability to define old problems in new ways" (Abbott, 1988, p. 30).

In terms of professionalization, the legal profession is particularly interesting for studying marketing of professional business services. In many countries, the law industry has long exhibited a relative absence of mass marketing in comparison to other providers of professional business services (Abbott, 1988). One reason for this is probably the tradition of the legal trade in the civil law (also called Roman Law) system, a meta-legal code existing in German, Napoleonic and Nordic variants in Continental Europe and the Nordic countries. Within this legal system, lawyers are not supposed to act like "star lawyers", that is, like the lawyers in the Common Law system predominant in Britain and its previous colonies in the new continent and elsewhere, such as in India or Australia, where lawyers rise to celebrity status with high-profile legal cases handled in the courtroom and often also in the media.

The requirement in civil law countries is that lawyers are to present themselves as representatives of the collective of professionals, not of their own individualism. This is more than empty rhetoric. The requirement is closely monitored and related directly to the practice of the legal profession in these countries. "Discretion", in the sense of an almost total silence as to the achievements of law firms, is an institutionalized aspect of the operations of law firms, especially when it comes to the top or corporate law segment of law firms in civil law countries.

Most legal disputes in civil law countries between leading corporate clients of top law firms are settled through arbitrage, or out of the courtroom, rather than in the courtroom. A corporate client will often denounce allegations that they have used any law firm in the first place. As a result of having participated in the "low-profile" resolution of the dispute, the top law firms acting as mediators on the opposing sides of a legal dispute between leading corporate clients are thus restricted in how they can secure references or enhance their reputation through media exposure.

This low-profile professional culture is a highly institutionalized part of the professional system of lawyers and law firms in many civil law countries. In Sweden, law firms have traditionally been very hesitant to be aggressive about marketing communications (Winroth, 2000). In Finland, the Bar Association explicitly prohibited the advertising of legal services from its members until 1997. Still today, while the code allows a law firm in Finland to advertise, the content of advertising has been restricted to "objective content", such as the law firm's name, address, telephone and fax numbers, etc. All subjective qualifiers and emotional content are no longer (since 1997) strictly forbidden, but they are still discouraged. Similar norms or restrictions have existed in other civil law countries. This has restricted the marketing tools available to law firms. In the following, we will turn to the services marketing literature in a search for a deeper understanding of how marketing still takes place in Finnish corporate law firms. Some of this literature will make direct sense in this context, while other parts must be translated into the context of law firms.

The author was able to access marketing practices in top law firms, and selling practices in particular, through discussions and observation of the negotiation, selling and service-delivery practices of seven leading Finnish legal practitioners. Of these seven lawyers, four were partners in top-five corporate law firms, two partners in other top law firms, one a lawyer in the law services unit of a global auditing firm, and one a corporate lawyer. The author's intent was not to collect data that would be statistically significant, but to develop insight and foresight of marketing practices in the field of business law services.

Marketing business law services

What kind of relevant knowledge can we find in the services marketing literature on the topic of marketing in law firms? We find very few studies other than generic guidelines that focus on the marketing of "pure" professional services. Many of the studies about marketing of legal services have either been at very high levels of abstraction in terms of marketing, such as findings about principles of general management (Maister, 1993; Winroth, 2000) and organizational templates (D'Aunno et al., 2000), or at very detailed levels, such as those about pricing (Uzzi, 2004). While the odd exceptions to the rule may be found in terms of mapping the marketing techniques or practices that are generally available to law firms (e.g. Sipilä, 2000; Shostack, 1992; Bitner, 1992), they have failed to make a distinction between a business law services firm and other specializations or non-business law services, such as the handling of family inheritance or criminal cases.

Making a distinction between business law firms and non-business law firm is important for at least two reasons. First, most top law firms are business law firms. Second, the top business law firms differ from other business law firms. The top law firms are influential drivers of change in the rules of the game in their profession. Their business is most closely intertwined with international business where challenges of globalization and changes in the rules of the game are most acute (cf. Vähänäkki, 1991).

To study what makes top business law firms qualitatively different, we find plenty of generic literature on services marketing beyond our focus on the legal profession. As will be argued below, this generic literature provides useful insights that may enhance our overall understanding of services marketing in law firms and business services firms.

The central point of departure for the services marketing literature is the distinction between goods and services. Services are in this literature generally distinguished by the greater involvement of customers in the production process, greater difficulties in maintaining quality control standards, the absence of inventories, the relative importance of the time factor, and the structure of the distribution channels (Lovelock, 1984, p. 4).

As shown in Figure 4:1, the distinction between goods and services is a gradual one, with some goods having strong service aspects and some services having a lot of "goods" characteristics. Figure 4:1 also shows how, in services, the production and delivery processes are generally more integrated than in the case of manufacturing or distribution of physical goods. Just as there are many kinds of goods, there are also many kinds of services, with the distinction between "experience" and "credence" being the most important difference (Zeithaml, 1981). While service industries may in themselves be quite heterogeneous (ranging from restaurant meals to medical diagnosis), they do exhibit a number of common characteristics about which it is useful to generalize (Berry, 1980). Rather than being products that can be "searched" and found, services exist when and where they are experienced and believed to exist.

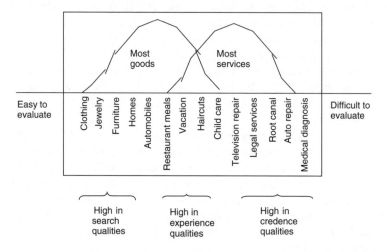

Figure 4:1 Differences in evaluating various types of products and services (Zeithaml, 1981)

Below, we make an attempt to break new ground by first reviewing and then translating the general literature on services marketing to the marketing practices of law firms. As originally identified by Berry, the salient characteristics are that, in contrast to physical goods, services are (Berry, 1980):

1. More intangible than tangible.
2. Produced and consumed simultaneously.
3. Less standardized and less uniform.

We will focus on how these peculiar characteristics of intangibility, inseparability, and variability shape the marketing of business law services.

More intangible than tangible

To understand the challenges of intangibility, a review of physical-goods marketing provides a counterpoint and perspective. To attract the attention of consumers, marketers of physical goods approach customers by enhancing the core physical object through abstract associations. Visual, verbal and aural associations with authenticity and youth surround the bottle and contents of Coca-Cola, for example. Customers make mental connections between a tangible product in reality and abstract images that it serves to trigger. In contrast, when it comes to evidence of the physical core, the marketing of services is turned 180 degrees. Clients make mental connections between a product that is already intangible and images that this and other service characteristics trigger.

Service marketers are often challenged by the fact that the product is not fully tangible at the core. Lack of tangibility becomes the starting point, rather than the goal, as in the marketing of physical goods. The marketers of most services enhance and differentiate "reality" of a service through creation, production and manipulation of physical and tangible cues. The focus is on things that the consumer or client can comprehend with his or her five senses (Shostack, 1977). Successful restaurant marketers often have to work hard at making services "real". At McDonald's restaurants, for example, the main *service* element – that is, fast-food preparation – is tangibly distinguished from other similar services by uniformity of environment, color, style of graphics, consistency of delivery (young employees), and the ubiquitous golden arches. In turn, the tangible food *product* is associated with intangible properties such as "nutritious" ("two all beef patties" etc.), "fun" (Ronald McDonald), and "helpful" ("we do it all for you", "you deserve a break today"). In other words, a McDonald's meal becomes a hybrid between a physical hamburger and other physical food products and a series of services that make and deliver the meal for consumption either on site or take-away. As a result of this design of the sense-making experience of the consumer on the part of the services marketer, McDonald's has become a case example in the services marketing literature of how services are abstract to begin with, and require concrete evidence that cue their quality (Shostack, 1977). This implies that a services firm's products and outlets need to display both abstractions and evidence in about equal proportions. In fact, as a result of the power of display in many service industries, what is and what is not a tangible service element is not always clear.

Several techniques of stressing physical cues can be observed in the ways Finnish law firms market to business clients. In recent decades, the signaling of distinction with *physical and graphical cues* in the form of accreditation, letterheads, newsletters, person-based evidence, and brands has spread. It has long been widely recognized that any law firm's or lawyer's membership in the Finnish Bar Association and carrying the credentials *"AA"* (*asianajaja*) is "descriptive of competence and a brand." The visibility of the Bar Association's logo can be enhanced "in line with the modern principles of design management, by encouraging its use in the law firm's letterheads, web pages, and other graphic design" (Sipilä, 2000, p. 29).

Until the 1980s, it was customary that a client would never argue about price with a law firm carrying the *"AA"* seal of accreditation on its letterhead. Then, in the 1980s, managers in Finnish corporations internationalized to a point where they learned that their peers in London, England, for example, sometimes negotiated prices with the law firms, or even changed law-service suppliers, in order to raise the price-quality ratio they were getting. In response to the potential threat of price competition diffusing into the Finnish market, top Finnish law firms began to differentiate themselves from rival law firms in Finland and elsewhere. They began to use letterheads that carried the names of all of the lawyers in the firm, in order of seniority, in the top left-hand corner of the first page. This practice, openly imitating the practices of leading British and American law firms, has since spread widely in the top and second-tier Finnish law firms.

The services marketing literature generally suggests that an important marketing vehicle is the client's ability to *connect to real people* who represent the service. Depending upon what kind of service "reality" a service marketer wishes to create, the human representation of any service can be encouraged to display conformity or nonconformity (Shostack, 1977). Relational aspects, in particular those between individuals, have also long been central aspects of business relations involving management advisory services. While professionals in the "creative" departments of advertising agencies may make a point of not wearing a tie when wearing a suit (often, they do not wear suits at all), lawyers adhere to the other extreme.

Lawyers build an "appropriate" legal case by attracting the client's awareness and developing that awareness into interest about the further particulars of the service entity. Lawyers make a conspicuous point of wearing a suit and tie, both of conservative style. In fact, in most countries of the world, lawyers are known for their pinstripes and vests (see, for example, Shostack, 1977). The goal of such vestitures is to signal credibility and help or guide the client to make decisions and take actions in terms of purchasing their services. The involvement of a real person of apparently high credibility – in the contact, presentation, negotiation and production processes related to the sale and delivery of the service entity – is thus an important part of services in business law firms.

In addition to stressing physical cues and presence, other options of services marketing by which to reduce intangibility generally include such strategies as encouraging personnel to communicate with customers, using personal sources of information, stimulating word-of-mouth communication, and creating a strong corporate image (Kurtz and Clow, 1993, pp. 10-14). One lawyer in Finland is known by her friends for habitually inviting them, and their friends, to social events such as the theater. She makes a point of saying that "anybody can come, and why don't you also ask that friend of yours to come, too. Her husband works for … doesn't he?" This type of discourse enables her to weave her way into a hub of a social network where she stimulates word-of-mouth, as well as creates an image of being more interested in helping out her friends than she is in increasing the revenue stream of the law firm in which she works. Even when she had just had a baby, she was in a hurry to get back to work because "friends depend on her to solve their legal problems." The importance of personal relationships with clients is precisely the reason why top legal firms in Finland have traditionally carried the names of their partners. As the "rainmaker" partner of another law firm revealed about creating opportunities for transforming social occasions into arenas for sourcing in "legal cases" and, in turn, business for his firm: "I make presentations at various clients and on other occasions. After almost every one of these presentations, somebody approaches me to talk about a [legal] case, bringing a client to me. It is amazing to me how it works."

To leverage the importance of relational aspects with clients, the names of the top law firms in Finland (e.g. *Roschier Holmberg*; *Peltonen, Ruokonen and Itäinen*; *Hannes Snellman, Dittmar and Indrenius*; and *Borenius and Kemppinen*) have long carried the names of their partners. The brands in turn have, in part, become so strong as to become decoupled from the names of the partners in the logotype of the firm's documents.

The top law firms are no longer family-owned firms with "one man and a law book."[1] Professionalism has in most cases taken over, with partnership no longer being hereditary. Some top law firms in Finland

---

[1] There have also been many new firms with partners whose names derive from less prestigious families or, in any case, family names that have less of a distinctive clang to them than is the case of many established firms. This has to do with issues of identity and language, as many of the rising top law firms have come from the Finnish-speaking majority of the populace, while the older law firms tended to represent the Swedish-speaking minority.

that are relative newcomers have detached themselves from the tradition of having the family names of partners represented in the name of the law firm. This is especially the case for firms established from about 1990 and the years after with brand names as *Fennica, Forum Partners* and *Astrea*. The brands of these firms have had no direct risk of suffering, if a partner has left for whatever reason.

In addition to the persistence of physical cues and presence, sediments and new forms of relational aspects, and symbolic cues such as the new trend of depersonalized branding, the service outlet or office is clearly an important source of signals to the prospective client who might otherwise be unable to determine the quality of the intangible product s/he was to purchase. Any service outlet is sensitive to specific characteristics of the local surrounding area, such as the presence or absence of other service outlets that cater to the same clientele in a complementary manner. The historical, current and future volume of demand, and prestige of prospective clients; complementary service providers; and competitors in the city's service-trading area bring the location social cohesion and prestige. Service managers across industries weigh all the criteria with respect to the type of operation they plan to operate. Their criteria for determining location of their service outlet typically include: Can the area serve as a source of supply of employees? Does the client base work nearby? Is the population density of the area sufficient? (Corman et al., 2005, pp. 178-180).

The optimal environment for the delivery of a service to a client is believed in the marketing discipline to generally depend on the typical emotional landscape of the customer or client. Experience-type services of the entertainment variety, such as cinema, or vacations that involve adventures such as rafting, will want to operate at the exciting end of the emotional landscape. In experience-based services, there will be all kinds of merchandising and special effects intended to appeal to all the senses. In contrast to cinema or adventure, law firms operate in a gloomy sector of the emotional matrix. Many clients may exhibit anxiety and be hesitant about going to a lawyer; they go only as a last resort after all other means of negotiating a settlement have been exhausted. Within this context, lawyers will want to provide a "servicescape" that lifts clients out of their state of stress. The environment should strive to make the experience pleasant and comforting. It must reduce the feelings of gloom and hopelessness (Shostack, 1992, pp. 210-211; Bitner, 1992).

Within this context, the specific office building in which the office is situated is important. Concerns such as office rental costs are, in turn, less important for top law firms. These firms are not discount stores but sell exclusive services to a selected audience (Bitner, 1992). Besides the office and its milieu, the choice of which city to open in – and which country, upon internationalization – becomes important.

In summary, similarly to other providers of services, lawyers face a challenge in the intangibility of their offering. Several techniques, by which this challenge could be overcome, were identified above, including the use of physical cues, the establishment of interpersonal connections, branding, and the choice of physical location.

Simultaneous production and consumption

A second characteristic of services is that of their simultaneous production and consumption. This means that the service exists only during the time when it is rendered to the customer or client. "Inseparability" refers to the simultaneous production and consumption of a service. A service will "perish" if not consumed on the spot since it cannot be stored or kept in the form of inventories. Routine jobs that sometimes threaten to pile up cannot be put off in wait of slow periods. For this reason, marketers in many professional service industries have developed techniques to cope with fluctuating demand.

Service quality is always a process rather than an outcome, that is, quality management becomes a series of interim struggles towards a goal that is pursued constantly, equally as much when profits are up as when times are bad. Quality is "everyone's job": everyone has customers, either external or internal customers. Responsibility for producing quality and for quality control cannot be delegated to one single person or, for example, a staff office. This also means that quality is intertwined with leadership and communication. Quality benefits from a corporate culture that emphasizes integrity and treating both customers and employees with respect, dignity, and courtesy (Shostack, 1981, pp. 221-229). These are generic guidelines for delivering excellent service that ought to be useful for any service firm.

Techniques for dealing with the challenges of simultaneous production and consumption include building a quality image and blueprinting. According to Berry (1988), the first technique for dealing with simultaneous production and consumption is building a quality image:

Quality is keeping the service promise. More than anything else customers seem to expect service providers to do what they have promised to do. If promises are not kept, or if some critical part of

> *the bundle of promises given is not kept, quality deteriorates.*
> *(Berry, 1988; quoted in Grönroos, 1990, p. 262)*

Because quality lies in the eyes of the demanding client, top law firms have discouraged any appearance of inconsistent behavior. The entity's "true reality" has been orchestrated to take place experientially in a way that has included the client, rather than in engineering terms that would have excluded the client (cf. Shostack, 1992, p. 42; Pine and Gilmore, 1998).

Within this context, service quality is a "design issue", that is, the concept of service quality can be designated at the front end before the service delivery's "details, petty in comparison to the intellectual insight," are developed. Sometimes this is a façade maintained for the sake of making the clients feel important. As one partner in a corporate law firm said, "I always have to say to the client: 'No problem, we can do it.' And then I have to make sure that we keep that promise, no matter how difficult this is, in reality."

The "one man and a law book" tradition in Finland is still vibrant. Top lawyers maintain an appearance or image of aloofness whereby they are gentleman experts, akin to university-based medical diagnosticians who have a "practice" for intellectually stimulating cases.

Blueprinting schemes will differ across service industries, but they will also always share some important commonalties. Blueprinting is the process of diagramming the service operation for purposes of signing up the support staff that will provide support for experienced expert lawyers who can then act as rainmakers. Blueprinting the service operations for quality service and efficient support allows firms to locate and clear "capacity bottlenecks" (Shostack, 1992, p. 140).

In a service process, capacity bottlenecks are points in the operations that restrict the maximum output of a service operation. If not handled efficiently, these bottlenecks will tie up the time of the senior staff, which represents a most valuable resource for the law firm. Thus, airlines, for example, have worked hard to develop techniques by which to board planes quickly and efficiently. Another example is Disney World in Florida, which is famous for how it has organized lining up so that visitors to the theme park do not grow restless in the slow-moving lines. The guests never stand in line for very long in the same place, because the lines keep on moving so that there is an illusion of progress.

How does building blueprints apply to top law firms? For one thing, law firms, in Finland at least, have for more than a decade been catching up to other service industries at a rapid pace. In this respect, they can in fact be said to blueprint in terms of both productivity and image. Many top business law firms have not accepted client relationships below a minimum monetary or strategic threshold value. At the same time, partners in the law firm have tacitly recognized and shared a view that the threshold is not to be interpreted rigidly. The partners may make it a point of sticking to a rule of "corporate clients only, please", but have seldom hesitated to take on individual clients when these individuals have been affluent owners of family firms. The partners have not communicated this option of flexibility in the interpretation of the threshold rule to their assistant lawyers, receptionists, or other support staff. Neither would the traditions of the Civil Code have encouraged such communication. Delegating too much discretion to employees would have complicated control of the consistency of actions throughout the organizational levels of the law firm and of the meeting of client expectations in terms of quality experiences and credence. Thus, the threshold rule of control is a case in point of a blueprint somewhere between a rigid standard to dictate and a tacit rule to guide customization of service offerings within the law firm.

One advantage of blueprints is that they help to renegotiate professional boundaries. Another is that they help to sign up the support service staff with appropriate levels of skills and competences (cf. D'Aunno et al., 2000).

Less standardized and less uniform

A third characteristic of services, as opposed to goods, is that they are less standardized and less uniform. Variability is primarily caused by the human element, although machines may also malfunction causing a substandard service delivery. Clients bring to the service process a variability of knowledge and experiences that cannot but affect operations. High variability is always a potential threat of unwanted or random levels of service quality that customers may experience when they patronize a service provider. Techniques for creating and sustaining flexibility by overcoming these barriers include design of strategy and procedures, as well as controlled media relations.

Generally, organizational barriers to marketing and growth include that good service and a sound service culture can effectively be destroyed by an "organizational structure inherited from yesterday's society" (Shostack, 1981, p. 273). The norms of modern highly advanced industries and societies include a clear design strategy that enables one to "design the company's responses to failure so they will exceed customer expectations" (Davidow, 1989, p. 155). Effective design for service calls for accommodating customer behavior, even when customers behave in quirky, unpredictable ways.

Designing products and service systems to maximize customer value goes against the grain of designers in most professions (Davidow, 1989, p. 155). This problem was very much true also for the one-man-and-a-law-book tradition in the legal profession, whose members have generally internalized the social codes of conduct of their offices of employment even better than most other professions (cf. Abbott, 1988). Recently, design strategies in this profession have nonetheless begun to change. One reason is that a clear design strategy constitutes a "great simplifier of many challenges for designers in any service industry" (Davidow, 1989, p. 153).

The benefits of a clear service strategy include that it helps to elicit a clear understanding within the organization of how the core product or service can break down. This makes it possible to pay special attention to the ways in which customers may cause unexpected failures. Such attention serves to create a service culture "where giving good services to internal as well as ultimate external customers is considered a natural way of life and one of the most important norms by everyone" (Grönroos, 1990, pp. 243-4).

Since the 1980s, the design of structures and processes in top Finnish law firms has been increasingly influenced by the example set by British and US law firms. The law firms have become a model to imitate in terms of larger size of the firm, economies of scale and experience, client relationships, and automation. Consequently, Finnish law firms' operations have come to include a built-in tension between Anglo-American models and the civil law tradition.

Finnish top business law firms have traditionally tackled the challenge of the conflicting demands of these legal traditions, in terms of the lacking degree of standardization and uniformity of business law services, by controlling the media presentation of these services. In fact, this has been supported by the guideline coming from generic services marketing literature that one ought always to remember that effective representation of complex intangibles is a function of establishing non-abstract manifestations of these intangibles, rather than of raising the levels of abstraction and complexity.

At first glance, there would appear to be reason to believe that law firms would thus remain conservative in terms of advertising, as well as in terms of increasing media exposure of legal services in general. However, closer study of the issue reveals that this principle of services marketing has in fact recently begun to erode in business law, as evidenced, for example, by 1997 modifications in the rules for advertising and marketing by the Finnish Bar Association. The reasons for the change in rules may, again, be traced to the potential challenge coming from international competition.

Discussion and conclusion

Business law services have traditionally been dependent on personalized exchange, in spite of, or because of, their backing by a highly articulated and well-protected profession. In this chapter, the selling practices of top law firms in Finland have been examined and discussed in light of the services marketing literature. This investigation has indicated that a new and more sophisticated set of institutional rules of the game by which legal services may be marketed has started to emerge. Top law firms in Finland have quite systematically established non-abstract manifestations of legal services to provide sensibility and credibility to their services. These manifestations have included certification, letterheads, and brands.

Noteworthy in this context is that even members of a "pure" or strong profession, such as those of the legal profession (cf. Abbott, 1988; Maister, 1993), which can have traditions of built-in institutional constraints on marketing practices, can ultimately be seen to act as suave marketers of their services. Neither differences across legal codes nor the rules of the local Bar Association have hindered lawyers from supplying various marketing cues to their clients by which they can influence client search processes for services, client experiences of good service, or client perceptions that the lawyers represent professional credence.

Marketing practices have been more highly developed in common law countries of past or current British influence than in civil law countries, and there would appear to be development in that direction also in a civil law country such as Finland. The local legal discourse has traditionally not favored active marketing by members of the Finnish legal profession. Nonetheless, although the application of the services marketing literature has in practice been constrained by the differences between the common law and civil law traditions, the generic principles of services marketing appear to function as a robust "grammar" for understanding how top law firms sell their services.

To recap, the practices of selling business law services incorporate elements from both contingencies of personalized marketing of professional business services and those of depersonalized marketing. Several propositions for further research may be formulated against this background. Firstly, it would appear that the selling of legal services has been depersonalized where the professional system and domain of service delivery exhibit signs of stability, while personalized marketing exchange has persisted as the norm where there remains flux. Secondly, changes in the institutional rules of the game about marketing have not been discrete events, but incremental and contingent processes. Finally, marketing of professional business services has appeared as a robust grammar for a rich language, with many possibilities for more or less open-ended development of both the language and the underlying grammar itself.

With these propositions about a robust grammar underlying the selling of business law services, this chapter has perhaps opened up new directions in how and why providers of professional business services carry out what can be called "marketing" or "selling" activities. Further research ought to elaborate and expand on how law firms signal client experience and professional credence. It ought to explore the extent to which the kind of grammar of services marketing identified in this chapter may be valid in the marketing of professional business services more generally. Studies based on interprofessional, international and intertemporal comparative research designs would serve to contextualize the findings of this inquiry, based on a single unique context. In these and other ways, further research ought to reveal the full potential of the marketing of professional business services, as well as specify the ultimate limits of such activities, given that these will always be embedded in systems of professions and their particular local and global contexts.

When the purchase of management advisory services is studied in more detail, the potential insight to bear in mind from this chapter may be that the so-called "pure" or strong professions, such as the legal profession, may be characterized not only by criteria such as authorization by the collective system of their profession, but also by their peculiar emphasis on their marketing activities. If representatives of the legal profession are given credence or trust not only for belonging to a professional system in general, but also for the way they market their services, what implications does this have for the study of other professions that provide advisory services to client managers?

CHAPTER 5

Properties of Expertise

Constructing the product and need for
corporate finance services

KARIN SVEDBERG NILSSON AND
KARIN WINROTH

Complex services are no off-the-shelf products. The characteristics of these services and the needs they fulfill tend to be uncertain and ambiguous. They are subject to an ongoing negotiation primarily between seller and buyer, but secondarily also between "others" who provide the context for sellers and buyers.

The interaction between buyer and supplier in determining the character and need for a product or service has been discussed, for example, in the relationship marketing literature, as illustrated by Normann's (2000) "prosumer" concept. In this chapter, we take a more explicit constructivist perspective. We aim to describe and analyze how properties are ascribed to the product of corporate finance services including the construction of the needs it fulfills.

The empirical part of the chapter is based on an interview study with providers of corporate finance services. It is part of a larger project examining the organization and practices of Swedish investment banking (see e.g. Winroth, 2002). We begin the case discussion with a description of how the product of corporate finance services comes into being. We then proceed to our first analysis, where we find extravagance and necessity to be two important features of corporate finance services. In the section that follows, we return to the issue of selling corporate finance services and give a more detailed account of the sales process. This section is followed by an analysis of the sales approach being utilized in the case of the investment bankers.

Constructing product properties

There exists a diverse set of perspectives that can be defined as more or less constructivist (e.g. Berger and Luckmann, 1966; Gergen, 1991; Knorr-Cetina, 1994). One common denominator among different constructivist perspectives, however, is the idea that many of the things we consider natural and real, such as business firms, markets, the state, unemployment or schools, are social accomplishments. They are the results of processes of social construction where we, and people before us, have done similar things in a similar way over an extended period of time – an idea usually attributed to Berger and Luckmann (1966). For example, over time, people have not only learned what a school is, that it includes things like teachers, pupils, classrooms and learning, they have also come to take the meaning of "school" for granted. This means that in everyday life there is no need to ponder what a school might be in order to be able to deal with it as a parent, pupil or teacher. We already know. As Berger and Luckmann emphasize, social reality is perceived as objective reality. It is taken for granted.

The "taken-for-grantedness" of social reality might lead one to believe that it is static. And, according to Berger and Luckmann, things considered to be real do not usually change dramatically or very quickly. But one also needs to keep in mind that one important aspect of the process of construction is that it is ongoing. Reality has not been constructed once and for all. It is dependent on the activities of people. If the activities of people change, social reality will change too. That is, although we tend to regard social constructs, such as markets, as self-evident and objective, they are social accomplishments. They will whither away or be reconstructed in alternative ways unless we keep on referring to them, treating them, and acting in accordance with them as markets.

Sellers, buyers and products

Placing this thinking in the context of selling and purchasing, makes it evident that what a specific product is and what needs it satisfies may not be as self-evident as one might think. Rather, people are expected to be involved in shaping their attributes or properties. The constructed character of products is apparent, e.g. in the case of cars. For most people, a car is not just a car, although, of course, it is common for cars to be constructed primarily as a means of transportation. But a car may well be constructed as an expensive toy and as a means to show affluence, or, alternatively, as a fuel-thirsty threat to the environment. Properties of products such as cars are thus not simply something that these products have. Specific properties are attributed to specific products. What areas of usage the car primarily is for – transportation, showing off or pollution – is also a matter of construction, as are its price-worthiness, image, brand and so on.

In a basic sense, this is, of course, a topic covered in any marketing textbook worth its salt. It is standard marketing knowledge that there is a difference between the concrete attributes of a product and the benefits a particular consumer will expect and experience from that product and those attributes. The present perspective does not necessarily contradict this knowledge. Rather, it complements it by looking into some implications of the understanding of products as being more or less constructed, rather than purely "objective", entities. Thus, what we would like to draw particular attention to here is two features of the process of construction involved in ascribing properties to products. Firstly, the buyer cannot single-handedly decide for himself what he has bought. But neither can the seller decide for herself what she has sold. They do it together. The construction of the product is a joint effort (Callon et al, 2002). The sellers, or providers, of products are often central actors in processes of product construction, especially so in the early stages of the process. That sellers are important early on can have several reasons. For one, sellers are often involved before buyers as they advertise the existence of products to potential customers and thereby pre-construct the kinds of needs the product is meant to fulfill. This is not to say that customers are not important, on the contrary. Customers do participate in constructing the products and services they buy, although they may not be involved as early on as sellers. Callon et al (2002) also draw attention to a third type of actor that may affect the process of construction – external audiences. Products are often constructed in settings where they are visible to external audiences, such as the media, which may lead to the inclusion, or exclusion, of particular product properties.

The second feature of the process of construction involved in ascribing properties to products that we would like to stress is that it is just that – a process. This second feature implies that one cannot simply state beforehand what the properties of e.g. a car are even when it is sold to a very specific customer segment. These properties and the needs they fulfill for this particular segment may be equally difficult to establish after the fact as well. Consequently, what really needs to be analyzed is the process of need and product construction whilst it is going on, making the analysis of the process of selling/buying the product in question of particular importance. Hence the focus on the selling of corporate finance services in this chapter.

Before turning to our main topic, two main categories of product properties also need to be outlined. First, there are functional properties and their consequences, as in the car being a means for transportation but also a cause of pollution. Second, there are what can be denoted "image properties". That is, properties of a symbolic character, like status symbols or identification with a certain group. These properties can be interpreted in various ways by different audiences to an even larger extent than the functional ones.

Constructing expert services

All kinds of products can be regarded as being constructed, but it is even more evident in the case of services, and in the service economy, than in the case of material goods. According to Callon et al (2002), one reason this is so, is that services tend to involve a greater degree of reflexivity. To know, or at least to take for granted that one knows, what a product such as a car is, is easier than to be sure what qualities the service of e.g. top management consulting involves.

Although a division between goods and services can be criticized as being too simplistic a distinction to make, services tend to be defined as intangible and difficult to identify before they have been bought (Grönroos, 1990). Furthermore, expert services may be conceived as a special form. When considering expert consultation as a socially constructed product/service, one needs to look into what "expert" stands for in this setting. First, expert services are a type of service that is demanded under specific circumstances. In day-to-day routines, the knowledge and advice of external experts is not necessary. It is rather in critical matters, and under changing or otherwise extraordinary circumstances, that the demand for expert services arises. Consequently, expert services are wanted in situations that customers cannot handle all by themselves. Second, expert products or services are hard to evaluate for outsiders. Fully judging the content and value of proposed analyses, advice, and recommendations is not possible. The signs and symbols of expertise expressed by service providers therefore come into focus. The customer becomes bound to trust her knowledge about how experts behave, their manners, logic of reasoning and the like. Of course, this is not to say that expert services cannot also come to contain more tangible elements, like a contract, that are closer to the product end of the product-service continuum. What we would like to draw attention to here is that the customer's situation is complicated by the fact that she cannot fully evaluate the advice of the experts. When discussing expert services, the signs of expertise intertwined with this service become crucial for understanding the relationship between buyer and provider of expert services.

Lately, there has been an increased interest in using a constructivist perspective in the study of markets (e.g. Fligstein and Mara-Drita, 1996; Knorr-Cetina and Bruegger, 2000; Velthuis, 2003; Helgesson et al. 2004). This chapter in particular follows the tradition of taking a particular interest in the cultural construction of products (e.g. Kopytoff, 1986; Callon et al. 2002; Winroth, 2004). To recapitulate, one important implication of a constructivist perspective for studies of sales and purchasing is that in order to understand what a specific product, such as corporate finance services, is, and what needs it fulfills, one needs to look into the sales process. However, in order to understand the sales process, one also needs to look into what kind of product is being sold and how this product is linked to the needs of the buyer. This is what we will do in the next section.

Corporate finance services

An obvious trend in today's economy is the increased amount of expertise being bought by large corporations. The expanding industry of financial advice is an apparent example of this trend. Within this industry, the investment banks play an important role in carrying through the transactions on the Stock Exchange and by supplying financial advice to managers as well as (the wealthier segments of) the general public.

The financial industry has evolved all over the world in the last decades, and this is also the case in Sweden. Earlier brokerage houses have developed their services to include corporate services advice, meaning that they have mirrored the large international investment banks, which are usually of American origin (see Eccles and Crane, 1988). Parallel to this change, the number of Swedish banks has increased considerably. Thus, the industry as a whole has evolved dramatically during the 1980s and onwards. One factor that has made this development possible is increased interest in the Stock Exchange. Financing corporations by emissions has become a more common solution for financing enterprises today, and investing in the Stock Exchange has grown to become a more general interest among Swedish citizens.

This chapter focuses on one of the most prominent expert groups of the investment banks, the "bankers", who offer top managers advice on financial restructuring of corporations and have become important consultants in the Swedish as well as the international economy. We focus on the bankers because we find them an intriguing example of how the sales process among consultants has developed. The bankers are trendsetters for how selling practices are to be performed in the economy today and, in Scandinavia, other consultants follow in their steps, adopting their terminology and manners. Before the reader is introduced to the service practices the bankers offer, the products that they supply the top managers with will be presented.

Offering financial expertise

According to bankers, the insights of top managers regarding the need for professional advice in strategic financial matters have increased considerably during recent decades. It is legitimate to consult experts in the financial area nowadays, and has even become considered a necessity when it comes to crucial strategic decisions. As a consequence, the market for financial services was one of the fastest growing industries during the 1990s. In parallel with this development, the top managers of corporations have drawn increasing attention to exploiting the possibilities of the financial market. According to bankers, ten years ago, new ventures were often financed by capital offered by banks. Nowadays, however, managers have gained better insight regarding the usually favorable terms of financing investments by emissions in the market. As the supply of capital has grown over the last decade, the market, as a financial opportunity has become even more attractive.

According to bankers, top managers in general have gained better knowledge when it comes to financial strategy concerns. There is a more general awareness of the considerable amount of capital now floating within the system. This in turn has supported the interest in investments, making professional investors important actors. Opportunities for profitable investments are continually evaluated and investment portfolios more carefully estimated. Thus, if a firm is perceived as an interesting prospect for the future, professional advisors will analyze the offer and later inform prospective investors about the proposal. That the financial industry as a whole has become more sophisticated could be one explanation as to why the services of financial experts, and especially bankers, have become in great demand.

The service the bankers offer involves strategic financial advice for top managers. There are some strategic matters in which bankers are almost always involved. For instance, this tends to be the case when discussing mergers or acquisitions. The bankers specialize in various industries and therefore become competent in judging the various major competing firms in an industry. With this background knowledge, they can advise clients to offer mergers or make an acquisition of a competing firm, all in an aim to create a preferable market situation or more profitable financial structure for a corporation.

> *You try to cultivate customer relations, we call it "pitching", a form of marketing. What you actually do, is try to come up with interesting new ideas for them. This could involve an acquisition or selling parts of a company. Or ideas for making adjustments in liabilities, for example, repurchasing shares. If they are in need of capital, it could involve issuing new shares or, in other cases, private placement. Also the splitting of a firm can come into question, which could actually be seen as a trend now - to focus on the main essence of the business. (Banker)*

One of the more prominent services offered by the bankers, is the introduction of firms on the Stock Exchange. This means introducing the firm as an investment product, making it possible to invest in the firm on the public market. To be allowed this introduction, certain conditions concerning the financial situation of corporations have to be fulfilled, as well as matters of stability. Later, new emissions could also provide capital for acquisitions or other investments. In both cases, the bankers become important co-operators for realizing the intended financial solutions.

Making introductions or new emissions are rare activities, and the timing and packaging of these solutions are described as being of vital importance for the possible success of the offer. Many kinds of services have become more specialized in the financial industry, and therefore also expectations for all financial documents have increased. This is the case, for example, for the listing prospectus of a firm on the Exchange.

> *Nowadays the expectations on offers are considerable. Expectations about how they are communicated, presented, the pace of the services – there has been an unbelievable professionalization of everyone involved. Just look at what a listing prospectus looked like in the 70s! It has made all the difference in the world! (Banker)*

Although the Exchange Commission prescribes what information is to be presented in a listing prospectus, consequently making the prospectuses rather uniform, it is seen as crucial to have high-status advisors involved in producing these documents. As introductions or new emissions are infrequent activities in a firm, the financial analysis and involvement of bankers becomes something of a guarantee for high quality. The bankers are experts in financial analysis and the estimation of value, and are therefore trusted in their judgment and in their handling of the process. High-status investment banks convey an image of a high-status offer. There is usually more than one investment bank involved in an introduction at the Exchange. When introducing firms of international interest, there is generally at least one international investment bank and one Scandinavian bank involved in the procedure. In addition, the services of other investment banks may be requested for a "second opinion" (a second review of the data and analysis made by yet another firm). As the bankers' credibility is important for the judgment of the text and numbers by prospective investors, the investment banks are consequently presented with high visibility on the prospectus – on the front cover.

The vital task for the bankers is to present a product for the market that has the power of attraction – a product that investors will be willing to risk their capital for. The firm has to be perceived as a promising investment, more seductive and exciting than other offers at hand. Still, it also has to be trustworthy, not too risky, to suit prospective investors.

Finally, a few words on the structure of authority among bankers. The senior banker (also referred to as the "director") is the person primarily involved in the "pitching" of clients. More about this process will be presented later in the chapter. For support the director has three categories of subordinates. Newcomers start off as "analysts". Then, if successful, they advance to become "associates", and later "associate directors", before finally gaining the full status of "director". The three subcategories support the directors with the more detailed financial analyses of corporations and industries. They prepare the material to be presented to clients or for documents, which is later approved by the director. Although this work is a prerequisite that makes the pitch possible, this chapter will focus on the directors' task, as it is primarily directors who perform the selling process.

A product with the properties of extravagance and necessity

How, then, can the products that the bankers offer be characterized? What are the specifics of this offering? One aspect, related to all expert services is that their advice is needed only in complex situations. The experts are considered as having knowledge that the top managers are perceived to lack. As the cases also involve a considerable amount of analysis, every product sold has to be specifically tailored for the case at hand. Though the ideas behind the products are rather similar, the timing and the corporations involved are crucial choices, and therefore each case requires in-depth scrutiny.

The cases are complex products and the purchase of them is rather infrequent and involves high risks. The infrequency and risks involved in buying the services mean that they are bought by the top managers themselves, and not through any special department within the company. As the buying procedure is rare, there is no standard procedure for assessing the offerings made by the bankers. The purchasing of financial products must therefore be seen as buying an item not easily evaluated. This also makes the branding of the products important. A bank of good repute becomes the guarantee that the product delivered will be of the quality promised. The "signs" of expertise, meaning the expected manners of the bankers, the established practice when interacting with clients, the exclusive suits worn, an address in the more prominent financial district, etc, all contribute to the assurance of a competent advisor. The complexity of the product makes this the only security that the top managers will be granted.

As with many expert services, the risk involved in a case is high. To handle this risk, experts are needed. The financial changes that are involved in the products are considerable and are, of course, meant to result in a financial surplus. High-risk products involve potentially high benefits, which is the ultimate goal for the deals. As the scenarios tend to be complex, the future is difficult to foresee. However, as long as the right experts are involved, the financial restructuring is supposed to yield considerable benefit. As in all branded offerings, however, a special name also commands a special price. The price of these products is very high, even from the perspective of large corporations. The uniqueness, the complexity, the branded product and the high price give the financial products sold by bankers a distinguished mark of extravagance, giving the buyer status and membership in an exclusive category of firms.

In the language of marketing theory, the product of the bankers could be described as a "specialty good" (Brassington and Pettitt, 2000). This refers to a category of products that are usually presented as luxuries. From the perspective of the client, these goods are expensive, high-risk purchases, aimed at satisfying a need of high priority. It is usually a product that is seldom bought because of its exclusiveness, but as for all real luxuries, the price tag is high. As buying decisions concerning specialty goods are rare, the customer is often highly involved in the process, both psychologically and emotionally. It is supposed to be a rational decision, but as branding becomes of high importance, the image of the producer may be just as important as what the item bought actually brings. Furthermore, specialty goods tend to be sold in high-end boutiques.

Our case thus illustrates that characteristics of a specialty good are expressed in the services of the bankers. However, there is one characteristic of the bankers' services that is usually not related to specialty goods – nowadays, their services are seen as a necessity when implementing large financial restructurings in corporations. It is hardly legitimate today to make an IPO or large merger without having consulted the large investment banks. Even though their advice is far from always profitable, and their services expensive, the legitimacy they bring to their customers and cases is hard to substitute today. Thus, there seems to be no other way of handling a large financial restructuring, than by consulting these selected advisors. Consequently, the products that they sell can be seen as both extravagant and necessary. However, rather than being contradictory properties, they support and enforce one another. Extravagance, as a symbol of success (and by assumption expertise, reliability and quality), is an important part of what is bought, which is the provision of legitimacy. As uncertainty rises with the increasing level of activity of financial advisors, suggesting increasingly complicated deals, the need for legitimacy provided by extravagance increases further, thus creating a situation in which extravagance becomes a necessity.

The case continued

For bankers, the process of selling is highly integrated in the process of producing a service. As with many professionals, the service is not produced until someone is willing to buy it. However, the bankers are more involved in the preparatory work for a production than is usually the case for other consultants, as for instance lawyers or auditors. This is because lawyers and auditors are usually contacted for a specific task or problem. The bankers, however, make the contacts themselves and are also the ones who suggest a solution to what they consider a possible inefficiency. Consequently, the bankers not only supply the solution, but they also define or suggest the "problem" the top managers might have. They are thus strongly and directly involved in the construction of the need for their services. This means that the bankers must know as much about the financial state of the firm as the top managers controlling it, and thereto more than the managers know about the financial state of the industry and the competitors. This knowledge is acquired in close contact with top managers of the Swedish economy and with the support of financial analyses carried out by the director's subordinates.

"Pitching" clients – The practice of offering financial advice

The practice of the Scandinavian bankers has developed considerably over the past decades. Parallel to the changes in the financial industry as a whole, also the service provided in corporate finance is described as having become professionalized. The relationships between buyer and seller have followed evolutionary patterns, according to bankers, meaning that as the seller has become more specialized so has the buyer, and vice versa. In this development, clearer expertise roles and career patterns have evolved among the bankers. A source of inspiration for this development has been American international investment banks. The appearance of these banks on the Scandinavian market in the 1990s forced Swedish bankers to adjust to international practices, and also served the business by supplying a model to imitate. As mentioned earlier, to be able to perform as a director takes considerable competence in the economy as a whole, in the specific industry of the client, and having the ability to "read" and draw conclusions from economic analyses. A prerequisite for making a call to a client is to have an idea about a financial restructuring that the client might take an interest in. Hence, the director has to discuss and do the initial brainstorming with his (unfortunately seldom her) colleagues at the bank. When having decided on the idea to suggest, the next step is to contact the client. It is, however, necessary to already be involved in a network of the top managers to gain access to the valuable time in their schedule. As the managers will have a number of bankers calling them wanting to meet, earlier contacts with the top managers are seen as prerequisite for a meeting, though may not necessarily lead to closer contact even so. Thus, the directors invest a lot of time and effort in keeping in touch with their potential clients. They call them continually, inviting them to lunches, dinners, and meetings to discuss suggestions or ideas. In banker terms this courting is called "pitching".

This contact with prospective corporate clients is a very time-consuming activity that precedes the actual sale of a case. One rough estimate, confirmed by the directors, is that they spend around 90 percent of their work time in meetings with possible future clients. Only the last 10 percent of the work time is spent producing actual services.[1] However, the selling procedures also include constructing an idea of what to sell. The quotation below illustrates this.

> *It is often quite hectic, you run from one meeting to another. It's always tight, in terms of time running out, meetings, and different projects running in parallel, so you have to be effective. You can't go around thinking about things, you have to get them done right away. (Banker)*

'Pitching' involves a lot of phone conversations to discuss changes in the business and ideas for interesting financial solutions. If a suggestion is found exciting, it can be discussed in more detail over lunch. If a top manager's interest in the discussion continues, a more thorough presentation will take place. For this, the director will involve the analysts and associates, who contribute more detailed analyses and presentation material. At the actual meeting, the director will likely also be assisted by an associate director.

In cases where this meeting is perceived as important for the final acceptance of an idea (which could also be some meetings later), the bankers will invest considerable time in the analyses and the presentation. This then becomes a crucial time of the pitch, as it will decide whether the case, will actually be purchased or not. If the case is accepted, an intense period of work follows. The depth and breadth of the analysis are intensified, and a detailed scrutiny of the corporations involved is carried out. If the pitched case is not accepted, the bankers continue as before, staying in touch with the top managers and trying to convince them that they have interesting suggestions for the firm's future.

The bankers are well aware that good relations are the key to their business. To maintain access to the top managers, which enables them to arrange meetings, they need good relations. As many bankers will try to keep in touch with the managers, wanting their attention, there is a very close competition.

The bankers do not only help in financial matters. If cases are accepted, the bankers also assist their clients by acting as intermediaries. In deals involving other corporations, the bankers can be involved in the negotiations with the other party. The analyses of the deal might be of considerable interest also for the managers of the

---

[1] This estimation was made in the first years of the 21st century, before the bear market of the Exchange. Information from 2004 shows that also now a large part of the directors' time is spent on pitching, but the number mentioned now was about 50 percent of the time. This is in line with the fewer introductions at the Exchange and an overall more cautious strategy to change in the economy.

other corporations, informing them of the situation and the advantages of the deal at hand. The bankers might also handle administrative matters with institutions or legal instances, as they are familiar with their routines and practices. In some deals, additional consultants may be needed, for instance lawyers. Usually, the bankers handle these contacts as well, as they must cooperate closely with those consultants involved. Thus, the bankers perform the various roles of idea generator, negotiator and intermediary when serving their clients.

It is competence and specialist knowledge that counts. To be a good businessman, a really good negotiator and a respected advisor, that is what is most important – and also what is most rewarded. (Banker)

Selling conformed to producing

In the previous sections, we have shown that relationships in the business tend to extend across time. They last longer than the duration of a single transaction and can be defined as ongoing rather than one-off. One finding in the case of the bankers is thus that longevity is a main characteristic of the supplier-buyer relationship. Due to its longevity, the relationship between sellers and buyers could be defined as a kind of long-term, relationship-oriented approach to purchasing as discussed by Axelsson and Wynstra (2002). Even more so, as Axelsson and Wynstra (2002; see also chapter 3) argue that the relationship-oriented approach is appropriate when the focus is on qualitative aspects of products rather than on minimizing the price, a finding which is in line with our previous analysis of corporate finance services as a specialty good, where attributes such as brand name are more important to customers than a low price.

Courting-Engagement-Courting

A main finding concerning the relationship between sellers and buyers is that there was no direct link between longevity and intensity. That the intensity of interaction varied over time is a distinguishing characteristic of the relationships studied here. Though there is usually an ongoing relationship between bankers and clients, most of the time this relationship is characterized by a low level of intensity. Long phases of courting alternate with periodical phases of mutual engagement and intensified interaction. Then a new courting phase begins, which in turn can evolve into a phase of engagement, as shown schematically in Figure 5:1.

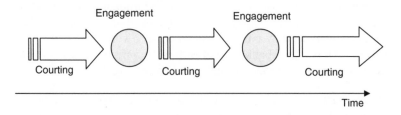

Figure 5:1 Alternating phases of varying intensity in relationship selling

Initially, in the courting phase, sellers are active, striving to catch the interest of current and prospective clients, but client involvement is relatively low. When the bankers have received an acceptance, "a contract", the hard work of the engagement phase begins. A number of junior bankers are engaged in the tasks of conducting more detailed economic analyses of the deal, and interaction with the client intensifies. When the contract is fulfilled, sellers once more slip back into the courting role.

The courting-engagement-courting nature of the relationship further means that it is not until the client has actually accepted an idea, that the specific service/product properties are attributed. During the initial contacts, the framework for the construction of a more concrete product and a need for this product is beginning to be put into place. These contacts work to create trust between the banker and the top management of prospective client corporations, and the parties discuss the situation and needs of the corporation in question. Based on an arising mutual understanding of the problems at hand, the bankers can then go on to develop ideas that can actually be sold to the management. In this way, ideas are gradually turned into real cases that are presented to clients – or discarded for new ones that have a better fit with the client's simultaneously emerging needs. It follows that previously engaged sellers may be replaced by other courting candidates with more attractive ideas.

An additional finding concerning the relationship is that it fulfilled several functions for sellers – and for buyers. Importantly, the seller-buyer relationship enabled continuous contacts between bankers and clients, i.e. it made it possible to keep the process of need and product construction going over time. Furthermore, the relationship made it easier for the bankers to keep up to date with the clients' views on what was going on in the field, i.e. the relationship worked as an information channel. But information did not only go one way. In the case of the bankers, the relationship constituted a meeting place for dialogue and for building shared constructions of the situation at hand and the problem to be solved by the financial services product. Thus, although the chapter has focused primarily on sellers, we would, once again, like to stress that both sellers and buyers were involved in constructing the needs for and the properties of the products in the bankers' case.

Conclusions: Management advisory services under construction

When buying products and services, it is, of course, an advantage to know what one is buying and why. It makes it easier to decide, for instance, what supplier to use or what is a reasonable price for a particular service. But knowing what one is buying and why is not always that easy, especially when the product being bought is an expert service. One reason for this is that products and their properties, especially products such as expert services, are the results of processes of construction involving several types of actors and activities. One aim of this chapter has therefore been to increase the understanding of the construction of such products by analyzing how financial services products are constructed in the sales process.

In this chapter, we have shown how properties attributed to certain services do not have to be ascribed in direct words, but rather can be understood as subconsciously expressed. Given by the nature of the product, the properties therefore become seen as obvious and, consequently, do not need to be stated explicitly. In our analysis, we have underlined how the properties of necessity and extravagance are simultaneously being ascribed to corporate finance services. As mentioned earlier, properties ascribed to products can be presented in two categories: functional aspects and properties related to image. The functional aspect of necessity is expressed most explicitly in how larger financial transactions and IPOs are not accomplished today without the help of bankers. Among top managers there is an expectation that the need for bankers is given – a need based on the perceived and generally taken-for-granted expert knowledge of the bankers. The bankers have a plethora of experience from different sorts of transactions, and this, complemented by detailed knowledge of various industries, enables them to offer solutions to a variety of (financial) problems, many of which are constructed in the interaction between sellers and buyers of the bankers' services. Given a certain feeling of ignorance by the client in the financial consultants' rapidly evolving field of expertise, an important functional aspect of the bankers' offer is legitimacy. This legitimacy may be divided into two parts – one that relates to the deal as such and one to the buyer of the service. First, a number of transactions today are expected to involve bankers for realizing the deal. In order to attain legitimacy, e.g. for an IPO or a stock offering, the involvement of an investment bank is often needed as a seal of the quality for the deal. But second, after the realization, the bankers themselves can also be used to legitimate the actions of individual top managers. Even if the transaction leads to financial loss rather than revenue, the managers can always legitimate their action by referring to the advice of well-reputed bankers. Thus, top managers need bankers to help them in financial restructuring of business. This need is based both in the generally accepted, institutionalized idea that certain kinds of activities, such as mergers and acquisitions or IPOs, require the involvement of external experts, as well as in the very local interactions between buyers and suppliers in the pitching process as bankers try to convince managers of the beneficial nature of their ideas and suggestions.

The property of image, as we have pointed out, is one of extravagance. This is expressed in various symbols used in the bankers' professional culture. Their offices are located in first class districts and also their interior decoration shows signs of wealth. The furnishings, the art on the walls, the cut-glass chandelier – all represent signs of capital and success. The material setting is followed up in the dress code of the people working there, who wear expensive suits and jewelry. But it is not only the material symbols that signify prosperity, the action symbols do too. The manner in which the client is met also exudes the image of extravagance, being treated to expensive lunches and dinners, and reports and suggestions presented in elegant design. The relation with the client is developed over long periods of expensive "courting", when there is no discussion about monetary reward for the financial suggestions made. When there is a decision to buy, the extravagance also appears – in the price of the bankers' services. Consequently, the attribution of extravagance appears in most material and behavioral symbols of the bankers. As we have shown, the properties of necessity and extravagance in the context of financial services reinforce rather than contradict each other. The increasingly complex solutions and possibilities in the corporate finance world have created a need for experts to provide legitimacy to uncertain managers.

This turns extravagance, as a symbol of expertise and quality, into a necessity in the domain of financial advice.

This chapter has highlighted the constructed nature of the properties of financial advisory services, and investigated one of the central processes in which needs and properties are constructed – the sales process. Viewing properties as being "under construction" contributes to the analyses of management advisory services in general by underlining the importance of a more complex understanding of products, services, purchasing – and needs. It also opens a perspective that highlights the culture we use to understand everyday life, as well as a specific product and the process of buying (or selling) it.

CHAPTER 6

Taking Control of Need Construction

On the organizational needs that drive the use of consultants

ANDREAS WERR

From an individual to embedded view of management consultant use

Management consultants, like many other management advisory services, are based on a diffuse and heterogeneous knowledge base. Consequently, as illustrated in the previous chapter, the characteristics as well as the needs that MAS fulfill may vary between situations as the result of negotiations, primarily between buyers and suppliers of these services. Based on observed differences in the use of management consultants, including both the reasons why consultants were hired and the emerging consultant-client relationship, this chapter will investigate in more depth the organizational aspects that may help us to understand such differences.

It may be argued that the use of management consultants is a "make or buy" decision similar to other such decisions, calling for an analysis of the strategic importance of the product or service, the organization's capabilities in the area, the market conditions necessary for the service to be made or bought, control and influence aspects, etc. (see e.g. Axelsson and Wynstra, 2002). However, most literature on management consulting has dealt with the use of consultants as an individual decision, focusing more on the individual manager's needs than on the organization's needs. In both the normatively oriented- and the critical literature on management consulting, the buyer of consulting services has been more or less explicitly pictured as an individual manager and it has been his/her personal needs for cognitive or psychological support that have been in focus as reasons for hiring consultants and as central in the formation of the consultant-client relationship.

In the normative literature, the main reasons for hiring management consultants are generally said to be related to a deficiency in either knowledge or resources of the manager or his/her organization. Here, the manager's and organization's interests are generally seen as identical when it comes to reasons for hiring consultants. The individual focus, however, becomes salient once the consultant-client relationship is discussed. Hiring consultants is described as an emotionally stressful task, placing strong pressures on the individual manager (Maister, 1993; Schein, 1988). In the critical literature the use of consultants is further individualized, and it is here attributed to the buyers' identity needs. Clark and Salaman (1996) describe the providing of a positive managerial identity and the building of a manageable organization as the central contribution of management consultants. In much of the current literature, the need for management consultants, as well as the formation of the relationship between consultant and buyer, is thus discussed on a personal and interpersonal level. It is the managers' knowledge or resource deficiencies, psychological needs and anxieties that are described as drivers of both the need for consultants and the formation of the relationship with them.

Recent research on management consulting and the consultant-client relationship has, however, called for a more open-ended understanding of the client and the consultant-client relationship allowing for a wide range of different uses and relationships (see e.g. Fincham, 1999; Salaman, 2002; Sturdy, 1997a). Attention has been drawn to a number of contextual factors on different levels of analysis including the societal- and the organizational level.

On a societal level, a number of different factors conditioning the use of consultants have been pointed out, including economic and social structures (Sturdy, 1997b), attitudes towards receiving help (Schein, 1988), and the nature of the managerial role and managerial issues (Bäcklund and Werr, 2003; Kipping, 2002; Werr and Styhre, 2003). On an organizational level, the organizational context of managers has received some (although limited) attention. Formative aspects of the organizational context in the use of advisors pointed out include the size and competence level of the buying firm (Fincham, 1999), managerial power structures and interests (Gammelsæter, 2002), and the organizational culture (Hislop, 2002). Details of how different organizational characteristics condition the use of consultants, however, remain to be explored and provide the focus for this chapter.

In the following, we will turn to two cases of large organizations, Alpha and Beta, and their use of management consultants. In trying to understand the differences in both the extent to which consultants were used and the ways in which they were used, two aspects of the organizational context are identified as central – the decision-making culture and the organizational self-confidence. The relation of these factors to the use of management consultants is then discussed.

In the following, we will thus look closer into the different uses of management consultants in two large multinational organizations.

Alpha – A self-confident buyer

Alpha[1] is a large Sweden-based engineering company. It has about 70,000 employees worldwide and a turnover of € 19 billion. During the years 1998-2001, the company spent about € 1.5 billion on management consultants or about € 40 million/year. A large merger and the implementation of an ERP system are single large projects that account for a considerable portion of the consulting costs during these years.

Alpha has a divisionalized structure with rather independent divisions. Decisions to hire consultants could be made by the managers within the limits of their budget. The managers could also purchase the consultants of their choice, so a large number of different consultants were used within the company. The choice of consultants was generally based on earlier experiences or recommendations. An evaluation of alternative suppliers for a specific consulting project was rather rare.

Management consultants were used in a wide range of projects within Alpha, including strategy projects, reorganizations, process reengineering, marketing projects, product development projects, etc. A common denominator of many of the occasions when consultants were used, however, was a large recent merger. Initially, this merger required considerable consulting support, but also after direct

---

[1] Data was collected through interviews and the study of secondary material. Interviews were carried out with managers and members of consulting projects in Alpha (24 interviews) and Beta (20 interviews). Interviews ranged between 60 and 90 minutes and were taped and transcribed.

completion of the deal and the first integration, the use of consultants to realize the desired synergies continued.

Reasons for using consultants

Although the motives for using consultants within Alpha varied widely, a common denominator of the largest projects was a perceived lack of resources and ability to coordinate and execute organizational change. As a typical engineering organization, Alpha had highly skilled engineers. In some divisions of the company, however, management competence was less developed and decision processes were described as slow and complex. Individual managers would not always implement decisions made by higher level management if they did not believe in them. Decision-making methods were described as participative, and involved seeking the approval of, in particular, informal leaders with long-term experience. The decision-making structure was often informal. Being an organization in which people had traditionally made life-long careers, seniority and experience was important – sometimes more important than one's formal position in the company. Making things happen in this culture was described as rather tedious:

> *That might be a small difference between Alpha and Epsilon [a major competitor of Alpha]. In Alpha making decisions takes a little more time. We are much more focused on getting consensus here than they are in Epsilon.*

Consultants were therefore valued for their drive and ability to make things happen in the organization, which was the most commonly claimed reason for using management consultants in Alpha. This ability to coax the organization into action was attributed to both the consultants' working style, and their analytical and presentation skills. Management consultants in the organization were generally known for working very hard and thereby keeping issues on the agenda:

> *The consultants are incredibly pushy. Their drive can almost become too intense. They drive both themselves and others to death, but OK, they get things moving.*

By collecting, analyzing and presenting data, they were able to support the creation of consensus and sense of urgency within the organization, and put pressure on it to make decisions:

Yes, if we go back to the project with CC consulting last year, I believe that the consultants made it clear that we had to make a decision. They were pushing quite hard, which I definitely thought was positive.

The ability of management consultants to make things happen in Alpha was also linked to their contribution of extra resources. Several managers within Alpha described the organization as rather lean after a number of years of downsizing. This had led to a lack of free resources to devote to future-oriented and developmental issues. Recent mergers and acquisitions had also generated an increased need for change projects to release operational synergies.

Against this background, the extra, dedicated resources that the hard working management consultants represented were very welcome. Use of consultants was especially prominent in projects related to analyzing the potential synergies of mergers and acquisitions, and in designing and implementing new processes and procedures to realize these potentials. Several large projects involved issues regarding operational structures and processes (e.g. restructuring the dealer network, analyzing the production network, refining the procurement structure, etc.). A large majority of projects were done in the areas of strategy, organization, marketing and IT (including ERP system) and were motivated by a need for resources rather than specific expertise. Using management consultants for other than resource reasons was regarded with some scepticism by most managers:

You have to be aware, that when you hire management consultants, in a sense you disavow your own management and problem-solving capability.

However, there were some exceptions to this view that consultants should be used only as resources. These included the use of consultants in financial matters, such as the preparation and execution of the financial aspects of mergers and acquisitions.

Key issues related to the use of consultants
The use of management consultants within Alpha was however not unproblematic. The most frequently recurring critique of consultants was their lack of knowledge of Alpha and its industry as well as the specific premises for the day-to-day operations:

Consultants know nothing. They don't know our industry. They don't have a clue. That's the way it is. It is we, who have spent our lives in this industry, who have all the knowledge.

I want value; I want consultants to add value on my balance sheet. But for that to happen, I am not helped by an overly theoretic collection of models.

Managers felt the consultants lacked a detailed understanding of the client organization and its context. As a result, the consultants' contributions were perceived as "theoretical", i.e. not sufficiently realistic. They also felt that the consultants did not always understand their situation. The consultants that were described as "good consultants" were appreciated for their ability to "enter the world of the managers" and refrain from theorizing:

They don't engage in too much theorizing. They're willing to enter reality rather than staying in their theoretical models. They have a realistic approach. They don't stake out goals and directions that we see right away are unrealistic, that there is no way to reach. These upward going curves they present are amazing sometimes. Realism, a willingness to found solutions in the real world, is very important.

Besides the consultants' lacking knowledge of and willingness to engage in the managers' day-to-day problems, a second recurring problem was the organization's commitment and buy-in in projects run by/with consultants. Managers in Alpha told about numerous projects in which management consultants had been hired without having ensured the mental- and resource commitment of the affected organization. Such projects generally led to failure in the sense that resistance was considerable and no lasting change was achieved:

You can't change an organization by asking a consultant to do it. Change must come from within, from your own management structure. You have to agree internally. When you have drawn up your new structure, 35 percent of the job is done. Then it gets difficult. If you don't have buy-in then, you're going to stumble. We have many examples of that.

If an organization hires consultants because it lacks resources, it might be living a bit dangerously. If you don't have the resources

> *to engage in the project, the output may end up being one-sided,*
> *representing the consultants' view. Then we get the standard*
> *slides we've seen before.*

The use of management consultants as resources in large organizational change projects was thus seen as problematic, though recurring within Alpha. It created problems of buy-in and commitment to the process and often led to failure to achieve the objectives of the consulting intervention.

In summary, consultants in Alpha were generally hired as extra resources in order to "make things happen", to push the organization to decisions and implementation by keeping issues on the organizational agenda. This was achieved by providing analysis as a basis for decisions, by pressing the organization to make decisions and by providing the experience and resources to run large organizational change processes. This specific use of consultants also generated a number of issues in the relation between managers in Alpha and the consultants however. These issues concerned the consultants' lacking understanding of Alpha's operations and the industry, a sense that the consultants delivered "theoretical" solutions without relating to the managers' reality. Another issue concerned a lack of commitment from the client organization in the consultant-supported projects. Both these issues may be viewed as consequences of the specific use of consultants as resources "to make things happen" in Alpha, which will be discussed in more detail later in this chapter.

Beta – An unconfident buyer

Beta used to be a public organization, and was transformed into a state owned corporation a number of years ago. Its operations are to a large extent constrained by laws and regulations. The company is organized into a number of rather independent business and support units. The transformation to a private corporation put pressure on the organization with respect to efficiency and profitability. These pressures have been driving a number of different change efforts to reduce costs as well as increase revenues. During the IT boom at the end of the 1990s, the organization became engaged in numerous projects to create new types of IT-based services in order to replace a drop in the demand for its traditional services.

Beta has a turnover of € 2.5 billion and employs about 40,000 people. In the three years covered by this study (2000-2002), management consultants were employed for an average of € 28 million a year with an increasing trend, from € 21 million in 2000 to € 36 million in 2002. The management consultants were to a large extent employed by top management and its staff functions. The use of management consultants in the different business units was rather limited. A large driver of consulting costs in 2002 was the initiation of a company-wide ERP implementation as well as large-scale changes to the organization's distribution network.

Reasons for using consultants

A frequently recurring motive for using management consultants in Beta was their ability to act as neutral outsiders and thereby provide a "second opinion" on important issues. The consultants' neutrality was especially important in the decision-making climate dominant in Beta, which was described as participative and consensus-oriented. In this context, consultants were needed to "eliminate all the feelings," to create an "objective" image of reality:

> *When you do these analyses internally, emotions always get involved. A business manager is still a manager of that business wanting to defend it. Now all our analyses have gone through Strat consulting [an international strategy consultancy] and been stripped of all the feelings, so now we have a very very clear picture of future volumes and Beta's financial situation.*

In addition to providing an objective picture of the organization, consultants were also valued for their ability to provide new and different perspectives. Although these might often seem self-evident once they have been presented, they are still regarded by the organization as important:

> *Even if you have the knowledge and competence to do it yourself, new eyes from the outside can see things you might miss which can be valuable. There's a cliché that "consultants only say things that stand to reason," but that's not always so bad. Once someone has said it, you say: "That's obvious. Why should you pay him several million for that?" But one shouldn't underestimate the importance of this.*

Managers in Beta were anxious to make the right decisions and did not want to rely exclusively on their own judgment and that of their colleagues. Rather, they perceived the need for a second opinion to confirm their interpretations and plans:

> *Beta is too important a company for Sweden not to solicit a second opinion, not to hire qualified consultants to look at our conclusions and see whether they have a different analysis or arrive at different conclusions.*

Consultants were thus to a large extent valued for their analytical abilities and their expert knowledge. This expert knowledge was sought in areas where the organization itself lacked sufficient experience due to a lack of exposure to the questions at hand. Examples include knowledge on how to develop an international trademark strategy or how to coordinate large, organization-wide change processes:

> *... What we bought from Implementation consulting was their method. Their method and support, because we had no knowledge whatsoever of this in Beta. It included everything from how to work with training of our own personnel, of the personnel of our partners, etc. A lot of communication issues were also involved.*

Statements like the above, in which managers in Beta openly admitted their lack of knowledge and experience in certain areas of management, were widespread. Consultants were often described as the remedy to this problem. The confidence in the role of expert knowledge and the consultants' ability to provide this knowledge, and thereby contribute to a successful solving of the organization's problems, was large. Especially when it came to large financial transactions such as acquisitions or divestments, the use of consultants as experts was uncontested.

Against this background, managers viewed consultants as a source of increasing the organization's level of competence. Knowledge transfer and learning were vivid elements in Beta's thinking about how to manage the relationship to consultants (in Alpha, knowledge transfer from consultant to buyer was regarded a non-issue). The active involvement of the company's own personnel in consulting projects was seen as the main vehicle for this transfer of competence. A recent project had been organized with an explicit rule that consultants could not exceed 40 percent of staffing, and no consultants were allowed to hold managerial positions in the project (in practice, this meant that project management positions doubled, consisting of a project manager from Beta, and an assistant project manager from the consulting company).

In many instances, consultants had become a taken-for-granted element in the organization's problem-solving structure, which was seen as a problem by some of the managers:

... We have used consultants too much to run the business and possibly also to interpret information. It should be the responsibility of management to interpret the information that comes up and back the remedies to be taken. You can't let consultants do this – change in the organization needs to take place organically.

A recurring reason stated by managers in Beta for what was perceived as an excessive use of consultants was the organization's lack of self-confidence:

I think we often underestimate our own competence. There is an underdog feeling in Beta. Time after time, when we ask for help, we get proof that our little knowledge is often better than that available outside. It might be a question of culture or maybe also image - how we are perceived, the belief in our ability.

I guess it's the company culture that provides the basis for this low self-confidence. In order for something to happen, you need to involve an external consultant.

The only area where the organization demonstrated considerable self-confidence was in relation to the industry and the actions of competitors. In these areas, consultants were seldom hired.

In addition to providing "second opinions" and expertise, the consultants were also appreciated, as in the case of Alpha, for their ability to make things happen in the organization. Based on their commitment to deadlines, the consultants were said to have been important in maintaining momentum and focus in the processes they were involved in.

Key issues related to the use of consultants

As in Alpha, the list of issues expressed in relation to the use of management consultants was long. Some were mentioned more often than others however. These involved the consultants' ability to make their clients dependent on them, a perceived lack of competence in purchasing consultants, and the consultants' limited understanding of the managers' reality.

Consultants' tendency to work their way into projects was the single most mentioned issue in Beta's use of consultants. Managers spoke repetitively of the consultants' efforts to sell the company more consulting and Beta's inability to resist these efforts:

> *They are extremely skilled at creating tentacles and additional work ... The more tentacles they get, the more difficult it becomes to discontinue their assignment. It's difficult. They see things, and they have the resources and methods to tell you what you need to do – "this is what we could do" – and before you know it they're doing it.*

Also linked to the consultants' dominant role in Beta, is their perceived reluctance to transfer knowledge (in opposition to Alpha, knowledge is seen as an important element in the relation between consultant and buyer in Beta). Numerous examples were given of projects in which consultants were said to have avoided transferring knowledge to Beta in order to make themselves indispensable. Rather than transferring knowledge, managers in Beta perceived consultants to drain the organization of existing knowledge, thus making the company increasingly dependent on the services of consultants.

These perceived problems were to a large extent attributed to Beta's lack of competence and confidence in the processes of purchasing and managing management consultants. Beta managers generally viewed their own- and colleagues' handling of consultants as too naïve, giving consultants too much freedom and influence:

> *I think Beta should be a little tougher when buying and managing its consultants. ... All management in Beta should be carried out by people employed by Beta. Consultants are a support business. But I've seen several examples where consultants started taking over management positions and Beta must be able to stop this. We are very bad at this I think. We let the consultants take over. In the end, they begin to dominate certain parts of the organization, which is not good.*

The managers' control over consulting assignments and their occasional abdication of managerial responsibilities to consultants was repeatedly criticized within Beta.

Furthermore, as in Alpha, consultants were criticized for their reluctance to really become familiar with the details of the organization's operations and take responsibility for the advice given, which made their solutions and suggestions at times "theoretical" and difficult to apply in practice:

> *If you're hired as a consultant, it's easy to say: "Yes, but this is not my responsibility. I can support you, but only this far." But if you are part of the organization, you're held accountable in a different way than if you're a temporary consultant.*

The above thus indicates a feeling among managers in Beta of being in the hands of consultants, with limited confidence and ability to take control of the situation, to place specific demands on the consultants. The consultants dictated the terms of their involvement and the managers in Beta were depicted as rather passive expedients of these demands.

In summary, the use of management consultants in Beta showed a rather different profile than in Alpha. Whereas the main reason to use consultants in Alpha was a lack of resources, arguments for consultant use in Beta were dominated by references to the consultants' knowledge and expertise. To verify the managers' own analyses and to provide a second opinion were recurring motives for the use of consultants in Beta. This use of consultants was increasingly viewed as excessive, however, and linked to a lack of self-confidence within Beta.

The lacking self-confidence was also reflected in the issues perceived when using consultants. Here, managers generally critiqued the consultants' way of expanding their presence in the organization once they had a foot in the door. The managers questioned their ability to resist the consultants' agenda and act as competent buyers of consulting services. Again, the specific use of consultants is seen as driving a specific set of challenges for the client organization.

Understanding the use of consultants in an organizational context

The use of management consultants in the cases of the two large companies described above shows that organizations' need for and use of consulting services is by no means homogeneous. The two cases indicate large variation in a number of dimensions, including the extent to which management consultants are bought (0.2 percent of turnover in Alpha vs. 1.4 percent spent on management consultants in Beta), the reasons for which they are bought (resources or competence) and the way in which the relationship evolves (the kind of issues faced in the relation to the consultants).

While individual differences between managers' use of consultants in the companies were of course present, the systematic differences between the organizations were striking. While the use of consultants as resources in Alpha was generally accepted, this was not the case in Beta. Here, the main justification was the consultants' contribution of competence and expertise – something which was frowned upon in Alpha as it was interpreted as a sign of managerial incompetence. Furthermore, the kinds of issues faced in the consultant-client relationship and the perceived power relation between consultant and client differed between the organizations depending on how and why they used consultants.

Rather than discussing the use of consultants and the consultant-client relationship in relation to individual managers' needs, as has been common in the literature, the above empirical patterns suggest a change of the level of analysis to an organization level and to the "organizational needs" that drive and shape the use of consultants. As argued by Fincham (1999, p. 347):

Consultancy can be thought of as a kind of parallel management divided from the main body by the organizational boundary, and by the division between internal and external expertise, but not by any fundamentally structured relationship.

This calls for an understanding of management consulting in relation to the managerial structures and processes in the buying organization. Depending on the characteristics of these, the boundaries between the regular management and consultants' "parallel management", as well as the division between internal and external expertise, may vary considerably. As with other goods and services, managers have a "make or buy" choice (although they may not explicitly consider that choice) when it comes to activities in the management process. Two aspects of the managerial structures and processes emerge from the above cases as important in forming the choices made in relation to management consultants – the decision-making culture and the management's self confidence.

Decision-making culture

Viewing management consulting as a kind of "parallel management" (Fincham, 1999) identifies the key managerial process of making and implementing decisions potentially important in understanding the use of management consultants. Different ways of making and implementing decisions may create different niches for consultants to fill. Pfeffer (1981) e.g. identifies four different decision-making models – rational, bureaucratic, decision process/organized anarchy, and political power – and it may be argued that the potential roles of consultants differ between the different processes (Skjølsvik, 2004). Saxton (1995) also argues, that consultants play different roles in different phases of the decision process and that their potential contributions vary depending on the composition of the decision-making team. For example, he proposes that there is larger need for legitimizing roles, the more heterogeneous the management team is.

Although the potential links between the way in which decisions are made and implemented in an organization and the use of management consultants have been established by previous studies, empirical illustrations and elaborations are to a large extent lacking. The above cases, however, provide a basis for such a contribution, as the needs for management consultants were to a large extent formulated in relation to the organizations' ways of making and implementing decisions. "Making things happen" – i.e. making and implementing decisions – was a central reason for hiring consultants shared by both organizations. However, due to different decision-making cultures, this translated into rather different uses of consultants in the two organizations.

In Alpha, the decision-making was described as democratic and decentralized, with a large focus placed on the consent of informal leaders. This made decision-making slow and posed problems for the manager attempting rapid implementation of decisions. In this context, management consultants were described as important to see that important issues were kept on the agenda and that implementation projects did not lose momentum. The consultants' dedicated and hard work pressured the organization to make decisions and the consultants were viewed as supporting a fast implementation by providing extra resources.

Also in Beta, the decision-making culture was described as democratic. In addition, it was described as conflict-avoiding and somewhat risk averse, resembling what Pfeffer (1981) characterizes as a rational decision-making model. The "second opinion" of consultants was often solicited before decisions were made in order to establish what were regarded as safe and neutral grounds for decision-making and to ensure that no aspect of information was missed. In contrast to Alpha, where the consultants' provision of resources was emphasized as a way of overcoming the perceived inertia of a democratic decision-making culture, in Beta, the consultants' knowledge was in focus, providing "objective" grounds and expert advice based on which decisions could be made. Although the contributions of consultants were regarded for the most part as confirming the analyses made in Beta, their input was still regarded as an important contribution.

However, using consultants to overcome the perceived barriers to implementation and decision-making was not necessarily very successful, as indicated by the key issues cited for the use of management consultants. The specific use of consultants as resources or knowledge providers embedded in the organization's decision making-culture had a tendency to create its own, new problems.

In Alpha, where consultants were hired as resources in order to keep momentum in the decision-making process by actively driving the process and acting in it, the consultants and their work were perceived as disconnected from the organizational reality. Viewing consultants mainly as resources limited the client organization's involvement in change initiatives, as the work was perceived as delegated to the consultants. Once the consultants reported back, frustration was common with the results, however, as these were perceived as insufficiently adapted to Alpha's specific reality and lacking broad buy-in, which made them hard to realize. The consultants' efforts were often described as taking place "next to" rather than in the organization, and resistance to the consultant-driven initiatives was at times strong.

In Beta, management consultants were generally framed as neutral "experts", speeding up decision-making by providing expert input. This use of consultants seemed to be associated with a different set of issues related to the consultant's relation to the client. In Beta, managers felt helpless in relation to the consultants. Their faith in consultants' expert knowledge was perceived as exaggerated and unrealistic and they perceived themselves as victims of the consultants' control over the selling process and the consultant-client relationship. This feeling of inferiority led in turn to the second factor conditioning the use of consultants indicated by the above cases – organizational self-confidence.

Organizational self-confidence

Management consultants are often described as being in the market of providing ideas and knowledge to their clients (Bessant and Rush, 1995). The above cases indicated that the need for such ideas may be understood in terms of an organization's general perception of its own- vs. other actors' knowledge. Hiring consultants for their expert knowledge may not be so much the result of "real" knowledge deficiencies in the organization (given that such deficiencies can be identified) (e.g. Greiner and Metzger, 1983; Kubr, 2002) nor individual managers' strategic use of consultants' expert power (e.g. Clark, 1995; Clark and Salaman, 1996a), but of a collectively shared valuation of the company's own knowledge vs. other actors' knowledge. Following the lead of the managers in Beta, we will call this feeling "organizational self-confidence". Several of the managers in Beta characterized the organization as lacking confidence in its own knowledge.

In this respect, Alpha was quite different. Managers in Alpha expressed considerably less confidence in consultants' expertise and seldom used them for knowledge reasons, but instead viewed them as readily available resources. Given the strong confidence in their own expertise, managers in Alpha enacted a rather strong position in relation to the consultants. A general scepticism about consultants was common in Alpha, and managers were not easily impressed by the consultants' models and concepts. Rather, they strongly criticized these for being too theoretical and thus void of practical value.

The observed differences between Alpha's and Beta's self-confidence may be linked to their respective backgrounds. Alpha is one of the largest companies in its industry globally, and its technical abilities are highly regarded. Many of the managers in Alpha have spent their entire careers in Alpha, thus giving them a feeling of deep knowledge of the company and the industry.

In Beta, the situation was different. Although Beta managers had also often risen to their managerial position by climbing an internal career ladder, since Beta had a tradition of recruiting internally and providing people with education as it was needed, several of the managers in the company lacked formal academic education. In Beta, this internal experience was regarded as less of a strength than in Alpha, however, and being a former state monopoly faced with a shrinking market, Beta placed great hopes in the managerial practices and models of the private sector (c.f. Brunsson and Sahlin Andersson, 2000).

The repeated use of consultants as "second opinions" may be the best illustration of this. Managers in Beta did not trust their own knowledge. They felt a need to have it validated by "experts". The confidence in the internal knowledge of Beta was thus considerably smaller than in Alpha, providing a possible explanation of the extensive hiring of consultants for knowledge reasons.

While organizational self-confidence is of course partly linked to the business challenges faced by an organization – moving into a new industry, as in the case of Beta, will reduce the managerial self-confidence of the organization – it may also be linked to other factors, such as the status of the organization and the business sector it operates in (DiMaggio and Powell, 1991). Beta's background as a former public organization may be seen here as a possible explanation for its strong belief in management consultants and their "expertise". The private sector has for the last decade been touted as the main model for how organizations should be run (Brunsson and Sahlin Andersson, 2000). With management consultants seen as the "experts" on private organizing, Beta's high faith in the knowledge of management consultants is understandable. For Beta, management consultants represent the knowledge it needs to go from an unprofessional public-sector organization to a professional and efficient private organization (however, Beta managers repeatedly expressed their disappointment in the realization that the consultants' knowledge was often less advanced than their own).

Although the variations in what were perceived as legitimate areas for consultant use were rather large between Alpha and Beta, there seemed to be some areas of use perceived as universally legitimate in the sense that they were seldom questioned by either organization. These were those areas of consulting related to major financial transactions such as mergers, acquisitions and the selling of companies. In such cases, the use of consultants was seen as self-evident and thus not in need of legitimation. Consulting services may thus have different degrees of "self-evidence". Some services may at any given time be attributed universal legitimation based on a generally shared understanding that this specific service is indispensable (see also Chapter 5). These views on what can be regarded as universally legitimate services may change over time.

The organizational construction of the consultant-client relationship

The power relation between consultant and client has been debated in the literature for some time. As discussed in Chapter 1, positions vary as to who is the more powerful party. Some argue that it is the consultant, based on his expert power and the client's anxiety (e.g. Bloomfield and Best, 1992; Clark, 1995; Clark and Salaman, 1996a), thus rendering the client a victim of consulting rhetoric and persuasion. Others argue that the client holds the power based on his/her power to hire and fire the consultants (Kubr, 1982; McGonagle and Vella, 2001). More recently, however, among others Fincham (1999) and Sturdy (1997a) have argued for a more situation-specific understanding of the consultant-client relationship, which will be the argument in relation to the two cases in the following.

Comparing the client managers' perceived power position in relation to management consultants between Alpha and Beta reveals some substantial differences. Whereas managers in Alpha implicitly viewed themselves as in control of the consultants, (the lack of) control over consultants in Beta is a main concern of managers, who often saw themselves as victims of the management consultants and their ability to "work themselves into the client organization."

The differences in the perceived power position of the client in relation to the consultant may be related to the differences in the use of consultants discussed above. In a context (as in Alpha) in which consultants are framed mainly as "resources", the buyer implicitly establishes a position of control. The notion of "resource" to "get things done" also implies the existence of an "exploiter" of the resource who determines the use of the resource and knows what needs to be done. It also implies that the client is at least equal to the consultant in terms of knowledge. Resource consultants are generally opposed to expert consultants, with resource consultants providing more of the knowledge the client already possesses (e.g. Kubr, 2002). This (perceived) equality of knowledge makes the client confident to formulate, supervise and follow up the consultants' assignments. Uncertainty regarding what the consultants should do, whether they deliver good quality or not, etc, is strongly reduced since the consulting service is constructed as based on a technical knowledge base shared by the client organization (Reed, 1996).

In Beta, consultants entered a different context, shaping a rather different consulting-client relationship. In this context, where consultants are mainly used as experts and knowledge carriers to support organizational decision-making and implementation, the power relation tips in favor of the consultant. With consultants as "experts" and providers of knowledge, client managers are implicitly placed in a position of "non-experts", lacking knowledge, a position that creates a sense of lack of control over consultants (c.f. Bäcklund and Werr, 2003). As discussed in Chapter 1, this perceived imbalance in knowledge created considerable uncertainties among the client managers with respect to both the quality of the expertise and the "professionalism" of the consultants. Neither relationship-building, nor overall efforts towards professionalization seem to have been especially successful in dealing with this uncertainty on an organizational level. Managers in Beta were genuinely uncertain whether the use of consultants benefited their organization.

The above suggests the importance of the client managers' collective construction of their knowledge and role in relation to the consultants' as an important factor forming the consultant-client relationship. The boundaries drawn between the management of an organization and, to use Fincham's (1999) term, the "parallel management" of consultants are locally constructed within the context of the client organization's specific management and decision-making culture. Who provides "knowledge" and "expertise" and who provides the "resources" in this system seems to be a matter of negotiation between client managers and consultants. (c.f. Reed, 1996)

The outcome of this negotiation is an important one in terms of its far-reaching consequences. As illustrated above, the position taken on the role of consultants in the organization not only affects the power relation between consultant and client, but also the processes and procedures by which consultants are used and ultimately the outcomes of the use of consultants. This relationship between the negotiated role of consultants and their consequential use and the outcomes of that use, adds further complexity to the discussion of the power relation between consultants and their users. Based on the above cases, it may be argued that a strong power position for the client may actually be counter-productive to a (for the client) beneficial use of management consultants. The low valuation of consultants' knowledge implied in their use as resources fosters a use of consultants "at arms length", creating in turn a number of specific issues concerning the integration of the consultants' work with the organization's work. It also leads to a disregard of learning opportunities in consultant-supported projects. In the long run, this may increase a company's need for and dependence on consultants, thus weakening the client managers' collective self-confidence and position in relation to the consultant (see also Werr and Linnarsson, 2002).

Conclusions

One of the central questions posed in this book concerns the construction of needs for management advisory services. While the needs for these services in the literature on management consulting have been primarily related to the individual buyer, this chapter has argued for the need and fruitfulness of adding an organizational level of analysis when trying to understand the use of management consulting services by client organizations. As indicated by the analysis of the use of management consultants in two different organizations, consultants may be seen as integrated parts of an organization's decision-making structures and procedures. In the case of the two organizations looked at here, the role of consultants was constructed in relation to perceived organizational needs in the making and implementation of decisions and client-managers' confidence in the internal knowledge of the organization. Depending on the needs constructed in this context, consultants were used for different reasons and in different ways, influencing both the power relation between client and consultant and the outcomes of the consulting process in terms of perceived key issues

By focusing on the organizational context of consultant use, this chapter breaks with the tradition of analyzing the consultant-client relationship as an interpersonal one between an individual consultant and an individual manager. Earlier explorations of the contributions of consultants as well as the character of the consultant-client relationship have generally focused on the manager's cognitive, social and socio-psychological needs. While I do not deny the existence and importance of these needs in shaping the use of consultants, the argument put forward in this chapter suggests that these needs may be formed and conditioned by the organizational context, i.e. the decision-making culture and organizational self-confidence. The exploration of the detailed links between organizational context and individual needs lies beyond the scope of this paper, but may provide an interesting area for further research.

CHAPTER 7

The Organization of Expertise

Swedish organizations' production, subcontracting and purchase of interactive media solutions

FREDRIK AUGUSTSSON

Interactive media as an emerging field of expertise

Organizations are embedded in ongoing flows of constantly evolving ideas, knowledge and expertise that alter opportunity structures. Now and then, new areas of expertise emerge, requiring responses from organizations as to how to relate to this new expertise. Is it a knowledge area that is important for the organization? Is it an expertise to be developed internally or is it better purchased from an external market? What is the nature and structure of this expertise, etc.? Simultaneously with these reflections, in some potential user organizations, other organizations begin reflecting on the practice of realizing the expertise in concrete products and services: Can these be provided by the existing organization? Can new businesses be started based on it? What is the scope of the expertise and its associated products, etc.? Situations involving the emergence of new areas of expertise may be well suited for study in order to understand the nature and emergence of needs for MAS in organizations.

The current chapter focuses on one such situation, the area of interactive media production, which largely emerged in the middle of the 1990s. Organizations at that time had very limited tradition of either purchasing or producing these services. There were no groups of actors that could easily claim expert status in the production of interactive media. It was further not given that interactive media was a form of expert knowledge that firms should purchase rather than produce internally. In the following, the emerging content and structure of the demand and supply for interactive media services in Sweden is studied. The first area studied is the extent and organization of interactive media production and purchase among larger Swedish companies and government agencies and, second, interactive media production as performed by experts, including external IT/management consultants. Based on the above, it will be argued that the purchasing of MAS is a fundamental and complex process, involving central "make or buy" decisions impacting on the organization and provision of expert knowledge, and thereby the division of labor within and between firms (Augustsson, 2001).

The chapter is structured accordingly. After a brief discussion of the nature of interactive media solutions, a description of the organization of production and purchase of these services within larger Swedish firms and government agencies will be provided. This is followed by a description of the actual activities produced and purchased, the reasons to produce, subcontract or purchase interactive media, and the kind of relations purchasing organizations develop with their suppliers. The chapter then turns to a discussion of the construction of expert knowledge within interactive media production and concludes with a discussion of purchasing as part of organizing, with a focus on the extent and ways in which the production and purchase of interactive media solutions constitutes expert knowledge.

The socially constructed nature of interactive media

Interactive media solutions are socially constructed, tailored technological artifacts, often packaged as part of a wider IT, computer and management consulting solutions, and hence made up of both services and goods (including design, construction, maintenance, updating, etc.) (Pavlik, 1998). Most interactive media solutions are not ready-made goods, and usually do not exist at the time of purchase, meaning that buyers cannot always see what they are actually buying. This leads to certain problems regarding issues of trust and confidence discussed later in the chapter.

The said social construction not only involves the solutions themselves, but the meaning of what interactive media is, what needs it fulfills, how it should be produced, and the activities and actors involved. The outcomes of these constructions have implications on whether or not organizations will use interactive media, whether they will produce it or not, and, if not, whom they will turn to for help. Although this means that the meaning of interactive media as solutions and practice differs between actors and over time, the meaning is not arbitrary; some consensus needs to exist (Hacking, 1999), and when organizations and solutions have been constructed, they exist as structures and artifacts that limit and enable actors' opportunities (Archer, 1995). A technically founded definition based on the current understanding of those involved is: "digital solutions that incorporate several media (sound, images, etc.) that the user can interact with." The solutions are either off-line (CD-ROM, DVD), on-line (Internet/intranet solutions), wireless (WAP, 3G), or a combination thereof. Examples of such solutions are websites, computer games, e-business solutions and information kiosks.

The organization of interactive media production

Against this background, the organization of the supply and demand for interactive media services emerges as an uncertain field in which numerous interrelated forces may create rather different outcomes – both on an industry- and organizational level where different organizations may construct different interpretations and needs for these services. Thus, in the following, we look at the organization of both the supply side and the demand side of the business. The empirical data used originates from two firm-level surveys conducted within the MITIOR program. The first one was conducted in 2001 and was aimed at managers of Swedish firms that produce interactive media for external customers. The second survey, conducted in late 2001/early 2002, targeted managers responsible for IT in a sample of Swedish firms and government agencies, with more than 200 employees, that purchase, maintain and/or produce interactive media in-house for their own use. Roughly 350 firms responded to the first survey and 370 to the second. Additional data was collected through a visual analysis of interactive media producer websites and a study of Swedish media coverage of interactive media related topics. The design of the empirical studies is described in more detail elsewhere (Augustsson, 2004; Augustsson and Sandberg, 2004a; Sandberg and Augustsson, 2002).

The supply of interactive media services

The growth of interactive media production is commonly equated with the number or total revenues of companies that produce such solutions for external customers. But interactive media production cannot be reduced to a certain type of organization or organizational setting and, in official statistics, companies that produce interactive media for external customers are not defined as a single industry. If interactive media production is instead viewed as a practice aimed at creating a certain type of solution, it becomes clear that it can be organized in different ways and carried out by a variety of organizations. It is something that organizations can do by themselves, in cooperation with other organizations, or purchase as a service.

Firms that produce interactive media for external customers can be divided into: 1) newly started firms that only produce interactive media; 2) newly started firms that produce interactive media as well as providing other goods or services; 3) previously active firms that have moved into interactive media production that either continue to produce other things; or 4) those that do not. The results show that 36 percent of firms that produce interactive media for external customers were previously active ones that moved into interactive media production, and 74 percent of the firms are also active in other areas. Less than a quarter (23 percent) of the firms are newly started for the sole purpose of producing interactive media solutions for external customers, i.e. devoted interactive media experts.

Producers of interactive media for external customers do not only differ horizontally, i.e. having different scope and combinations of business areas, there is also vertical differentiation based on outsourcing of interactive media production to other firms acting as subcontractors to interactive media firms. Roughly two thirds (65 percent) of the firms that produce interactive media for external customers outsource part of this production to other firms and over half (54 percent) of the firms tend to function as subcontractors for other firms producing interactive media solutions. Further, 42 percent both function as subcontractor *and* outsource production, and less than one fourth (23 percent) are full-service providers that always handle all production internally. Thus, it is not only that firms are engaged in several business areas, they frequently also have different positions within interactive media production.

The above-described diversity and alternative and shifting positions of firms that produce interactive media solutions for external customers can also be seen among larger Swedish firms and government agencies, in terms of their internal interactive media operations. Nearly 40 percent of Swedish organizations with more than 200 employees produce all or parts of their interactive media solutions internally. Of these, 8 percent produce all of their solutions internally, and 32 percent produce parts of solutions and subcontract the rest to other firms. Another 37 percent purchase all of their interactive media from external producers, leaving 23 percent that claim not to use interactive media at all (see Table 7:1).[1]

	Firms	Government Agencies	All Organizations
Produce all	6 (12)	12 (18)	8 (30)
Produce some	28 (63)	36 (54)	32 (117)
Purchase	43 (95)	29 (43)	37 (138)
Do not use	23 (50)	23 (35)	23 (85)
Total	**100 (220)**	**100 (150)**	**100 (370)**

Table 7:1 Types of organizations and their involvement in interactive media. Proportions and (base numbers)

Seen as a whole, the above situation creates a more complex and dynamic picture than the traditional idea of buyers and sellers on a spot market. Buyers and sellers are not easily identified and separated groups of actors since both can be, and often are, producers, buyers and sellers. Rather, interactive media production constitutes a complex web of temporary horizontal and vertical structures (Augustsson, 2002b). Firms that produce interactive media solutions for external customers consist of a number of networked adhocracies characterized by flexible specialization with respect to both tasks and positions (Augustsson and Sandberg, 2003b), and organizations in general show a variety of involvement in interactive media ranging from more or less non-use to handling everything themselves. The latter further vary in how they organize their internal operations into separate departments, networks between departments or projects, etc. From this follows that make or buy are not black and white decisions, and that the purchase of interactive media expertise is an integrated part of the overall organization.

Sourcing interactive media services

Having briefly described the organization and structure of the supply of interactive media solution services in Sweden, the chapter now focuses on larger Swedish firms and government agencies with in-house operations, i.e. production, subcontracting, maintenance and purchasing of interactive media solutions, and how these organizations manage the sourcing of these services.

---

[1] According to a study by SCB, almost 100 per cent of larger Swedish companies use the Internet and have their own website (SCB, 2003). The major reason for the lower figure for Swedish organizations with interactive media solutions, 77 as compared to nearly 100 in the SCB study, is mostly due to a limited knowledge of interactive media and differences in terminology (Augustsson and Sandberg, 2004a).

Involvement in the development and purchasing process

As a part of IT solutions in general, interactive media solutions are becoming more central features of organizations' structures, especially with regard to information and communication flows. This means that the design of certain interactive media solutions is of crucial importance for organizational efficiency and the working situation of employees (Augustsson and Sandberg, 2003a). Since interactive media solutions are not usually standardized, as opposed to packaged software like Microsoft OSs (Operating Systems), their features and functions may differ even if the type of solution, e.g. website or intranet solution, is the same (Manovich, 2001). It is therefore of importance to identify the types of actors responsible for choosing production and collaborating partners, as well as the design of the solution, since different actors can maintain different perspectives on- and interests in the functioning of a technical solution (Latour, 1996).

The results show that the most common types of actors involved in the process of purchasing the latest interactive media solutions are representatives of IT and information departments and top management, who are involved in more than 50 percent of cases (see Figure 7:1). Least involved in these processes are end users and their representatives, as well as unions. Findings from organizations that produce their interactive media internally differ somewhat: the information department, managers of affected units and end users and their representatives are involved more frequently, whereas top management is less often involved.

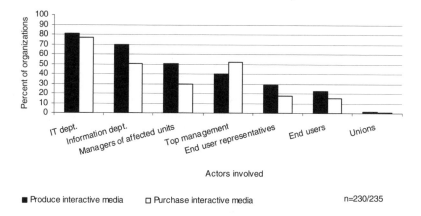

Figure 7:1 Groups involved in the development and purchase process of the latest interactive media solution in organizations, respectively

Three conclusions can be drawn from these findings. First, both production and purchase of interactive media solutions is a collective process that usually involves more than one type of organizational actor, meaning that devoted interactive media purchasers often do not exist (although some are probably more involved than others). Second, the decision-making process is more centralized when an organization chooses to purchase an interactive media solution than when solutions are developed internally. Users and other organizational members probably find it easier to demand influence over the design of solutions when they are produced by co-workers within the own organization than when they are developed by external experts. Further, purchase is most likely seen as more of a financial decision than in-house development and as something that mainly internal "experts" of technology (the IT department) and economy (top management) need or should be involved in. It is uncertain what role the external expert knowledge providers, the interactive media producers, play here. They may have an interest in limiting the number of actors they collaborate with since more participants usually implies more opinions on the design of the artifact, which may lead to communicative confusion and conflicting demands (Law and Callon, 1992). The third conclusion drawn is that even when solutions are produced internally, and even though the end users are the ones who are supposed to work with the solution, the involvement of the actual end users and their representatives is very limited. User involvement thus seems to exist more in discourse than in practice (Oudshoorn et al, 2004).

Distribution of activities

In our study, the practice of producing interactive media solutions was divided into 15 inherent central activities in order to investigate in more detail what is produced and purchased. These activities need not, but may be included in interactive media solutions, as indicated by the "not relevant" alternative in Figure 7:2. The point is that the production process can be divided and thereby performed by different actors, both inside and outside an organization, creating a division- and integration of labor within and between organizations (Augustsson, 2002a). The most common activities performed by the customer organizations themselves are content research, concept and storyboard, and graphic design. The activities organizations are least involved in are providing actors, video/film and sound/music, mainly because they are often not relevant for the solution being developed. Still, when they are relevant, more than half of organizations subcontract these activities. Excluding these activities, the least common are systems development, education of customers and strategic consulting. All of the latter represent specialist competencies that, for the most part, only experts have.

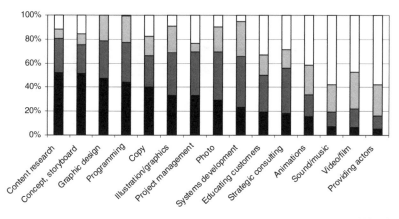

■ Yes (usually perform) ■ Sometimes (can perform) ▨ Subcontract □ Not relevant   n=143-147

Figure 7:2 Swedish organizations' performance and subcontracting of different activities related to interactive media production

An important finding is the variation regarding what each organization chooses to handle internally and what they subcontract to external experts. The proportion of organizations that perform an activity "sometimes" is in many cases as high or higher, than those that usually perform the activity internally or subcontract it, respectively. It is thus not only a question of whether to get involved in interactive media production or not, but also of what to do in specific production situations, and of organizations generally having a broader knowledge of interactive media than they take advantage of in each individual project: they can do it, but choose not to. Make or buy decisions, through which an organization's needs for external services are defined, thus seem to be repeatedly (re)negotiated and, in some cases, never settled, creating temporality and dynamics in the organization of production.

Reasons for making and reasons for buying

What, then, are the reasons for organizations to either produce interactive media solutions in- house or buy parts of- or total solutions from outside providers? Figure 7:3 shows the relative importance of different factors in user organizations' choice to keep interactive media production internal, and Figure 7:4 presents the reasons to outsourcing to other organizations according to a 5-point scale, where 1 is "not important at all" and 5 is "crucial".

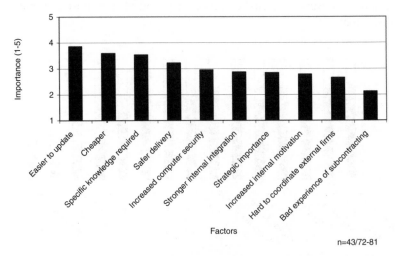

n=43/72-81

Figure 7:3 The relative importance of different factors in organizations' decision to handle interactive media production internally

The most important reasons to keep interactive media within the organization is the simplicity of updating, the belief that the functions require specific knowledge about the organization, that it is cheaper to produce internally and to secure delivery. The most important reasons for outsourcing interactive media production are the ability to focus on the organization's core competence, to gain technical and design competence, and to improve service for end users (Figure 7:4). The above-defined list of reasons for keeping the operations inside the organization differs somewhat from the reasons for outsourcing them, mainly because it made little sense to ask all types of organizations about certain factors. Nevertheless, it is possible to identify clear differences in the reasons organizations give for choosing one way of supplying interactive media over another.

Differences in the valuations of these factors may also help us understand why certain organizations prefer to buy interactive media services, while others develop internal capabilities. Organizations that produce everything internally cite a need to maintain control over the development process and seem to have less of a need to acquire external expert knowledge. Organizations that subcontract parts of production and those that purchase everything strongly emphasize the importance of focusing on core competencies, which apparently do not include interactive media production. They also stress the need to acquire expertise in technology and design, in part to improve security and ensure smooth operation of their interactive media solutions. These organizations do not have sufficient knowledge to produce all or parts of interactive media solutions or view such knowledge as their core competence, and hence turn to external providers to obtain solutions that work properly. These organizations seem more willing to accept the cost for this, both economically and in terms of security.

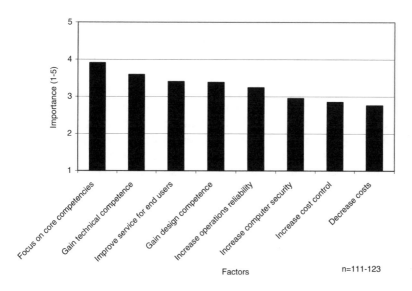

Figure 7:4 The relative importance of different factors in organizations' decisions to outsource interactive media operations

In essence, this means that organizations purchase what they lack the knowledge or willingness to produce themselves. This is almost a tautology, or at least an unsatisfactory answer that calls for further investigation. The view taken in this chapter, that interactive media services are socially constructed, introduces questions about how the expertise and practices involved in interactive media production become established as a specific kind of expert knowledge, which can be defined either as a core competence, implying its internal development, or as peripheral competence, implying its purchase. We will return to this question later in the chapter. Before doing so, however, we will take a look at the kinds of relations formed between providers of interactive media services and their buyers.

Relations with collaborating partners

As stated, tailored interactive media solutions are not bought as ready-made goods over the counter, often meaning that the relation between supplier and customer can become quite close and longstanding. This is especially the case for organizations that produce some interactive media internally and subcontract the rest to other organizations. Around 70 percent of organizations turned to their previous provider of expert interactive media knowledge the last time they outsourced interactive media production. Of these organizations, 37 percent of those that subcontract parts of interactive media production had some form of framework agreement, as compared to 29 percent of those that purchased everything. A plausible reason for the difference in the prevalence of framework agreements is that organizations that "only" purchase a solution might do so less frequently and see less reasons for a formal agreement with their suppliers, whereas organizations that subcontract parts of their interactive media operations view it more as an ongoing activity in which contact with suppliers is more important.

Another measure of the strength of relations between organizations is their perceived relative dependence. This is analyzed by asking organizations how they think that they, as well as the organization they collaborate with, would be affected if the collaboration were to cease. It is a hypothetical question, but elicits a picture of the subjectively perceived relative dependence between actors and serves as a predictor of how organizations will behave towards each other. 38 percent of organizations that subcontract parts of production state that they would have no problems if collaborations ended, as compared to 46 percent of organizations that purchase all of their solutions.

This means that more than half of organizations believe that they would have at least transitional problems if collaborations with their current providers of expert knowledge ceased. Again, it is organizations that produce some of their interactive media internally that feel more dependent on the external actors, showing that they have tighter connections with their collaborating partners than organizations that purchase entire solutions. Also interesting to note, given the troubled state of the IT sector at the time of study (the major IT crisis in Sweden started in late 2000), is the belief held by organizations that the companies they purchase solutions from or subcontract to would have fewer problems than themselves if collaborations ended. This suggests that the firms producing interactive media for Swedish organizations have been able to convince many purchasing organizations that they do provide a form of expert knowledge that is not easily replaced. In the following, we will take a closer look into the strategies applied in establishing the new and emerging practices and expertise of interactive media production as an expert service to be either developed internally or bought externally.

Constructing interactive media production as expert services

New areas of practice are constantly emerging in the business world. Some of these may be easily incorporated into ongoing areas of practice, while others provide the basis for the emergence of new areas and groups of experts. It is in the latter cases that make or buy decisions for organizations become salient. Given the emergence of a new area of expertise, organizations need to make decisions on whether this is a kind of expertise the organization needs, whether the organization should develop it internally or source it externally, etc. The construction of a specific area of expertise is thus a key prerequisite for organizations' constructions of needs for advisory services and will be the focus of this section.

Interactive media production is not a profession, although some of those involved, e.g. civil engineers and journalists are "semi-professionals" (Mähring, 2002 p. 65; Abbott 1988 pp. 83-84), new professionals (see Chapter 2). Common for all firms producing interactive media is that they have no certified or legitimate claims of being professionals experts since there is neither a previous history nor official, accredited education in interactive media production. It is more correct to speak of interactive media producers as self-proclaimed experts who attempt - and sometimes succeed in convincing others, both internal and external actors (Augustsson, 2004), of their expertise status (Robertson et al, 2003). Interactive media producers are thus knowledge-intensive firms (Alvesson, 2004). There is a lack of certification, i.e. an exclusive right to perform a certain practice in a differentiated society through the protection of the state's monopoly of violence. Anyone who wants and has the necessary knowledge, or at least can convince others that they have it (Augustsson and Sandberg, 2004b), can produce interactive media. With the lack of certification and thereby professional status, coupled with the generally limited knowledge of interactive media, and thereby purchasing skills, on the part of the customer (Wiklund and Shepherd, 2003 p. 1309), as well as the Klondike gold rush-like quality of the new economy, means convincing others of one's expert status has had to take on other forms (Sanders and Boivie, 2004). Such forms include building trust in this expertise by presentation and association, organization, and social relations. The need to be seen as a trustworthy provider of expert knowledge is particularly acute since firms are not only supposed to give advice, but actually deliver a working solution, with no finished good to show at the moment of purchase.

Trust by presentation and association

For interactive media producers, a fundamental aspect of trust building is how they present themselves to those outside the social field, which is done via their websites and through the media. The companies have to present an image of themselves as trustworthy and competent developers of interactive media. Given the novelty and known turbulence of the IT sector, they must also convince potential purchasers that they are in fact a serious and actually existing company, i.e. that they are providers of expert knowledge. On web pages, this is done visually by referencing a combination of aesthetic, technological and economic skills, and the use of institutionalized attributes characteristic of "serious" companies (Augustsson, 2004).

The media also play a role in the presentation of interactive media firms as providers of expert knowledge (Petterson and Leigard, 2002) and it is a form of presentation that firms can only partially control (Fombrun and Shanley, 1990). Since most media coverage of interactive media producers has focused on e.g. share values, rather than firms' quality as expert knowledge providers, the extent to which the media has been an avenue by which to build trust is uncertain. Increases in investors' and analysts' firm valuation may be a sign of high quality, i.e. of expertise and trustworthiness, since potential buyers might think it is more likely that firms that perform well financially are good at what they do. Reports on firms that win high prestige accounts appear in specialist media such as Computer Sweden, but potential purchasers probably seldom read them.

Since customer knowledge of specific interactive media firms and the social field and development process in general is limited, an important factor in a firm's self-presentation is trust by association: even if potential customers might not know of the firm per se, they might be familiar with other firms that it is- or has been associated with. Thus, many interactive media producers present the names of current and previous customers and development projects. This is a way of showing that they can in fact provide the expert knowledge they claim, and that other firms have preferred them as expert providers or collaborating partners. The more widely known one's current and previous customers and collaborating partners are, and the higher their status, the more effective this form of trust creation is. For potential customers, this can be a rational strategy; having faith in others means that the costly process of trying to make informed rational decisions can be shortened. This does of course create risks, since one's faith in trusted decision-makers may not mirror their real capacity to make informed decisions. Citing well-known previous customers as a sign of one's expertise and trustworthiness similarly occurs in areas such as management consulting (Micklethwait and Wooldridge, 1996) and fashion photography (Aspers, 2001), where some accounts or clients are valued more for their ability to lend status to the seller rather than their value as actual customers.

One form of trust by association is the "semi-certification" that some interactive media producing companies have. For instance, they might be certified deliverers, installers or maintainers of hard- and/or software from Microsoft, IBM or Sun. The idea behind this form of trust creation is that major, well-known IT firms like those mentioned would not risk their reputation and brand name by making low quality or irresponsible companies certified providers of their products and services. For this to work, however, there must be a sense of exclusivity attached to the certification, at least as perceived by customers: if everyone who wants to can be a certified provider, then certification's role as a trust-creating tool diminishes. Coca-Cola is one of the strongest brands in the world, but any hotdog vendor who wants to can sell Coke, so whether or not a particular vendor does sell Coke or not says nothing of the quality of the hotdog or the vendor's business performance.

Among interactive media producers, it is mostly smaller and more local actors that explicitly state their status as certified providers. It would seem that larger and more well-known firms are not in need of it; it is more or less taken for granted that they can get certification if they want it. Certification as a provider might have a negative effect for more high-status firms, since they may be potential competitors to the firms whose solutions they provide and "should" not need the support of others. Rather, they ought to develop standardized solutions of their own. Jonas Birgersson, co-founder and previous front figure of Framfab, publicly challenged Microsoft's dominance by throwing a brick through a glass window at a press conference, the brick representing Framfab's program – "Brikks", and the window Microsoft's OS – "Windows" (Willim, 2002).

Trust by standardization

Customers' knowledge of interactive media technologies and development processes is generally quite vague. This can lead to a sense of insecurity among customers who may view the technology as unstable and the development process as characterized by an ad hoc- or lack of clear organization (which might no be far from the truth). A way to overcome this insecurity and to create an image of being a trustworthy provider of expert knowledge is to present the technology and/or development process as standardized (Sigma, 2000). The company can thereby present itself as being in control and on top of things. In reality, however, the development process need not be as structured as the idealized models, as the rational unified process (RUP) model depicts them. An example, which also involves trust by association, is the IT company Adstream, whose website reports that "Adstream has won the trust of delivering the web content management system for the Swedish Children's Ombudsman (BO), based on Adfinity™" (Adstream, 2004). In some cases, this standardization can be demanded by prospective customers (Räisinen and Linde, 2004, especially p. 106). Several interactive media firms do point to the standardization of either technology or the development process. In general, this standardization would appear to be a result of the codification of previously tacit and experience-based knowledge that is specific to the firm. Firms that have developed a number of interactive media solutions develop routines that are transformed into prescriptions (Mackenzie and Wajcman, 1999). Although not based on actual comparison of alternative development methods, these routines work in practice and are kept until further notice.

Organizing trust

There is no central authority that can issue certificates for interactive media production and thereby legitimize claims to expert status in the field, but there are a small number of Swedish professional and trade organizations related to interactive media production, the most well-known and influential of these is "IT-företagen" ("IT Companies"), with roughly 550 member companies. By covering the entire IT sector, it is broader than interactive media production. On its website (www.itforetagen.se), IT-företagen claims that membership entails a "seal of quality," which shows that a company is serious and trustworthy. To what extent this actually holds true in the eyes of interactive media customers is far from certain: although the IT-företagen organization is fairly well known, it is unclear whether membership is seen as a sign of quality and trustworthiness. Further, membership in IT-företagen is based on approval, which signals some form of exclusivity. Still, it is unlikely that interactive media customers are aware of this, and having roughly 550 member companies from one sector in a country the size of Sweden does not really make it an elite organization (of organizations). Some, but far from all, of the member firms present themselves as members of IT-företagen on their websites, indicating that, in relation to potential customers, it is hardly crucial for trust-building and construction of expertise status.

The trade organization Promise (Producers of interactive media in Sweden), www.promise.se, focuses directly on interactive media producers and had roughly 40 member firms in 2004. Considering that the total number of Swedish firms producing interactive media was estimated at more than 700 at the time, their coverage is limited. Further, customers of interactive media solutions in general seem to have limited knowledge of the existence and purpose of Promise (as it is rarely mentioned in the media, for instance). As a result, Promise's role as a source of constructing status is highly limited, despite claims of being "a strong support for you [firms] and an engine for the industry" and that "Promise membership is a sign of quality" (as translated from Swedish). Moreover, few of the member firms explicitly state their membership in Promise.

Thus, even though membership in trade and industry organizations is a potential source of status and trust, it is not one that is used to any greater extent by firms that produce interactive media, nor does it seem to have any greater impact on their customers. Still, both IT-företagen and Promise do have an impact on producer-purchaser relations and the construction of trust through limitation of insecurity. Both trade organizations have developed standard agreements and contracts that they offer their member firms, as well as prospective customers. These standardized agreements, which generally require some modification and specification, is a way of specifying the activities included in the practice, i.e. what expert knowledge to provide, as well as the division and integration of labor between the parties involved.

Social relations

Given that most expert knowledge provision is affected by interpersonal communication and that the purchase of interactive media solutions usually requires repeated interaction between producer and purchaser over a period of time, the role of social relations in the construction of trust would seem to be important. From the producers' viewpoint, there is clearly an interest in establishing longstanding relations with purchasers since this increases the opportunities for future contracts and sales. However, there was quite a large proportion of purchasing organizations that turned to a new producer the last time they purchased a solution even though many claimed that they were dependent on their suppliers for the provision of expert knowledge. Media sources frequently report on interactive media producers that have lost contracts, so customers do seem willing to cut ties with firms despite the potential problems this might cause. It would thus seem that social relations do play a role, albeit a complicated one, in the establishment of trust for the expertise involved in interactive media production.

Discussion: The organization of expert IT knowledge

The above description of the emerging expertise of interactive media production, its legitimization, its organization in terms of how it is structured, by whom it is needed, and by whom it is provided, illustrates considerable variability in how different firms chose to react to this emerging expertise and thus how the expertise and its buyers and suppliers become organized.

By defining the activities inherent in a practice and examining who performs them, as has been done in this chapter, it becomes possible to ask how production and consumption is organized, i.e. how expert knowledge is constructed and provided. It has been argued that practices are socially constructed, meaning that what they consist of, what needs they fulfill, who should be involved, and how they should be performed, are not given. Instead, they are repeatedly contested and at times the source of open conflict. As a result, it is not always clear what should be included in a practice. This is perhaps more clearly visible in expert knowledge such as management consulting, but also in interactive media production: What does it mean to develop an interactive media solution? What is it that actually "should" be done? The inherent insecurity, partially based on differing interpretations and identifications of the actors involved (White, 1992), is one reason why actors have a mutual interest in specifying contracts in great detail (or ensuring that they cover "all" situations), or developing close long-term relations based on trust that offer flexibility and mutually forgiving attitudes towards differences in interpretation.

The social construction of expert provision and the division and integration of inherent activities between actors also involves those that are supposed to be involved, both in general, i.e. the *type* of actor, and specifically, i.e. the *particular* actors (White, 2002). When an organization comes to the conclusion that certain expert knowledge should not be provided internally, it has to make up its mind what other types of actors to turn to in order to acquire this knowledge, and what particular actors to approach. Further, the relations between different actors, e.g. in terms of formal and informal dependencies, have to be negotiated (Alter and Hage, 1993).

From this perspective then, an organization's purchase of expertise is an outcome resulting from a prior decision that a) some knowledge is needed, and that b) it should not be provided internally. In reality, the actual steps in the process may differ and change over time. From the point of view of the producing organization, it becomes natural to talk of different forms of organization and to view purchase and production as alternative ways of providing expert knowledge. This is in line with transaction cost economics as initially formulated by (Coase, 1937) and later operationalized and refined by (Williamson, 1985), although the reasons why organizations choose to either produce or purchase differ. Further, no goods or services are produced on markets, they merely act as a way of exchanging resources: that which is not produced in one organization is generally produced in another (Sayer and Walker, 1992). Thus, there is a division and integration of labor within and between organizations that creates complex webs of relations and interdependencies between a large number of organizations and a social structuring of markets (Granovetter, 1985). This is especially the case for expert knowledge since it is not an easily packaged and valued good. Instead of a "simple" make or buy decision, as described in transaction cost economics, it is rather one of "'make it yourself or hope that other known and trustworthy providers with sufficient knowledge, with whom you have particular forms of relations, will make it and sell it to you at an acceptable cost and quality in due time according to negotiated but imperfect agreements."

There is currently a growing discussion on the role of knowledge as a key factor in the limits of the division of labor (Becker and Murphy, 1992), as opposed to the role of e.g. markets and incentive structures/control (e.g. Alchian and Demsetz, 1999; Smith, 1952). The basic idea is that organizations cannot have all the knowledge they need internally, but are forced to get it in other forms, e.g. through markets or collaborations with other organizations (Kogut et al, 1992). Further, the availability of knowledge is seen as the most important factor in deciding the boundaries of the firm. This has been combined with the idea of success through a focus on the core competencies of the organization and outsourcing of practically everything else in a time of increased competition due to factors such as globalization and innovations in ICT (Barney, 1995; Prahalad and Hamel, 1990). This is an extension of the Tayloristic vertical separation between hand and brain (Braverman, 1974), whereby expert knowledge is externalized, making the purchasing of knowledge, rather than management of subordinates, a central tasks of managers.

There is justified criticism of the need for organizations to focus on their core competencies and outsource all support functions, but it is clear that these ideas have had a practical influence, e.g. through management literature (Furusten, 1999), and thereby affected the organization of knowledge provision. The idea of core competencies can also have financial consequences for firms since analysts and investors may punish firms that do not focus on core competencies, i.e. adhere to the institutions or management fads, by lowering share values (see Lee, 2001). In the case of interactive media services, the concept of core competencies was central in defining organizations reactions to the emerging expertise. A large proportion of respondents in this study stated that the focus on core competencies is one of the main reasons for not handling interactive media production internally. The need to focus on core competencies might be seen as a institutionalized, legitimate justification or rationalization of decisions related to expert knowledge provision, even though the decision-making process might not be especially rational or conscious, and sometimes both uncertain and ambiguous (March and Olsen, 1976). The idea of core competencies might not have any real organizational substance, but be real in its consequences as a held belief, a belief that may be rational to adhere to or by which to legitimize decisions.

The above discussion shows the importance of understanding the production and purchase of expert knowledge in a perspective broader than single organizations – a perspective that incorporates several organizations within a social field, the ideas governing this field, and the organization of activities within and between organizations engaged in a certain practice (White, 2002). The starting point is the actual practice, the service that is produced and used by organizations. Here, this refers to both the actual performance of practical tasks and the procedural knowledge, i.e. the knowledge of the procedures for how to do things (Knorr-Cetina. 1999), which can be hard to separate. The purchasing process is itself part of the practice and requires involvement and action. In IT development projects, the amount of the time spent communicating about the solution (talking, writing memos, etc.) may be greater than the time actually spent on actions such as programming and installing hardware (Robertson et al, 2003, p. 843). This communication is an integrated part of the development process whereby the relevant groups construct a closure on the meaning of an increasingly tangible solution (Bijker and Law, 1992); it becomes a node through which dialogue centers, and thereby functions as an actor in itself (Law and Hassard, 1999). The social construction of the technology through talk and action shows that the technology is not objective and hence cannot function, although presented as such, as a value-free basis for claiming expertise. Still, the technology and the methods of developing it are the epistemological bases for interactive media producers' status as experts (Knorr-Cetina, 1999).

Conclusions

This chapter has focused on the emerging organization of a new field of expertise – interactive media production – which largely emerged during the 1990s. Interest has been devoted to the emerging patterns of supply and demand between different organizations as well as the legitimization of the expertise of interactive media production as such. This investigation indicated that organizations reacted rather differently to the challenges posed by the new expertise. Some organizations developed internal capabilities, while others chose to purchase the expertise externally. A majority of organizations, however, applied mixed patterns of make and buy, which often change from project to project. One influential factor on organizations' decisions of whether to seek external advice rather than rely on internal expertise was the organization's view of the expertise as core competence as opposed to non-core competence. A common denominator of organizations that did not develop internal interactive media production was their perception of this knowledge as not being a core competency for the organization, a perception that needs to be problematized given that the idea of the existence and focus on core competencies function as powerful management institutions.

The chapter also indicates that choices concerning the sourcing of expertise implied different practices in terms of producing the service, e.g. as reflected in differences in user involvement. The buying of services implies a rather different involvement of stakeholders within the buying organizations than the internal production of the same services, thus rendering the make or buy decision more than a mere sourcing decision. Rather, it is a decision of what kind of product the organization wants. Finally, the chapter turned to the question of how new areas of expertise, such as interactive media production, were legitimated. Four different mechanisms were discussed, including presentation and association, standardization, organization and social relations, all of which were applied by the suppliers of interactive media solutions, albeit to different degrees, to enforce the expert status of the knowledge and thus the need for their services.

The emergence of new areas of expertise is thus a potential trigger for the emergence of new needs for external advisors. The establishment of the expertise as well as the organization of demand and supply are however complex processes. Individual organizations were found to have considerable freedom to react to the emerging knowledge in different ways, depending on their specific backgrounds and perceptions of their own (core) competencies.

CHAPTER 8

Needs and Interaction

How auditing firm services are purchased

NICLAS HELLMAN

Auditors represent what may be called a "traditional" profession in the sense that specifically authorized bodies tightly control their knowledge base as well as the quality of their services. Clear criteria stipulate the educational and experiential background of an auditor, and only those that have become certified in this way may engage in the auditing of organizations. Auditors thus have the kind of well-defined knowledge base that other services discussed previously, such as management consultants, financial advisors and providers of interactive media solutions, are lacking, and which complicated the purchasing process for the buyer, creating uncertainty concerning both the need for advisory services as well as the selection of providers. This chapter focuses on the purchase of advisory services from auditing firms and devotes special interest to the question of whether the more solid knowledge base of auditors creates different patterns in the purchase of these services as opposed to the other, previously discussed services.

Auditing firm services may be classified into "assurance services" and "other services".[1] The purpose of assurance services is to improve the quality of information to external users by improving the reliability or relevance of the information. Assurance services include *attest*

---

[1]   This classification originates from the American Institute of Certified Public Accountants (cf. AICPA, 1997; Elliot, 1997).

services (audits, examinations, reviews and agreed-upon procedures) and *compilation services* (preparing financial statements). The attest service implies that the auditing firm issues a written statement that expresses a conclusion about the reliability of, for example, the financial statements in a company. The primary attest service is the statutory audit. Other services include *technology services* (system analysis, information management, system security), *management consulting, financial planning* (tax planning, complex financial transactions, financial statement analysis, etc.) and *international services* (cross-border tax planning, international joint ventures, multinational mergers, etc.). The character of these services differs, and it will be argued that this raises different types of uncertainty in the purchasing situation.

In Chapter 1, Furusten and Werr describe two different ways for the buyer of management advisory services to reduce uncertainty: (i) professionalization (uncertainty reduction through productification, standardization, etc.) and (ii) interaction (uncertainty reduction through trust and mutual interdependence). Applying this terminology, the statutory audit, being an assurance service, could be classified as a service where the uncertainty of need and choice is reduced primarily by professionalization. Throughout the world, most local laws require public companies to have an auditor (see Needles, 2000), making the need for the service beyond doubt, and tough regulations and professional norms that surround this service set a standard for the quality, reducing the uncertainty concerning the choice between alternative suppliers. In Sweden, for example, authorized auditors are licensed and monitored by a regulatory state authority. This requires candidates to have about four years of post-graduate training, at least five years of practice and to pass an exam administered by the regulatory authority (KPMG, 1997, p. 30). While organizations are forced by law to purchase a statutory audit, their purchase of additional advisory services is up to them. Some clients may choose the legally required minimum version and refrain from using the auditing firms for other services. Other clients may view the auditing firms as key suppliers of both highly valuable audits and additional services. In the following, companies' purchase of additional advisory services from auditors will be examined in more detail. To what extent do organizations buy these services? How are they bought? How does the need for them arise? And how does the "professional" character of the statutory audit service influence these issues?

The chapter is organized as follows. The next two sections further elaborate on the different characteristics of audit firm services in terms of professionalization and interaction, including some quantitative descriptive results. Thereafter, empirical results from two studies are reported and discussed in three separate sections, and conclusions are provided in the final section.

Three sources of empirical data are used in the chapter: (i) a study of annual reports data regarding auditing firm fees in all Swedish listed companies 1999-2003,[2] (ii) an interview study of CFOs from large Swedish companies conducted in 2002 (16 companies) and (iii) a case study of the audit process in a Swedish listed company.

The characteristics of auditing firm services

As outlined in the introduction, an auditee must at a minimum purchase a standardized statutory audit, but has the opportunity of buying a "value added" version of the statutory audit and additional advisory services, both involving more interaction with the auditing firm. The relationship between these client purchase alternatives and the concepts of standardization and interaction is illustrated in Figure 8:1.

Figure 8:1 Relationship between client purchase alternatives and the concepts of standardization and interaction

Figure 8:1 illustrates that if the client only wants an audit that fulfills the minimum legal requirement (Service A), there is a market for relatively standardized statutory audits where the price competition is tough. In terms of the terminology used in Chapter 1, the buyer's uncertainty about the quality of the service is reduced by professionalization. However, if the client wants a more "value added" audit (Service A*) or additional advisory services (Service B), this will require more interaction with the auditing firm. The buyer's uncertainty about the quality of the service is then reduced through trust and mutual interdependence. There is also a fundamental theoretical difference between the statutory audit and the additional

---

[2]   The number of listed companies were 335 (1999), 346 (2000), 347 (2001) and 330 (2002).

advisory services in the sense that the former is formally ordered by the owners of the firm, while the latter are purchased by management.

The fundamental role of the statutory audit

An important aspect of auditing firm services is that the core service, the external audit, is statutory and subject to much regulation. This legal requirement automatically gives the auditing firm many clients, which, in turn, provide opportunities to also sell other services. This may give auditing firms incentives to offer the statutory audit at a low price when competing for new clients. This in turn may lead to initial losses for new audit assignments, since the costs and risks are particularly high with regard to new clients.

The purpose of the statutory audit is to increase the reliability of information for external users. Therefore, the auditor authorization process indicates the high competence that is required. Another key factor is the reputation of credibility and independence that is needed in order to sell assurance services. These factors are particularly important to the external users of company information, especially *auditor independence*.[3] If owners and creditors suspects that the auditor is refraining from criticizing his/her client for erroneous financial statements, because of friendship with management, economic dependence or for some other reason, the assurance service loses its value and the auditing firm loses its business. There is therefore much regulation concerning auditor independence. With regard to advisory services, one key rule is that an auditor should not first provide advice on a particular issue (for example, tax-related advice) and then audit the same issue.[4] Another measure taken by regulators in some countries is to require disclosure of the fees paid to auditing firms regarding the external audit and additional advisory services.

From a management perspective, it is important to signal to owners and creditors that the statutory audit is of sufficiently high quality. The choice of a Big Four firm is often used as a proxy for high quality audits in this context.[5] If management sees no further internal value of the statutory audit, there is little reason to buy anything more than such a (relatively cheap) standardized audit. In several countries, audit fees

---

[3] For a recent discussion on auditor independence, see Dopuch et al (2003).

[4] According to the Swedish Auditors Act, for example, an auditor should not accept the audit assignment under such circumstances.

[5] See Craswell et al (1995). The Big Four firms are PWC, KPMG, Ernst and Young and Deloitte.

are public and the minimum prices are quite easy to observe for other companies.

Purchases of standardized audits could be expected to make the relationship between auditor and the auditee relatively impersonal. In a way, this is in line with the basic idea of the independent audit, following from agency theory. However, this requires that the auditors are really independent. If management has much impact on the choice of auditors, it could replace auditors that are too critical to management.[6]

Purchases of additional advisory services

While the purchase of the statutory audit seems rather straightforward – it is mandatory and strictly regulated, reducing uncertainty concerning both the need and the quality of the service – the purchase of additional advisory services follows a different logic. The need for these services is created in interaction between the buyer and the seller, similar to management consultancy services. The starting point for the sale of additional services, however, is still the statutory audit. Thus, the key question is how to use the statutory audit in order to create interaction and subsequent sales of advisory services. The answer is that the standardized statutory audit needs to become a "value added" audit (see Figure 8:1) that the client appreciates on its own merits. If management finds the statutory audit useful, it will cooperate more with the auditing firm, which will make the client more dependent on its auditing firm. If the auditing firm succeeds in creating interaction, it has a competitive advantage in constructing needs for its services compared to other consultants in that the statutory audit gives them very good company knowledge. When a new problem comes up, the auditing firm has a short start-up time. Based on their knowledge of the buyer, the auditing firm may also identify problems that their clients have, and suggest solutions. But to what extent do organizations really buy advisory services from their auditors?

Since 2000, Swedish annual reports include information about (i) audit fees and (ii) fees paid to auditing firms for advisory services. A study of annual reports data for 2002 reveals that Swedish listed companies paid their auditing firms a total of 2.3 billion SEK. This corresponds to an average amount of 7 MSEK per company. A little more than half of the fees (56%) were reported as audit fees, while the rest (44%) were fees concerning additional advisory services. During

---

[6] See, for example, Chow and Rice (1982).

1999-2001, advisory service revenues grew faster than the audit fees, but in 2002 the trend changed quite dramatically as advisory services dropped by 13 percent compared to 2001. However, increased audit fees compensated the lower revenues from advisory services.

Focusing on large companies, the largest 10 percent of the listed companies paid, on average, annual audit fees of 76 MSEK during the period 1999-2002. The corresponding annual fees for advisory services amounted to 77 MSEK. However, although the average annual purchases of advisory services equaled the annual audit fees, there were major differences within the group. About half of the large companies (47%) purchased advisory services for significantly lower amounts than their audit fees (advisory service fees being less than 75 percent of the audit fees), while a little more than a quarter (27%) purchased advisory services for amounts that were significantly higher than their audit fees (advisory service fees being more than 125 percent of the audit fees). This further implies that the purchases of advisory services in the ">125% group" were particularly high since the total fees for audits and advisory services were about equal, on average. About 80 percent of fees for advisory auditing firm services in the group of large companies went to their largest supplier. In all cases, this auditing firm was also responsible for the statutory audit, either alone or together with another auditing firm.

Purchasing auditing services – A CFO perspective

This section presents results from an interview study of chief financial officers (CFOs) and other financial managers in high positions in 16 of the largest Swedish companies (15 of which are listed on the Stockholm Stock Exchange). The interviews were conducted in February-May 2002.

The procurement of the statutory audit

The procurement of the statutory audit is a starting point for selling additional services to clients. In Swedish limited companies, the auditors are appointed at the annual general meeting for four years at a time. In large companies, a tender process often precedes this appointment.

The procurement of the statutory audit had different status in the various companies. In many, there seemed to be a tradition of assigning low priority to auditing issues and auditors. In line with this view, the responsibility for auditor contacts and procurement was delegated from the board and the CFO to the internal audit department.

One of the interviewees responded as follows when asked about who was responsible for the procurement of the external audit:

> *That's what my boss asked me yesterday as well: "Are you responsible for this or is it the internal audit department?" I don't find it that fun to deal with the procurement of auditors; I want someone else to handle it. I'll see to that the internal audit department takes care of it.*

This quotation illustrates a relatively low status of the external audit, and one could expect that this will have implications for the purchase of additional advisory services. If the auditors have little contact with the top executives, it is probably more difficult to sell additional advisory services.

However, there seemed to be a general tendency of increased status for the auditors in response to the big accounting scandals (Enron and Worldcom), and there were companies who took the procurement of auditors very seriously. One of these interviewees described a recent tender process as follows:

> *The tender process lasted for about six months. The process started with a review of the present audit, leading to a specification of requirements. Thereafter, we made a tender invitation and received five offers. Then the auditing firms came here and presented themselves and their offers. We then started an extensive review process involving many people, including some specifically appointed persons from the board, the CFO, the accounting and finance department and the internal audit department. Both the CFO and the board members took active part in the review of the offers. The review resulted in five main criteria with many sub-criteria. The auditing firm's offers were rated with regard to these criteria. The five criteria were:*
>
> 1. *Functionality – global partnership: the ability to perform a homogeneous audit throughout the world managed by the Stockholm office.*
> 2. *Lead team and lead partners – what auditing firm staff would be in charge of the audit?*
> 3. *Audit methodology – what techniques did the firms focus on and how did this match the company's own ambitions in different areas?*
> 4. *Audit team organization in response to how the company was organized.*

5. *Price.*

Three firms were left after this review with ratings, and there was then another round of presentations. Thereafter, one auditing firm was selected.

In summary, this procurement focused on (i) what people were involved at the top (lead team), (ii) whether the auditing firm had the appropriate organization and techniques to conduct an efficient audit in a global company, and (iii) whether the price was competitive. This way of purchasing the statutory audit would seem to yield better opportunities for selling additional advisory services.

CFO attitudes and pricing

There were clear differences between the interviewees in terms of their *attitudes* towards the external audit and auditors. One group of interviewees was quite critical, and argued that the external audit was of little value to the client, partly because they perceived the audit to be too superficial. One of these interviewees made the following comment.[7]

> *Do you think that the external audit is made in the same way now as before [refers to ten years earlier]? No, they know as little now as they did then. They haven't got time to become involved in the business. They have their very specific task of auditing receivables and payables in the balance sheet and seeing if there are any material risks related to what management has achieved.*

With regard to the price paid for the statutory audit, almost all of the interviewees said there had been intense price pressure in recent years. The interviewees with a more negative attitude believed that this audit cost reduction was positive for the company, and that the auditing firms had to speed up and become more efficient. However, they were also aware of the great time pressure the low price placed on the auditing firms. One of the interviewees said:

> *We have squeezed the external auditors, "You get this fixed amount of money," and they just don't have all the time in the world [to complete the audit].*

This description of price pressure may seem inconsistent with the audit fee increases described above. A plausible interpretation is that the

---

[7]   Interviewer words are in bold type.

price pressure in Sweden refers mainly to the period before 2000.[8] From 1999-2002, prices were on their way up and this may perhaps be linked to the trend of an increased focus on auditors in companies and in media in response to the major accounting scandals. In a Swedish business newspaper (*SvD Näringsliv*) article from 17 January 2003, two high representatives of Swedish auditing firms (the CEO of Ernst and Young Sweden and the chairman of PWC Sweden) claim that audit fees would need to be further increased by 25-30 percent in response to the accounting scandals and the increased complexity of international accounting standards.

It was not possible to determine whether the companies with negative attitudes to their auditors also paid low audit fees and vice versa. The audit fee depends on many things, such as organizational structure (number of legal units, number of foreign units) and the quality of the company's internal control system. This makes it difficult to compare audit fees across companies and to determine what companies have purchased low-price audits.

CFO attitudes and purchases of additional advisory services

With regard to additional advisory services, there was no clear-cut correlation between companies with a negative attitude to their auditors and small purchases of additional advisory services. There was such a correlation for some of the companies, but not for all of them. However, with regard to companies with a more positive attitude to their auditors, there was a positive correlation with the purchases of additional advisory services. In particular, the companies purchasing much advisory services also had positive attitudes toward their auditors. What was decisive for companies that purchased much advisory services? First, they emphasized the *legitimacy* and *security* that the auditors provided with regard to the quality of the financial accounts. Some of these CFOs had also received public support from their auditors regarding controversial accounting issues. Another aspect was the *company-specific knowledge* that the auditor gained through the audit assignment. One interviewee made the following comment:

---

[8] There are no public data confirming lowered audit fees and tough price competition during the 1990s. However, there are a number of anecdotal observations in the mass media that indicate that the audit fees may have dropped dramatically. For example, in an interview printed 27 February 2001 in the Swedish business newspaper *Dagens Industri,* Reidar Peters (auditor for several listed companies during the 1990s) said: "I know a number of companies where the audit fee went halves. You get what you pay for, and there is a big risk that audit quality is markedly reduced." (translated from Swedish)

> *Being the auditor of the group, you get certain insights that are very valuable to us if we need help in terms of consultancy services.*

As indicated in this quotation, there were only certain people at the auditing firm, the lead team, that had this company-specific knowledge. It appeared to be very important for the client that these people had the *ability to interact with management*. One of the interviewees described this as follows:

> *One is very dependent on having the right people, that you have the right match between people. In our case, I think we have good conditions. I like the auditors very much and we use them very often for discussions. They're not the kind of auditors who work in isolation; they work with a sensitive ear. We can have breakfast meetings where we reason about things, so that you don't first do things and then the auditors come and tell you that "this was not good."*

Many of the interviewees emphasized that the use of the auditors was very dependent on the people that represented the auditing firm.

A basic difference between the companies concerned *the ways in which they used their auditors*. One interviewee, who had experienced two extremes, described this as follows.

> *I believe there's a major difference between how we work with the external auditors here [at company Y] and how they worked at [company X]. If you think about it afterwards, there was no clear difference between auditing and advisory services [in company X]. There, you sat down with the auditors and solved problems. Here we do our job first and then comes the external audit. After that, we have a discussion about what is right and wrong. In [company X] I sat down with [the engagement partner] and discussed it until we reached a solution. That's a significant difference compared to now.*

In company X, where the CFO used to work, there was no clear delimitation between the external audit and the additional advisory services. The external audit itself included advisory services and, in addition to that, company X purchased much advisory services. However, there were problems with the internal control systems in company X, and they needed the auditing firm to help them solve these problems. In company Y, the CFO had a positive attitude towards the auditors and they purchased relatively much advisory services. However, company Y had better internal control systems and the relationship with the auditor was very different compared to the one in company X. This implies that the interaction between management and auditors could work very differently depending on the quality of the client's internal control systems and financial reporting process.

In summary, there are some tentative relationships between the external audit and purchases of advisory services that should be emphasized. First, there is a tendency for companies with a positive attitude towards the audit to also be more positive towards purchasing additional advisory services. Second, the extent to which additional advisory services are purchased seems to depend on the specific persons that represent the auditing firm. Highly competent auditors with company-specific knowledge and the ability to interact with management seem linked to the purchase of additional services. It was particularly appreciated if the auditors helped their clients to improve the external legitimacy of their financial reporting quality. Third, it seems like the way the auditors are used during the external audit affects the clients' purchases of advisory services. On the one hand, high accounting quality (HAQ) companies with well-functioning internal control systems required less auditing effort. This led to less interaction with the auditors, which seemed linked to a reduced amount of advisory services. On the other hand, low accounting quality (LAQ) companies that involved their auditors more for internal control improvements at an earlier stage seemed more inclined to purchase additional advisory services. Of course, many of the companies fall somewhere between these two extremes. After this overview of CFO attitudes and uses of accounting-related services, we now turn to an in-depth study of the purchase of such services.

Purchasing auditing services – A case study

The results presented in this section are based on a case study of a listed Swedish industrial company, audited by a Big Four firm.[9] The data consist of (i) the audit memoranda (management letters and other documents) that the client received from its external auditors 1999-2001, (ii) in-depth interviews, based on the audit memoranda, with the company's financial managers at different hierarchical levels (16 interviews), and (iii) several informal interviews with the audit engagement partner. The case company will be referred to as

---

[9]   The case company is not one of the 16 companies in the interview study.

"CLIENTCO" and the auditing firm as "AUDFIRM". Audit fees as a percentage of sales, for the last four years, were lower in CLIENTCO than the industry average. This was due partly to the well-functioning internal control systems and the relatively simple organizational structure, and partly to price pressure (see below). The fees for additional services were at the same level as the audit fees, which means that the company was an average buyer of such services. CLIENTCO did not purchase advisory services from any other auditing firm, which implies a more dominant position for the auditing firm compared to the average.

The tender

AUDFIRM had won the tender for the statutory audit in CLIENTCO some years earlier. From CLIENTCO's point of view, three things had been decisive for choosing AUDFIRM: the specific persons that represented AUDFIRM, the internal control-focused approach to the audit, and the low fixed price. From AUDFIRM's point of view, the low price was motivated by the high standard of the accounting and the internal control systems in CLIENTCO, but a tough time schedule had to be imposed in order to meet the budget. It was also important that the audit team members charged extra fees if they did any work that was not included in the fixed price agreement.

Purchased advisory services

The types of additional services that were ordered from AUDFIRM fit well into the classification provided by the AICPA. With regard to *assurance services*, many of the interviewees referred to the need to purchase extra audits of sales subsidiaries, where the risks were not material but where CLIENTCO felt a need for better control. A number of interviewees also referred to the purchase of attest services with regard to insurance, government funds, written agreements, etc. With regard to *other services*, the interviewees referred most frequently to technology services, i.e. the development of internal systems involving information technology solutions. Other services mentioned by the interviewees concerned consultancy services regarding tax, accounting issues, organizational change, foreign joint ventures, cross-border transfer pricing, and international project management.

Interaction between the client and the auditing firm

All interviewees seemed to view the auditors primarily as critical scrutinizers of CLIENTCO. The auditors did not work proactively with selling additional advisory services. Overall, it would seem that it was

CLIENTCO who took initiatives regarding additional advisory services. The members of the audit team did not behave as sellers of advisory services. At the same time, the audit itself was of some value to the client, and the individuals at the auditing firm were very important. One of the interviewees described this as follows:

> *We regard [AUDFIRM] as an external consultant among others, but what is important is not [AUDFIRM] per se. We saw when we made the tender that the auditing firms are quite similar – the offers looked almost alike and the prices as well. It's about people. When you work together it's important to have the right, good persons – in the important factories and on the partner level. If things don't work, we have to find a way of changing [persons].*

What made auditing firm persons valuable to CLIENTCO had to some extent to do with their being technically competent, but also things like having good communication skills and being familiar with CLIENTCO's business.

Most of the purchases of additional services were made at the top level of the group and coordinated by a financial director in the accounting and finance department. In the cases where additional services were ordered at the business area- or business unit level, they were still typically coordinated by the financial director at the group level. The auditing firm was organized symmetrically with the client with regard to the additional services. That is, nearly all offerings of additional services were coordinated by the engagement partner at AUDFIRM.

Pricing

With regard to the pricing of additional services, some of the financial managers from CLIENTCO expressed the view that these were very expensive compared to the fixed price external audit. One interviewee made the following comment.

> *You notice that every extra assignment you ask for is very expensive. The fixed price for the audit has probably been set very low and then they try to compensate for that.*

The group level financial director and the engagement partner handled the price negotiations that occurred. In the case of attest services and extra audits, the typical procedure seemed to be that AUDFIRM gave CLIENTCO a fixed-price offer that they could either accept or turn down.

CLIENTCO's purchaser at the top level seemed very aware of prices per hour and the number of hours that were reasonable for different types of assignments. He also emphasized that CLIENTCO was very clear on the model they wanted to use for purchases from the auditing firm: a fixed price for the package including the statutory audit, and then offers from AUDFIRM for each extra assignment to be handled by the engagement partner and himself. The pricing model with centralized fixed prices implied good cost control for the client. The high prices for additional services seemed to make the client somewhat restrictive. However, there were some persons at AUDFIRM that CLIENTCO valued very highly, and that motivated high prices.

CLIENTCO's reasons for ordering additional services could be summarized as follows: (i) a need for an external second opinion on its internal systems and solutions to improve efficiency, (ii) the auditing firm offered specialist competence in areas where CLIENTCO needed such competence, (iii) CLIENTCO was required – or felt a need – to get attests from the auditors to ensure correctness of certain written documents, (iv) CLIENTCO perceived that the fixed-price package including the statutory audit did not give a sufficient scrutiny of sales subsidiaries. Thus, one type of additional advisory service involved specialist areas such as accounting issues and taxes (ii and iii), while another type of additional advisory service concerned improvements of the internal management control systems (i and iv).

In terms of the two (extreme) types of clients identified in the CFO interview study (HAQ and LAQ companies), CLIENTCO could be classified as a high accounting quality (HAQ) company. In line with this, there was a low level of interaction during the completion of the audit. The remaining, most important reason why CLIENTCO still purchased additional services for a significant amount each year was its need for the highly competent individuals on the lead team.

Discussion of the empirical results

This chapter aims to empirically investigate and analyze how auditing firm services are purchased and used, relating to the concepts of professionalization and interaction. So far, empirical data has been presented regarding the extent to which listed Swedish companies purchase additional advisory services from their auditors and how these purchases are carried out. In this section, these empirical findings will be discussed by comparing the purchase of professionalized standardized statutory auditing services with the additional advisory services demanding interaction and trust.

The statutory audit is the primary service that brings the auditing firm into a position where it acquires knowledge about the client and gains opportunities to sell its advisory services. However, the high degree of productification of the statutory audit, and the fact that it is difficult to sell advisory services when working as a scrutinizing auditor, would seem to make it difficult for the auditing firms to sell much advisory services. Still, they do, and advisory services account for a significant part of auditing firms' total revenues. There are three tentative explanations for this, which will be explored in this section.

1. Auditors with high competence, client knowledge and the ability to interact with management create a need for additional advisory services.

Despite the fact that the statutory audit as such is a relatively standardized product, the empirical results show that both the purchases of the standardized audit and the subsequent purchases of advisory services are dependent on personal relationships and trust in particular auditing firm employees. From the client's point of view, this means that the purchase of an audit that fulfills the legal requirements and creates the necessary external legitimacy may not be enough for creating internal certainty about the quality of the audit. It was important for CLIENTCO to get help from the auditors to improve the internal control. Many clients want audit partners that they can interact with in a way that reduces the uncertainty about quality, and creates the opportunity of purchasing highly valuable advisory services.

The way of organizing the relationship between the auditing firm and the client is an important aspect in this context. The advisory services seem to be purchased primarily at the top executive level, and the auditing firm adapts its client-specific organization to this. This was observed in the case company described above, where the sales of advisory services were handled by the engagement partner, while the auditors conducting the audit did not act as sellers of advisory services. This means that most of the auditors can concentrate on auditing rather than selling advisory services

The importance of audit partner competence, client knowledge and ability to interact with management has been emphasized in prior research. Grey (1998) points out the ability to handle the client as a key skill for advancement in the hierarchy and for ultimately becoming a partner. Grey uses the term "professionalization" to describe auditing firms' focus on employees who have good abilities with regard to handling clients. In fact, this was the core of being an "auditing firm professional" (*ibid*, p. 582):

> *...the definitions of professionalism articulated and reproduced is through the constant invocation of 'the client' as an explanation and justification.*

Applied to the case study, the most professional auditing firm staff would thus be people who interacted best with the client. This interpretation of professionalization is different from the classical use of the concept outlined above, however, where professionalization refers to uncertainty reduction through productification, standardization, regulation and protection.

It seems to be somewhat of a paradox that individual auditors' competence, client knowledge and social abilities are so important for the purchase of a service as standardized as the statutory audit. These are factors directly related to uncertainty reduction through trust and mutual interdependence. It would seem that an important reason for this result is that the clients have an underlying demand for the additional advisory services that knowledgeable auditors with interactive abilities can supply.

Two quite different explanations of the purchases of additional advisory services may be found in these services' ability to provide external legitimacy and to compensate for inefficiencies in the internal accounting and control systems:

2. The clients perceive a need for additional services in order to get more external legitimacy for their (low) accounting quality.

3. The client's internal management control systems and accounting functions are not fully developed, and the auditing firm is needed more or less continuously in order to solve problems as they arise.

The second and third explanations of why clients purchase advisory services from the same firms that scrutinize them represent the negative side of the interaction between auditors and their clients. Some of the companies who both had extensive "value added" audits and purchased much additional services appeared to threaten their auditors' independence. These auditors appeared to become involved in the production and external legitimacy of the financial accounts to an extent that perhaps goes beyond the auditor's scope. Beattie et al (2001) provide empirical case descriptions of such dependency in UK companies. From a theoretical point of view, Jeppesen (1998) argues that the Big Four firm's "value added" audit technologies have become so intertwined with consulting that the auditors cannot be independent anymore because the auditing is no longer independent.[10]

Conclusions

Auditing services, as opposed to most other advisory services studied in this book, represent a profession in its classical sense of being protected and based on a well-defined and exclusive knowledge base. One of the main purposes of this chapter has been to study how this impacts the purchase and use of these services, especially those services that go beyond the statutory audit. The study shows that the statutory audit can be purchased in a more detached way, rendering the interaction between buyer and seller, seen as so important in several of the other cases in this book, of less importance. This was however only true for the standardized statutory audit, in which uncertainty concerning the need for the service was low because it was required by law. As soon as additional services were involved, interaction again became critical as a means of establishing a need for the service. A trustful and close relationship between the auditors and the managers buying their services was a central prerequisite for the purchase of additional services, because it was in this relationship the needs for the services were constructed. The basis for these needs was found to be a combination of the auditors' ability to provide legitimacy and security to their clients and their superior knowledge of the buying organization, giving them a head start in solving emerging problems and identifying latent problems.

---

[10] Jeppesen uses the "value added" audit technology of one of the Big Four firms as an example.

CHAPTER 9

Doing Deals Despite Distrust

LARS ENGWALL AND CARIN B. ERIKSSON

Consultancy[1] services are sold on a promise that a certain value will be delivered – which emphasizes the importance for consultancy firms to avoid distrust. The very circumstance that management consultancy work is one of the most intangible types of work one can think of makes it very difficult for clients to choose a consulting firm for an assignment. As argued in Chapter 1 and by Clark and Salaman (1998), the immateriality, heterogeneity and interaction of management consultancy services imply that a buyer cannot pre-purchase a guaranteed level of service, and the production of consultancy services necessitates interaction between the consultant and the buyer (Clark, 1995). Since clients purchase an intangible service in which they subsequently cooperate, the matter of how to choose suppliers of MAS is essential. In the case of management consultancy services, uncertainty about the sustainability of the consulting firm, its professional background and the qualifications of its staff leads to a reduction of trust. Against this background, in the present chapter, we take a closer look into factors that are significant for the hiring of consultants.

1   This research is part of the programme The Creation of European Management Practice (CEMP). It has been supported by a grant from the European Union (TSER Contract SOE1-CT97-1072) and a grant from the Swedish Council for Work Life Research (Contract 97-0944). For further information, see the home page of the CEMP programme: www.fek.uu.se/cemp.

In order to provide a basis for the analysis, in the following section, we present a model that captures significant factors behind consultancy deals. This model takes its basic point of departure in the critical views of consultants expressed by both practitioners and scholars. This scepticism can be expected to be an important hampering factor when executives are considering consultants. However, despite this negative bias in attitudes towards the consulting industry, there is strong evidence that companies employ consultants (see e.g. Ernst and Kieser, 2002). To account for these circumstances, the literature provides explanations related to both demand and supply. In terms of demand, it is often said to be an effect of the wish to appear fashionable, but there is also evidence that consultants do indeed aid management. With respect to supply, on the other hand, we find arguments regarding both the product offered (price and quality) and trust in the consultancy firm. These arguments relating to demand and supply will be developed in the following section. A third section is dedicated to the description of our data collection, while the following three sections deal subsequently with attitudes towards the industry, demand and supply. In the concluding section, an extended model will be presented.

Significant factors behind consultancy deals

Distrust in the industry

There is a considerable amount of literature that points out the negative characteristics of the consulting industry. According to Kipping and Armbrüster (1998), this criticism takes two avenues. One questions the rationality of consulting services, another points out the failures of consulting projects. The first of these two criticisms targets management gurus, and their ideas, as well as consultancies. Among the works that present ideas in this tradition are Clark and Salaman (1996b), Huczynski (1993) and Micklethwait and Wooldridge (1996). The latter authors, who are journalists, take a particularly negative stance labeling the management gurus "witch doctors". However, even more academically oriented authors like Abrahamson (1996), Clark (1995) and Kieser (1996) put forward a rather negative view, implying that consultants are just working to impress management and carry out hard-to-sell services that companies do not really need. Ernst and Kieser (2002) describe the development as a "consulting explosion", concluding that:

Consultants sell a remedy for a situation that they have in part caused themselves – this becomes clear from the dynamics of differentiation in general, and in the consulting industry in particular. (Ernst and Kieser, 2002, p. 72)

The second type of criticism of the industry mentioned by Kipping and Armbrüster (1998) are critical remarks pointing out the weak contribution of consultants to corporate performance. Again Kieser has provided a critical analysis of the limited learning effects in the interaction between companies and consultants (Kieser, 2002a). However, the most widely spread criticism is also in this instance provided by two journalists (O'Shea and Madigan, 1997). Already the title of their book – *Dangerous Company. Management Consultants and the Business They Save and Ruin* – hints at its content. In the text, they then provide evidence of spectacular failures of consultancy projects. Needless to say, such accounts contribute to negative images of the industry.

In addition to the mentioned accounts, there is also a number of what Das and Teng (2001) refer to as "relational risks", where the consultants may have access to confidential information within a client organization. As part of the consultancy firm's knowledge management systems, client data may be collected, shared and used. Project reports may be saved in internal databases and downloaded when similar projects come up. The job mobility of management consultants also implies a risk for the client in that a consultant may work for a competitor in the foreseeable future.

All the above-mentioned accounts can be expected to contribute to a negative attitude towards the consultant industry. Among them, the journalistic accounts are probably the most influential for the negative image building we are discussing here. Thus, even if authors like O'Shea and Madigan (1997) and Micklethwait and Wooldridge (1996) may not always be entirely accurate and fair, their writing has more significance for the general attitude towards the industry than that of the academic scholars.

Demand: Needs of clients

The negative views of the industry summarized above are to a certain extent related to accounts of the demand side, i.e. what client needs the consultants are meeting. A common argument in this context has been that consultants sell only modern management solutions that vary over time. This has led some researchers to label these solutions "fashions" (Abrahamson, 1996) or "fads" (e.g. Hilmer and Donaldson, 1996; Shapiro, 1996), and others, like Kieser (2002b), to stress the herd behavior among clients. With reference to the theories presented by the neo-institutionalists (see for instance Powell and DiMaggio, 1991), it is argued that dominant actors provide role models for other actors in an organizational field, and thereby determine the rules of the game. They argue that rules, norms and – not least – imitation, tend to move institutions in the same direction. Since companies live in a very complex world, where a large number of factors influence performance, it is very difficult to establish a clear relationship between cause and effect. The views of appropriate measures to be undertaken can therefore be expected to be socially constructed. In this process, visibility is likely to become a vital characteristic. Visibility, in turn, appears to be closely related to size since, through sheer dominance, large actors have much greater opportunities to influence the opinions in a field. Thus, practices employed by the largest companies tend to become the model for their smaller competitors. In a world of uncertainty regarding appropriate actions to take, it may appear out of date for a company not to adopt the methods applied by the largest companies. Among the practices of the largest companies, employment of consultants is substantial, and can therefore be expected to spread to other companies. In their selection of consultancies, we may anticipate visibility to play an important role. As a result, we can expect large companies and large consultancies to live in symbiosis. At the same time, the largest corporations are also likely to have other relationships. This has to do with specialization, i.e. that some small consultancies may be able to work in fields such as human relations, IT, headhunting, mergers and acquisitions, and public relations, which complement the strategy advice provided by the large ones. This is in accordance with the prediction of Penrose (1959, pp. 222-224) that small firms may be able to successfully compete with large players by operating in the interstices between them.

However, although the arguments of herd behavior may be convincing, there is also reason to believe that consultants do more than just sell snake oil. There is indeed evidence that companies experience problems and that they not always have the competence and capacity to solve these with internal resources. This view would imply that the use of consultants should also be looked upon as insourcing of resources that have not been considered crucial to have internally on a permanent basis. Relating back to the fashion metaphor above again, we should expect client demands to be aimed at meeting both actual basic needs and the desire to appear modern.

Supply: Characteristics of the consultancy

Standard theory identifies two ways of competing: quality and price. For the management consulting market, Glückler and Armbrüster (2003) have pointed out that these two standard strategies for competition tend to be inadequate. The quality of consultancy services is difficult to measure – as the service is generated in co-production with the client and after the agreement is signed. Success is contingent on a wide range of variables, making quality hard to assess even after a consultancy project is finished. The price is not an adequate way of competing either, since it does not resolve the uncertainty perceived by clients, and service firms rarely pursue cost-leadership strategies (Lindahl and Beyers, 1999). Together, all this emphasizes how difficult it can be to choose a consulting firm for an assignment.

Under the circumstances mentioned, a respected reputation will separate and distinguish organizations. Reputation exists in the mind of each stakeholder and cannot be managed directly. According to Balmer (1998, p. 971), an organization's "image" involves the public's latest beliefs about that organization, whereas "reputation" represents a value judgment about the organization's qualities built up "over a period and focusing on what it does and how it behaves." Dowling (2001) further states that "corporate image" is the total impression an entity makes and that "corporate reputation" is the esteem in which the organization's image is held. Reputations make processing of new images dependent on retained past images (Gioia, 1986). The two terms – image and reputation – are thus closely connected elements, and development of either is dependent on the other. Image and reputation are also allied to the term "identity", which refers to an organization's unique characteristics, which, in turn, are rooted in the behavior of members of the organization. Identity answers the questions "Who are we and where are we going?" (Albert and Whetten, 1985). The perceptions of different stakeholders of the way an organization presents itself, either deliberately or accidentally, form the image of that organization. Since every organization of size and importance has many different identities and stakeholders, each with a variety of interests, it cannot be expected that an organization will have uniform and consistent reputation. Organizations are complex phenomena and can be expected to display different identities and images, adjustable and appropriate for a given audience.

The described significance of trust is to a large extent a result of the fact that management consulting is not a legally or institutionally protected profession. The sector has low barriers of entry and is potentially open to any individual or organization, a circumstance that leads to both high birth rates and high mortality rates. Uncertainty about the sustainability of a consulting firm, its professional background and the qualifications of its staff, leads to a reduction in market transparency (Glückler and Armbrüster, 2003).

In the same way as we argued above that visibility is important for corporations, visibility also plays a significant role for consultancies in promoting reputation. Large actors in the consultancy field are thus likely to determine the norms of behavior in the field. Efforts to differentiate oneself may meet considerable resistance (see e.g. Engwall et al, 2002). Large consultancies tend to become trendsetters, in the same way as men like Pierre Balmain, Pierre Cardin, Christian Dior and Yves Saint Laurent have influenced women's fashion. Just as film stars and other celebrities tend to promote the ideas of these fashion designers, large companies support leading consultancies by employing them. This symbiosis has positive effects for both the large companies and the large consultancies. As a result, the interaction between large companies and large consultancies can be expected to have a significant effect on the behavior of other economic actors. In other words: large consultancies become role models for smaller consultancies in the same way as large companies serve as examples for smaller ones (Dauphinais and Price, 1998).

A model for analysis

On the basis of the above reasoning we intend to investigate factors that influence the deals between companies and consultancies (Figure 9:1). In so doing, we will first look more closely into the distrust of the industry (cf. e.g. Kieser, 2002b). The basic question we want to ask in that context is whether or to what extent this is true. In terms of the impact on the hiring of consultants, we expect this variable to hamper the demand for consultancy services.

A second issue we address concerns the demand or the needs of the clients. This is particularly worth investigating since the literature, as pointed out above, to such a large extent includes writings that suggest that consultancy work is merely the selling of standard management tools on a large scale. We will contrast this view with the possibility that clients have very specific needs.

The third factor, the effects of which we intend to study, is the characteristics of individual consultancies, i.e. to identify which such factors have positive effects on the hiring of a consultancy. Here, we differentiate between "trust" and "product characteristics".

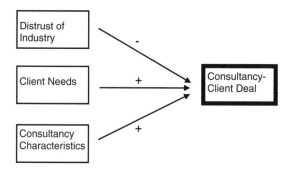

Figure 9:1 Factors influencing the hiring of a consultancy

Management consultants and top corporations

Management consultants

In our empirical study, we first delimited management consultants by using the definition provided by FEACO, the European federation for management consultants:

> *Management consultancy is the rendering of independent advice and assistance about management issues. This typically includes identifying and investigating problems and/or opportunities, recommending appropriate action and helping to impose those recommendations.*

Needless to say, this definition is rather open. This is also natural, since the boundaries between those who offer advisory services and those who offer management systems are blurred and constantly changing. In addition, major changes are taking place inside many consultant firms. Boundaries between strategic consultancies and IT consultancies are disappearing, as it has become common to bundle different kinds of services. An increased interest in enterprise resource planning (ERP) systems also explains part of the recent growth and the need for integrating different kinds of expertise. We also see that some firms are building alliances to penetrate certain industries.

Since our aim was to investigate the relationship between large companies and top management consultants, we derived a list of the ten most significant management consultancies in Sweden. This was done with the help of a consulting guide, published annually (*Konsultguiden*), which defines management consultancy firms as those having more than 50 percent of their sales within management consulting. From the consultancies listed in the guide, we selected the ones with the largest sales figures. This led us to the following top ten consultancies: Andersen Consulting (now Accenture), McKinsey and Co., PriceWaterhouseCoopers (PWC) Management Consultants, Boston Consulting Group, Carta Corporate Advisors, Ernst and Young Management Consultants, KPMG Management Consultants, Arthur D. Little, Gemini Consulting, and Arthur Andersen Management Consulting.[2]

Top corporations

In line with the introductory arguments, the corresponding selection of large companies has implied a focus on the ten quoted companies with the highest revenues listed on the Stockholm Stock Exchange.[3] In this group of companies, there is a wide representation of different industries: two producers of motor vehicles (Volvo and Scania), two companies in the forest industry (SCA and Stora Enso), one company in telecommunications (Ericsson), a construction company (Skanska), a pharmaceutical company (AstraZeneca), one ball bearing producer (SKF), and a special steel company (Sandvik). Significant industries that are missing include trade, transportation and financial services. Further, the focus on the quoted companies has excluded family-owned and state-owned companies.

The CEOs of the selected companies were contacted by letter and all, except the CEO of Volvo, agreed to give an interview, personally or through a colleague. For Volvo, the former CEO agreed to an interview. The interviews lasted about 90 minutes.

In the interviews, we tried first to find out whether the respondents were familiar with the above-mentioned top consultancies and whether they had used them. It was apparent that they were well aware of the top ten consultancies. All of them knew of McKinsey, Andersen (Accenture), Boston Consulting Group, Ernst and Young, and Price Waterhouse. However, for each of the other five consultancies – Carta, Arthur D. Little, KPMG, Coopers and Lybrand and Gemini – there was one of the executives who did not know about them. Nevertheless,

---

[2] Since the interviews took place, major changes in the field of consultancy firms have occurred. During the time for the study, Cap Gemini and Ernst and Young Management Consultants merged. Carta Corporate Advisors, the only domestic consultancy firm at that time, has since been bought and is now a part of the U.S. owned Booz, Allen and Hamilton. Arthur Andersen Management Consulting has disappeared from the market. Andersen Consulting has changed its name to Accenture.

[3] These companies are also among the largest in terms of employees.

all of the ten top consultants had been used at least by one of the top CEOs. The two most used consultancies of the ten were McKinsey (seven executives) and Boston Consulting Group (six executives), followed by Andersen/Accenture (five executives) and KPMG (three executives).

As expected (see page 152 above), in addition to the top consultancies, the interviewees had also used a number of smaller Swedish consultancy firms. In principle, the smaller firms used consisted of just one or two persons working as consultants. These are often used as personal advisors and the counseling is based on long-term relationships. In this way, these smaller consultants are trusted not to leak sensitive information, something that is feared in relationships with their larger competitors.

Yet another group outside the top consultancies that were mentioned in the interviews were investment banks. It was apparent that their role in consulting has expanded considerably and that this development is closely related to the merger movement observed in the last decade.

Finally, one executive used U.S. consultancy firms with no representation in Sweden. In this case, consultants flew in from the United States, collected data, performed their analysis, and offered strategic advice. After the initial consulting assignment, they have returned several times during the past year.

Thus, although the executives have also used other types of consultants, we can conclude that they have also had the relationships with top consultancies that we want to look more closely at.

The distrust of the industry

In order to investigate the attitudes towards the industry we confronted the respondents with twelve statements, six negative and six positive, regarding consultants in general. The six items expressing negative views were:

- Consultants diffuse the ideas of their clients.
- The fact that senior consultants sell the projects and junior consultants carry them out is a big problem.
- The work of many consultants is never implemented.
- Consultants are primarily loyal to themselves and their company.
- We are too dependent on consultants.
- There are too many junior consultants.

The following six items were used to capture positive views:

- With consultants you can do things faster.
- Consultants are useful because they present new ideas and perspectives.
- Consultants make a positive contribution to the development of their clients.
- Consultants are worth their salt.
- Consultants are very loyal to their clients.
- It is good to have a lot of junior consultants.

As we used these items in the interviews, we found some support for the expectation that CEOs have a basic negative attitude toward the industry. Thus, we are able to see from Table 9:1 that respondents generally tended to agree on the negative items. Only one of the items ("We are too dependent on consultants") received an average score below zero, while the scores for all of the others were above zero. The strongest support was obtained for the two items "Consultants diffuse the ideas of their clients" and "There are too many junior consultants" (0.7). The first implies that respondents fear that ideas developed for their own company will be used in other companies, while the second means that they consider the consultants they receive in the company too inexperienced. However, some of the interviewees appear to believe that they are able to handle this problem as a result of the size of their companies:

We are such an important customer for them so they always send us their best and most experienced consultants.

It is important to be clear about who we want to have in the project. They are very sensitive to our demands.

They are welcome to send us junior consultants, but we are not paying for inexperienced consultants.

A related item ("The fact that senior consultants sell the projects and junior consultants carry them out is a big problem") gets almost as high a score (0.6). For the remaining two negative items ("The work of many consultants is never implemented" and "Consultants are primarily loyal to themselves"), the average scores were 0.4 and 0.3, respectively. The average for the six items combined was 0.4.

However, we should also note that the respondents agreed with some of the positive items. On top were "With consultants you can do things faster" and "Consultants are useful because they present new ideas and perspectives" (both with an average of 0.6). Somewhat lower support was obtained for the related item "Consultants make a positive contribution to the development of their clients" (0.5). All three statements imply that respondents find consultants useful because they add resources and ideas.

Statement	Type	Agree (=+1)	Hesitant (=0)	Disagree (=-1)	Average
Consultants diffuse the ideas of their clients	-	7	3	0	0.7
There are too many junior consultants	-	7	3	0	0.7
The fact that senior consultants sell the projects and junior consultants carry them out is a big problem	-	6	4	0	0.6
The work of many consultants is never implemented	-	5	4	1	0.4
Consultants are primarily loyal to themselves and their company	-	3	7	0	0.3
We are too dependent on consultants	-	1	6	3	-0.2
Average for negative statements	-				*0.4*
With consultants you can do things faster	+	6	4	0	0.6
Consultants are useful because they present new ideas and perspectives	+	6	4	0	0.6
Consultants make a positive contribution to the development of their clients	+	5	5	0	0.5
Consultants are worth their salt	+	2	8	0	0.2
Consultants are very loyal to their clients	+	0	10	0	0.0
It is good to have a lot of junior consultants	+	0	3	7	-0.7
Average for positive statements	+				*0.2*

Table 9:1 Attitudes towards consultants

Thus, all in all, the respondents appear to have more negative than positive attitudes towards the consultant industry. They fear that ideas are transferred to competitors and that senior consultants leave the work to less qualified colleagues. Although they also see certain advantages in engaging consultants in their company, the negative views dominate. The average for the negative items is thus 0.4, compared to 0.2 for the positive items.

Demand: The needs of clients

In order to investigate the needs of clients, we first asked the respondents about their use of various modern solutions and to what extent they employed consultants in the implementation. In so doing, we were able to take advantage of a survey by Lindvall (1998). It identified fourteen significant management concepts clustered into four different groups dealing with: 1. investors, 2. human resources, 3. customers, and 4. processes. In the first group oriented towards *investors* were methods related to Shareholder Value, for instance EVA (cf. Stewart, 1998). Concepts related to *human resources* were Culture (cf. Deal and Kennedy, 1982), Intellectual Capital and Knowledge Management (cf. Edvinsson and Malone, 1997), Learning Organization (cf. Senge, 1992), Shared Service Center (cf. CEO Europe, May 1998) and Team (cf. Katzenbach and Smith, 1993). In relation to *customers,* the two significant concepts found were Time Based Competition (cf. Stalk and Hout, 1990) and Total Quality Management (TQM, cf. e.g. Cole, 1995), which aim at facilitating products of the right quality reaching customers on time. Finally, the fourth group, focusing on *processes,* contains the concepts of Activity Based Costing (ABC, Cooper and Kaplan, 1991), Activity Based Management (ABM, Morrow, 1992), the Balanced Score Card (BSC, Kaplan and Norton, 1996), Business Process Re-engineering (BPR, Hammer and Champy, 1993), Just-in-Time (JIT, Hill, 1991) and Process Orientation (cf. Schonberger, 1996).

Among the methods mentioned, it turned out that all respondents employed Total Quality Management (TQM) and Shareholder Value (e.g. EVA) in their companies (Table 9:2 below). However, just one had used a consultant to practice TQM and only one had used a consultancy in relation to Shareholder Value. Consultancies had been used mostly for implementation of Just-in-Time, Team, Shared Service Center, Process Orientation and Time Based Competition.

Learning Organization had attracted the attention of seven of the interviewees, but only one had used a consultancy to implement it. This was also the situation for Balanced Scorecard. At the same time, there were four of the fourteen concepts for which none of the companies had used consultancies. Consultancies had not been employed for the implementation of Activity Based Costing (ABC),

Culture, Activity Based Management (ABM), and Intellectual Capital/Knowledge Management.

Concept	Work With	Consultancies Used
Total Quality Management (TQM)	100%	10 %
Shareholder Value (e.g. EVA)	100%	10%
Team	90%	30%
Shared Service Center	90%	30%
Just in Time (JIT)	80%	30%
Process Orientation	80%	30%
Time Based Competition	80%	30%
Activity Based Costing (ABC)	80%	0%
Culture	70%	0%
Learning Organization	70%	10%
Balanced Score Card (BSC)	70%	10%
Intellectual Capital/Knowledge Management	40%	0%
Activity Based Management (ABM)	30%	0%
Business Process Re-engineering (BPR)	20%	10%

Table 9:2 Use of key concepts and consultancy involvement

The least used method was Business Process Engineering and respondents expressed a rather sceptical attitude toward this method:

It implies far too drastic changes – I don't believe in such things.

BPR – isn't that when you turn everything upside-down? No, we don't need to practice that here.

The interviews thus show that the CEOs use the popular solutions to a certain extent and some to a very large extent. However, to a very high degree, they do so without employing consultants. This means that there is only weak support for the idea that consultants are mainly diffusers of fashions or fads.

When we turn to other reasons for using consultants, our interviews show that the items "need for change" and "to solve a crisis" score high (2.0 and 1.8, respectively; see Table 9:3). However, as important as aspects relating to change are resource limitations: the staff has no time for it, or do not have the required competence (1.9). In the words of one interviewee:

You have a specific problem that requires a specific competence. The consultants have it. With our tight organization we can't maintain top competence in all areas.

Reason	Common = 2	Less Common =1	Uncommon = 0	Average
Need for change	10	0	0	2.0
The staff does not have the required competence	9	1	0	1.9
Need to solve a crisis	8	2	0	1.8
Support for internal processes	8	2	0	1.8
The staff has no time for it	8	1	1	1.7
Wish to learn from others	6	3	1	1.5
They often have good methods	4	6	0	1.4
It is a trend	2	7	1	1.1
Need to know the most modern solutions	1	8	1	1.0
By pure chance	3	4	3	1.0
You do not trust your staff	0	6	4	0.6
It is nice and pleasant	0	5	5	0.5

Table 9:3 Reasons for using consultants

Other common reasons are that it provides "support for internal processes" (1.8) and a "wish to learn from others" (1.5). A majority of the interviewees do not think it is common that consultants are chosen because "it is nice and pleasant" (0.5) or because "you do not trust your own staff" (0.6). One interviewee mentioned legitimization, which was not given as an alternative:

> *Another reason could be lack of self-confidence. It lends a certain legitimacy. It shows that you have tried. You choose a service firm with a top reputation – who can blame you?*

Supply: Consultancy characteristics

Thus far, we have seen that CEOs know of top consultants and that they use them, but that they look upon consultants with some suspicion. We have also demonstrated that they employ consultants in order to handle upcoming problems and to add capacity to their company. With this background, we will now turn to the consultant characteristics that are important in the selection of consultancies. As discussed above, we would expect trust and product arguments to play a role in this context. In our interviews, we employed the following seven indicators for *trust*:

- Competence
- Experience

- Personal Network
- Problem Understanding
- Recommendations from other Companies
- Reputation of a Specific Person
- Reputation of Consultancy

For *product arguments*, on the other hand, we used:

- Global Reach
- Methods
- One-stop Shopping
- Price
- Quality of Bid
- Quality of Presentations
- Tailor-made Solutions

As the respondents were asked whether these aspects constituted reasons for choosing consultants, it was evident that the trust indicators were particularly emphasized. The factor rated most important was "competence", with a maximum average score 2.0 (see Table 9:4). And, with respect to this item, it is particularly important to mention that the interviewees not only stress the significance of specific management competence, but all were also quick to underline the need for "social competence". As one of the respondents expressed this:

Sometimes the consultants don't function very well in the organization because they can't handle all the categories of personnel with which they get involved.

In the same vein, it is mentioned that an important characteristic of good consultants is that they have an ability to listen:

A consultant can't be like an alligator – with two small ears and big jaws.

Next after "competence" in importance among the trust items were "problem understanding", "experience", "reputation of consultancy", and "reputation of a specific person" (all with average scores of 1.9). The only two items of trust that obtained scores further from the top were "recommendations from other companies" (1.5) and "personal network" (1.0). Despite the lower scores of the latter two items, the average score for all of the trust indicators combined was 1.7 of a maximum 2.0.

Reason	Type	Important (=2)	Less Important (=1)	Unimportant (=0)	Average
Competence	Trust	10	0	0	2.0
Experience	Trust	9	1	0	1.9
Problem Understanding	Trust	9	1	0	1.9
Reputation of a Specific Person	Trust	9	1	0	1.9
Reputation of Consultancy	Trust	9	1	0	1.9
Recommendations from other Companies	Trust	6	3	1	1.5
Personal Network	Trust	2	6	2	1.0
Average for Trust					*1.7*
Quality of Presentations	Product	8	2	0	1.8
Price	Product	5	4	1	1.4
Quality of Bid	Product	2	8	0	1.2
Global Reach	Product	3	5	2	1.1
Methods	Product	3	4	3	1.0
Tailor-made Solutions	Product	1	8	1	1.0
One-stop Shopping	Product	0	3	7	0.3
Average for Product					*1.1*

Table 9:4 Reasons for choosing a particular consultancy

Only one of the product items, "quality of presentations", has a score above the combined average for the trust items (1.8). In terms of the item "price", half of the executives considered it *important*, while the other half found it to be *less important* or *unimportant*. Among the latter, one of the interviewees stated that:

> *The price is not of importance. If I need a consultant and the consultant is good, I never care about the costs.*

Among those who consider price important, a significant reason for this appears to be the difficulty of justifying consultant charges when they are running cost-cutting programs in their company:

In a cost-conscious company like ours, the fees of consultants blaze in the eyes of people.

The executives considered the other five product items even less important: "quality of bid" (1.2), "global reach" (1.1), "methods" (1.0), "tailor-made solutions" (1.0) and "one-stop shopping" (0.3). The weak significance of the last item is particularly interesting in view of the efforts of consultancies to integrate as many areas as possible in one company. Several interviewees were quite sceptical of this approach:

Nobody can be good at everything.

I think it is unethical. I do not think that you should have the same company giving advice and controlling your business.

On average, the product items clearly had a lower score than the trust items: 1.1 vs. 1.7. Another indication of this bias towards trust is that 54 answers to the trust items were *important*, while the corresponding figure for the product items was only 22. Thus, it seems that the answers of the respondents support the idea that trust is significant in the choice of consultants and that it is more important than product arguments. However, there is also evidence that the quality of presentations and price are considered important for the choice of consultants.

There can be no doubt that trust in a consultancy is to a large extent dependent on clients' earlier experiences. In this respect, the interviews show that the respondents have experienced both successes and failures. It is also evident from the interviews that consulting is an interactive process, which requires a fair amount of competence on the part of the buyer. According to the interviewees, it is very important for the buyer to know what to ask for and to provide distinct limits for the project. In the words of two interviewees:

Consultants are not better than the buyer. A bad buyer gets bad consultants.

Consultants can be very good – it all depends on the buyer.

Similarly, the respondents note that projects have failed because the customer was not sufficiently involved, was unclear about the purpose, or was generally careless. Of course, it also happens that the consultants have been the cause of failures, due to their not having sufficient competence or having been assigned a problem too difficult for them.

> *Certainly there are consultancy projects that are failures. There are occasions when we, as buyers, have not taken a sufficiently active part.*

> *Sometimes you meet consultants that don't understand their role. They don't have a sharp ear towards the organization but only like to show off. The work of such consultants, as a rule, ends up failing.*

These views on the use of consultants are consistent with earlier research in the area of industrial marketing (Håkansson, 1990 and 1994), which has shown that successful technological development is based on long-term interaction between buyers and sellers.

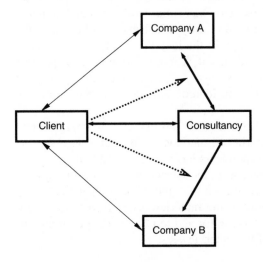

Figure 9:2 The building of trust through direct and indirect relationships

The cited literature also points out that companies are components of larger networks, in which trust can be built both directly and indirectly (see Figure 9:2). Needless to say, first-hand experience of a consultancy is a basic prerequisite for high trust (see bold lines in Figure 9:2). However, information from reference companies (represented by the thinner solid lines in Figure 9:2) may be equally significant, particularly for actors with limited personal experience of consultancies. In addition, we may also expect that the mere fact that a consultancy has a client relationship to significant actors (dotted lines in Figure 9:2) is important for the building of the trust.[4]

Conclusions

Although our empirical data is limited to ten top Swedish managers, it appears that we are able to draw certain conclusions regarding the interaction focused upon in the present chapter. It is evident from the interviews that the top managers know about the largest consultancies. There is also support for the idea of Penrose (1959), however, that small firms can successfully operate in the interstices between the large ones. The interviewees thus mention the use of very small, often one-man operations as personal advisors.

We have also found support for the basic model presented by means of introduction. That is, the respondents were inclined to support items associated with a distrust of the industry, particularly relating to the risk that consultants may diffuse the ideas of a client to other companies, and that they tend to send inexperienced people to carry out the actual project. We also found evidence to support the idea that client needs and positive characteristics of a consultancy stimulate deals between a client and a consultancy. There is therefore no reason to reject the model presented in Figure 9:1. Instead, it appears appropriate to use the evidence provided in the study to further develop it.

In developing the model (see Figure 9:3), we found that there are two basic client needs behind a deal: lack of resources and need for change. The first is simply founded in a restricted supply of resources, i.e. that the staff lacks the time and competence to undertake the necessary projects. The second, on the other hand, is based on the view that consultants can do things faster, and that they present new ideas.

As for consultancy characteristics (see again Figure 9:3) both trust in the consultancy and product characteristics play a role in the making of deals. However, the evidence provided by this study indicates that trust is more significant than product characteristics. Items used to capture the latter, thus scored lower than those oriented towards trust. Trust, in turn, appears to be positively related to three factors (see again Figure 9:3): the reputation of the consultancy, the earlier experiences of the client, and reference relationships. Of these factors,

---

[4] On the choice of management consultants, see also Clark (1995, Chapter 4).

we would expect reputation to be particularly significant, and for this to be to a considerable extent dependent on the visibility of the consultancy, i.e. that large consultancies would have an advantage over smaller ones. However, we have also obtained evidence in the present study indicating that different kinds of personal contacts may help smaller actors to be competitive.

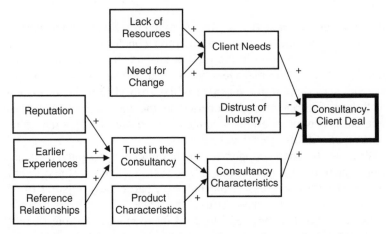

Figure 9:3 A model of successful consultancy-client relationships

The model presented is an attempt to provide a better understanding of the significant factors behind consultancy deals. Although, the empirical evidence provided is from a very small population of respondents, there is reason to believe that it has a wider application than just the ten Swedish top managers we interviewed. The main reason for this is of course that the basic features of the model have been developed from earlier studies. However, the strength of the model can only be assessed through further empirical studies. These should be directed towards larger populations from various contexts. This would enable us to make more sophisticated judgments and to develop the model even further.

Thus, it can be concluded that the explanations as to why deals are closed despite a distrusted industry are rather irrational. Factors such as the reputation and earlier experiences of the consultancy are important, as well as the belief that consultants represent new ideas and can do things faster. These observations are interesting to bear in mind when reading the next chapter, where an attempt by the state to rationalize the purchasing of management consultancy services for public organizations through launching a law on public procurement is in focus.

CHAPTER 10

Breaking Laws – Making Deals

*Procurement of management consultants
in the public sector*

NINA LINDBERG AND STAFFAN FURUSTEN

In the previous chapter, we saw that an important characteristic of large corporations in the purchasing of top management consultancies was that they tend to base their purchasing decisions on the reputation of the consultancy and earlier personal experience of the consultancy. As shown in Furusten (2003), reputation and previous assignments are also seen as important by management consultants in how they look upon their relations to potential buyers of their services. Working close to potential buyers, and assisting them in their definition of problems and need for services are seen by many consultants as crucial strategies, not only to do business, but also to be able to deliver professional services. Against this background, it is very interesting to focus on public organizations' purchasing of management consulting services since these organizations have to play by strict government rules when purchasing everything, management consulting services included.

In this chapter, we study what buyers in public organizations do when they hire management consultants. They have to deal with the dilemma of following the rule – the public procurement act – which is supposed to represent professional purchasing procedures, at the same time as the professional norm in management consulting is that choices are made on individualistic terms (Furusten, 2003). The question raised is what role the law plays when public organizations make choices about what management consultant to hire.

First, we will introduce the dilemma of constructing professionalism through national legislation, where we discuss the major principles for procurement practices stipulated in the Public Procurement Act (LOU, from the Swedish "Lagen om Offentlig Upphandling"). Second, we will see what public sector buyers of management consulting services, and management consultants who deliver to these clients, do in order to close deals. Finally, we will discuss the law in relation to the purchasing practices we have observed.[1]

Professionalism through law-compliance

The fact that purchasing procedures for public organizations are manifested in a law suggests that it can be expected to be a powerful instrument for states to regulate and control the effectiveness of public sector procurement routines. However, although the law has formal sanctions connected to it, it should not be taken for granted that it is LOU that rules the procurement process. The norms for professionalism in management consulting can very well give the consultants expert power in these relations, which can be more powerful than the power of law. The answer to the question of whether LOU has an impact on the selection of suppliers is where we will end the discussions in this chapter. Before we get there, however, it is useful to get a picture of the ideas behind this law that aims to stipulate professional purchasing procedures. Thereafter, in sections to come, we can discuss the extent to which the law has had any impact on the purchasing practice of management consultancy services in public organizations.

The Public Procurement Act (LOU) was launched on January 1, 1994. It is based on European Union public procurement directives developed between 1987 and 1993. These directives are, in turn, based on the World Trade Organization's Government Procurement Agreement for regulating procurement practices in public organizations. The first WTO Agreement on Government Procurement was signed in 1979 and entered into force in 1981.

Below, we primarily address the principles in the Swedish act (LOU), though we start with a discussion of the EU directives since they have served as the prototype for LOU.

---

[1] The empirical findings are primarily based on 25 interviews with buyers from public organizations and consultants experienced in offering services to both private and public organizations.

Non-discrimination, transparency and equality in purchasing

The purpose of the EU procurement directives is to remove restrictions on free trade of goods and services, and thereby create the conditions for a common market with open competition and a right to settlement.[2] Creating the conditions for competition is believed to be central in order to achieve rational allocation of public assets (EU Commission Green Paper, 1996). Free market competition is supposed to be secured through procurements made according to the principles of non-discrimination, equal treatment, transparency, proportionality and mutual recognition. In practice, this means that all suppliers should be given equal opportunities when bidding on public procurement of goods and services within the union. That is, they should not be treated differently because of nationality or location they must be given the same information at the same time, there should be a natural relation between qualification requirements and what is being purchased, and documents and certificates issued in one member state must be accepted in others (NOU, 2001). Concretely, a fair interpretation of the law is that it tries to prohibit nepotism, corruption, arbitrary judgments, or other phenomena that could result in an inefficient exploitation of the advantages of a common market and, in the long run, of taxpayers' money (EU Commission Green Paper, 1996).

The regulations most relevant for the purchase of consultant services (LOU 1992:1528, Chapter 6) state that public procurements must be officially advertised so that every possible supplier has a chance to inform oneself of upcoming and ongoing procurements. There are specific journals for this on the national- as well as European level and they are available electronically.[3] Announcements should clearly specify the demands relating to the assignment, and contracting entities must carefully design the documentation on which the procurement is based, the so-called "contract document". Contract documents must describe the assignment in detail, and should also list the criteria upon which the evaluation and selection of supplier will be based, preferably in order of precedence. All tenders should be subjected to a non-discriminatory evaluation process. The buyer must award the supplier who offers the cheapest or economically most advantageous alternative in consideration of quality, environmental concerns, technical features, running costs, or other predetermined

---

2   For a more detailed account of EU procurement directives, see:
    http://www.procurementsupport.com/templates/Page.asp?id=1861, 20/9/2002.

3   Ted.publications.eu.int/official/

evaluation criteria. The evaluation procedure must be documented and parts of it made public as soon as a deal is closed.

Most public organizations, including the state, municipalities and county councils must follow LOU when purchasing goods and services that exceed a certain threshold value.[4] Only state-owned firms and organizations that deal with the national security, such as the ministry of defense and affiliated organizations are excluded.

LOU makes little distinction between the volume or type of product or service to be purchased. With small variations, the principles of the law are supposed to be applicable to highly standardized products such as office material and building components as well as more specific, tailor-made services such as management consulting, as long as the total cost of the procurement exceeds the threshold value.

Non-compliance with the law may result in the purchasing organization having to pay damage claims or re-do their entire procurement procedure. Deals can be contested if a supplier has suffered- or perceived a risk of suffering a loss during a procurement process. A supplier who can prove that s/he has suffered a loss can claim damages for their loss.

In the next section, we will present a detailed account of our empirical findings on how public purchasers and management consultants say they manage to follow the directives regarding how they identify their needs and analyze possible solutions, develop and announce contract documents, and evaluate and select suppliers.

Identifying the need

Identifying needs is not always easy. The principle of equality requires that all potential suppliers are given the same opportunity from the beginning. Consequently, this obstructs the possibility to use consultants in the process of identifying and framing needs, since it might give them an advantage in the forthcoming procurement. The National Board for Public Procurement (NOU, from the Swedish "Nämnden för Offentlig Upphandling") points out that, if external consultants are to be used in the initial problem identification phase, the purchasing organization must make sure that these consultants do not benefit from their early involvement in the forthcoming procurement process (LOU, 2002).

---

4   The threshold value for services within the EU is about 1.7 million SEK. However, according to Chapter 6 of LOU (1992:1528), procurements under the threshold value must also adhere to the law as long as the total amount exceeds 2-4 times the basic amount, i.e. 80,000-160,000 SEK.

The barriers to engaging consultants already from the start have been sharply criticized by the consultants, who argue that engaging consultants in the problem definition phase is a prerequisite for delivering professional services. This is especially true in public sector purchasing where purchasing skills are generally lower than in the private sector.

A widespread notion among consultants is that, in procurements where the problem has been defined without the involvement of consultants, the specifications are often vague and problems ill-defined or even misinterpreted. Generally, they say, it seems as if the buyer does not know what s/he wants. "Vaguely defined needs makes the procurement a guessing game," one consultant commented. "LOU obstructs dialogue and problem definition, which forces us to guess what they need," another pointed out.

The notion that procurements in the public sector are to a great extent handled by less skilled buyers who have difficulty communicating what they need is expressed in other studies as well (SAMC, 2002). A consultant from a well-established consulting firm painted a descriptive picture of the perceived problem of unskilled buyers from public sector organizations:

A "procurement" was defined as the purchase of "organization development" services, proposing workshops and seminars as implementation methods. But, what exactly are "organization development" services? Organization development could involve anything from recruiting a new boss to restructuring or even downsizing the entire organization. And perhaps workshops and seminars do not solve their problem at all. As a bidding consultant, it is more or less impossible to formulate an appropriate offer on such brief information, let alone price it. So, if you try to get some more information by calling the procurement office, the only answer you get is: "We want you to propose different solutions, we won't say more than this."

It is difficult to prepare an appropriate tender for procurements as characterized in the above quote, especially since LOU, following the principle of equal treatment, obstructs one's ability to meet the buyer in person to further discuss needs and expectations. Consequently, consultants who are awarded contracts frequently either redefine the needs and change the specification during the consultation process (which, according to LOU, is illegal unless the procurement is recommended), or they end up tackling the wrong problem. Several buyers have found ways to solve this matter by adding to the contract that certain undefined services might be required if unforeseen problems occur.

The reasons for buyers being vague and refraining from giving too many details about an assignment, as in the example above, might of course be due to factors other than low purchasing skills. Another reason might be that the buyers do not want to prescribe the assignment. Too many details might result in a specification that offsets the principle of proportionality, i.e. that there is no natural relation between qualification requirements and what is being purchased. One public purchaser expressed the difficulty of balancing the need for detailed specifications and the risk of prescribing assignments as follows:

> *We were purchasing an investigation service in which we did not prescribe the methods we wanted the consultant to use. After selecting a consultant who suggested "interviews with employees" as an implementation method, we were criticized for selecting suppliers on grounds that were not stated as selection criteria in the specification. We had to start the entire process all over again and this time we included "interview with employees" as a required implementation method. Then we were criticized for prescribing the assignment and thus excluding a priori potential suppliers unable to offer that kind of service.*

The quote points out that it is far from obvious how to define a specification in accordance with LOU. The specifications should contain enough information for suppliers to be able to give appropriate offerings, but must not prescribe the assignments in such way that they discriminate against potential suppliers. The ambiguous directions on how to define the specifications might affect the quality of the consulting services. Statements such as "the quality of the service gets worse if consultants deliver what is ordered, since the solutions often don't correspond to the problems," and "the quality of consultant services deteriorate because they are based on regulations instead of needs," as pointed out by consultants, highlight the problem of delivering quality services based on inadequate specifications.

The perceived problem of ill-defined needs and vague specifications may, however, be a result of unfamiliarity on the part of the consultants. That is, it is likely that the perceived vagueness relates to the very fact that the consultant was not engaged in the process of framing it. This argument is supported by the fact that many public buyers do not believe that the needs and specifications are badly defined. On the contrary, they argue that one of the most positive advantages of LOU is that it has led to a more accurate problem definition. As one municipality buyer pointed out:

The law requires that we really analyze and think through what we need. Can we resolve this matter internally, or do we need to engage a consultant? LOU has in this way forced us to plan our purchases more carefully.

Developing and announcing contract documents

The second part of the procurement procedure, involving issuing contract documents, is strictly regulated by LOU. The contract document must be officially advertised and structured in such a way as to facilitate an objective comparison of the incoming bids. The document must contain a detailed specification relevant to the assignment, which carefully describes the assignment without referring to specific brands or methods that might exclude those who cannot offer such services (as described in the previous section). The document must furthermore include the administrative conditions, formal requirements (such as financial statements, records of technical resources, etc.) and evaluation criteria to be used in the selection of supplier, such as price, competence, prior experience and implementation method. The criteria should, when possible, be ranked in order of precedence.

As discussed in the previous chapter, it is common in the private sector that the buyer turns directly to a supplier whenever the organization needs consultation. Often the buyer already knows the supplier from previous engagements and they often have a well-established business relation already. Occasionally, consultants take the initiative and approach potential buyers when they believe that new consultation services might be needed, or when they have developed new ideas and concepts (Furusten, 2003). This kind of purchasing behavior is exactly what LOU is trying to offset, since it allegedly increases the risk of purchasing too much consultation at expensive costs.

In public sector procurement, there are mainly two separate ways to handle the issuing of contract documents – one in which the buyers strictly adhere to the rules of LOU, and another in which the rules are more or less ignored. In the first case, contract documents are officially advertised and consultants look them up in electronic databases whereupon they put together their bids and send them in on speculation. If the consultant fulfills the formal requirements, s/he proceeds to the evaluation process, so-called "step 2 evaluation", and may on rare occasions meet with the buyer to present his or her proposal. Many consultants perceive this process as uncertain and unpredictable. They say they risk putting a lot of work into preparing offers without getting the contract. The reason for not getting it might of course be that they do not meet the evaluation criteria, or because they are too expensive. Many consultants, however, argue that the main reason for not being awarded an assignment is because the procurement is rather illusively processed according to LOU. The buyer has already decided whom to assign the job to, and proceeds with the formal procurement only for the sake of the law. There are even cases when the evaluation criteria included in the contract document are developed together with a specific consultant so as to fit that consultant perfectly. Such procedures also carry a risk, however, since the consultant puts a lot of work into helping buyers to develop contract documents with no guarantees. One consultant describes this risk in an illustrative example:

> *We helped the client to analyze needs and develop a specification without getting paid since we thought we would get the contract. In the next step, the client had to procure according to LOU, and it turned out that we did not get the contract. They said they had to choose a cheaper alternative, but from what I heard they picked another consultant already known to some senior executives in the organization. This has made us very sceptical. Helping clients to identify needs and develop specifications does not guarantee you a contract. It just costs you a lot of resources.*

Many consultants point out that another reason for not getting a contract is misinterpretation of a project's proportions and objectives because of vague- or poorly defined specifications. Consequently, the consultants often "take a chance" and end up with maladjusted bids that are too expensive or suggest irrelevant solutions. In situations like this, potential suppliers must be rejected even though they might be the most suitable in terms of quality and prior experience.

In the second case, LOU rules are more or less ignored and the purchase is processed similarly to private sector praxis. This procedure is commonly used in cases when the buyer already has an established relation with a consultant s/he wishes to use again. Whenever a need for consultation occurs, the buyer turns to a specific consultant in order to discuss the matter, define the problem and analyze alternative solutions, as is customary in private sector purchasing. If the buyer has a framework agreement with the consultant, this kind of procedure is legal, so-called "direct procurement". In cases where there is no framework agreement, however, direct procurement is illegal, but nevertheless frequently practiced despite the threat of legal proceedings.

Evaluating and selecting a supplier

LOU put strict constraints on the process of selecting suppliers in order to maintain objectivity. The selection must be based on predetermined evaluation criteria stated in the contract document and must not take irrelevant factors into consideration.

Among the procurements investigated, in which buyers had followed LOU, specific evaluation methods were often applied. The typical method include a two-step evaluation process where the first evaluation step excludes those suppliers who do not meet the formal requirements put forth in the contract document. In the second step, the potential suppliers are evaluated according to the evaluation criteria. The complexity of the evaluation system varied from considering only two criteria, such as quality and price, to as many as ten criteria, adding prior experience, methods, tools, availability, number of consultants, etc. All buyers investigated in the study followed the predetermined criteria in their evaluation. A small majority of buyers used criteria ranked in order of precedence. The greatest weight was often given to competence and prior experience, and in some cases to implementation methods. Price levels typically ended up in the lower half of the criteria ladder, with a weighted importance of 10-50 percent. However, in cases where all other criteria were equal, the cheapest consultant was often awarded the contract.

According to the buyers, competence and prior experience are of greater importance than price when selecting suppliers, despite LOU's requirement for choosing the cheapest alternative. The law thus seems to be subjected to arbitrary judgments. The law says that the most economically favorable alternative is to be awarded. But economically favorable to whom? The buyer or the taxpayers? Balancing the importance of price versus quality seems to be a great challenge to many buyers, and perhaps one of the reasons why LOU is perceived as inefficient and unclear. The consultants argue that price levels are of greater importance in public sector than in private sector procurements. But they emphasize that the weight placed on price levels seems to deteriorate the further we get from the introduction of the law. Some consultants point out that it seems like some buyers use price levels as main determinants only to avoid having to defend decisions made on other grounds.

Professionalism through breaking the law

As argued above, in public sector purchasing procedures of management consulting, personal traits of single consultants such as the ability to cooperate and to establish trust also tend to be important success factors for all client projects to come about. From an LOU standpoint, however, consultants' personal capabilities are problematic. It is not only hard to measure these objectively and to textualize them in written contract documents, but the justification of choices based on personal capabilities is also problematic. Consequently, they are difficult to use as comparable criteria for the evaluation and selection of consultants. The only way to judge personal capabilities is through meetings and discussions in person. Following the principle of equal treatment, the law would require in this case that the buyer meet with every single possible supplier. If the suppliers are plentiful, it becomes an impossible equation. Consequently, procurements are often conducted without being able to meet potential suppliers in person.

The criminality of personal relations

Despite the fact that LOU obstructs the possibility of using personal relationships as evaluation criteria, many buyers are creative in finding ways to legally or illegally bypass the law. In several of the investigated procurements, personal meetings had taken place. About one third of the public buyers referred to procurements where they had met with several potential consultants in person. However, if these meetings result in selection of suppliers based on criteria not previously stated in the contract document, such as personal relationship factors, the process is against the law. One public buyer admitted that the consultant's personality had been crucial in the choice of supplier, although it was not specified as selection criteria in the contract document.

The problem of remaining objective according to the law, while also taking personal capabilities into consideration, is obviously a great dilemma. Many buyers commented that "LOU makes it difficult to evaluate personal traits," and "the law is not suitable for procurements were personal qualities are important." These buyers argued that management consulting services are dependent on trust and confidence between the seller and the buyer, and that confidence can only be achieved in meetings between individuals.

The *consultants* were also critical to the fact that LOU leaves no room for personal relationship factors. They say that personal factors are equally important in the public sector as they are in the private sector since the quality of the service is dependent on them. In the public sector, however, it is more complicated to state their importance transparently. For newly established consultants with no prior experience of public procurements, LOU has indirectly made it harder to win a contract. Since LOU obstructs the ability to meet potential consultants in the evaluation process, these consultants are never given the opportunity to establish confidence with the buyers. Instead, the buyers put more and more weight on factors such as prior experience and references in the selection process. Consequently, new suppliers have difficulty getting awarded contracts. One supplier commented: "In the public sector our international experience isn't worth anything. If you don't have prior experience of working with Swedish authorities, it's almost impossible to win a contract." Another consultant pointed out that "since you can't meet the buyers, it's difficult to gain credibility if you're not already known to them." It seems like the easiest way for buyers to assure (or at least estimate) suppliers' credibility is by relying on references from other public organizations.

For the consultants who already have an established relation with public buyers, personal relationships are already in place. These consultants do not need personal meetings to present themselves. In such cases, LOU becomes nothing more than a formality, an obstacle that has to be overcome.

Both buyers and consultants admit that the law can easily be ignored. "The law is easy to get around in order to maintain established supplier relations, but it costs a lot of energy," revealed a state authority buyer.

Methods for bypassing the law

The above accounts make it clear that, in the eyes of many public buyers, LOU is not well suited to the procurement of complex services such as management consulting services. Therefore, they try to find ways to bypass the law. The most common "legal" way to get around LOU is by using framework agreements. In framework agreements, the buying organization (sometimes in cooperation with other buying organizations) signs long-term agreements with several preferred suppliers. The buyer may then purchase directly from these suppliers whenever needed – without having to comply with LOU regulations, so-called "direct procurement". If the framework agreement itself is procured according to LOU, this is a legally permitted way to avoid following LOU in every single case.

Accordingly, framework agreements allow the buyer to procure consultants without having to set aside costly resources in order to procure services in accordance with LOU. "We use framework agreements because individual procurements according to LOU are far too costly, both in terms of time and administrative input" commented a municipal buyer. The process is faster and more cost efficient, according to both buyers and consultants. In addition, framework agreements typically extend over several years, enabling buyers to cooperate with specific suppliers over long time periods. This allows buyers to maintain important supplier relations.

About one half of the observed procurements were framework agreements. It is, however, remarkable to note that in most agreements no mention was made of how often, or to what amount, the consultants would be used within the time period. The agreements were often very vaguely specified and broad enough to cover several areas within the wide category of organizational- and business development. Compared to single procurements, these kinds of agreements are rarely based on specific analyses of needs. They are more likely to have broad delimitations that leave room for future consultancy needs in different areas.

Some suppliers, however, point out that framework agreements carry certain disadvantages as well. They make it harder for those who are not included to enter the market and, moreover, framework agreements do not guarantee any assignments.

Illusive procurements and other bypass methods

While framework agreements are a legal form of circumventing the law, public buyers commonly use other more "illegal" methods as well. As illustrated above, buyers quite frequently make illusive procurements for the sake of appearance only. In practice, they have already decided whom they want to work with. Either the buyer knows the preferred consultant from previous assignments, or the consultant was involved at an early stage (i.e. when the needs were identified). The buyer then tailors the evaluation criteria so as to fit the preferred supplier perfectly. As in a case described by a consultant, for example, the buyer might require that the consultant have a PhD, knowing beforehand that few other suppliers could live up to that requirement. The consultants interviewed explained that this illegal procedure is "very common". Tailoring requirements can also be used in the procurement of framework agreements, as described by a public buyer:

We formulated the requirements in the contract document so that supplier X would fit perfectly. Many of our framework agreement users wanted to work with supplier X. If X had not been included,

*the users would probably turn to that firm directly, and what then
is the point of framework agreements?*

Another frequently used method is to split whole assignments into
smaller parts so that the amount of each part falls under the threshold
value (and can be legally procured without adherence to LOU). One
consultant described a case where the public buyer asked the
consultant to divide the job into several 20,000 SEK assignments, so a
public procurement in compliance with LOU would not be necessary.

In following with the fact that there are many, frequently used ways
to bypass LOU, the consultants argue that LOU does not have any
considerable impact.

The power of law

Presumably LOU, supported by the EU directives and the WTO
agreement, would have much regulating power on practice. The fact
that it is a law means that offended suppliers are given a chance to
appeal. Perhaps it has presumptive effect, i.e. it might scare buyers into
compliance. Among the consultants in the study, however, none had
ever filed an appeal or a complaint. According to the suppliers, the
reasons for not filing an appeal or suing for damages are that suppliers
do not want to harm their reputation, do not want contracts awarded
under such circumstances, or because it costs a lot of resources to
appeal. NOU's report shows similar findings; 60 percent of the
suppliers in their report said there was a risk of being *"blacklisted"* if
they lodged an appeal.[5]

Moreover, only those buyers who have tried to purchase in
accordance with LOU risk punishment. If a buyer has purchased
services directly, without competitive tendering, there are no rejected
suppliers who might file complaints. A supplier who has not been a
part of the procurement process has difficulty arguing that s/he has
suffered harm through unfair treatment. A municipal buyer in the study
pointed out that "if you don't follow LOU, there is no risk of being the
subject of an appeal," and buyers in the NOU report (p. 41) said that "a
purchasing entity that tries to comply with LOU carries a greater risk
of being punished than those who ignore the law completely."

The problem with the sanction system, in other words, is that it
requires that a rejected supplier is able to appeal (which is not the case
if there has been a direct procurement) and that s/he is willing to

---

[5] Effekter av lagen om offentlig upphandling ("Effects of the Public.
Procurement Act), NOU, 1998. Page 41 (in Swedish).

appeal (which is seldom the case according to the empirical study). Thus, in the case of knowledge intensive management support services the law is not given much authority by those it is supposed to regulate.

To summarize one can note that the answer to whether LOU has an impact on the selection of suppliers differs considerably depending on whom you ask. According to the buyers, they adhere to LOU even though they do not necessarily select the cheapest supplier. Instead they argue that the supplier chosen is the most economically favorable, for example, in terms of quality. It is not too surprising to hear the buyers report their procurement procedures as in accordance with LOU, since they are obliged to do that by law. However, many of them also point out that the law is not easily applied to consultancy services since it does not allow buyers to take established supplier relations, confidence and personal trust into consideration when selecting suppliers. Since the consultants are not required to adhere to any law, perhaps their description of the actual procurement procedures is more revealing. For many consultants, LOU does not pose any threat to the maintenance of good business relations or the prospects of getting new contracts. Still, others may face the problem that the law makes it difficult to meet new potential clients in order to present oneself and thus establish trust and confidence.

One conclusion is that LOU's requirement for not letting prior relations be decisive in the selection process do not seem to have the intended impact. Several consultants criticized the law by commenting: "suppliers are awarded contracts thanks to their business relations anyway," or "the law is just bureaucracy, relations are crucial in the public sector as well." However, since LOU does have some impact on the procurement process, two ways of handling public procurements become evident here – one in which the buyers adhere strictly to the rules of LOU, and another in which the rules are more or less ignored. In the latter case, the parties have made an active choice not to adhere to the rules, which means that the law has an impact here as well. In both cases, however, the law has an impact other than what was intended. In those cases where LOU has a large impact, the process is perceived as extremely resource-demanding, not suitable for the procurement of management consultancy services, unpredictable and risky, and not focused on the problem at hand. In those cases where LOU has a lesser impact, that is, when buyers actively bypass the law, through framework agreements or other methods, LOU is perceived as bureaucratic and a waste of resources. In both cases, it is evident that established business relations direct the market. Whenever possible, buyers and consultants try to meet on a continuous basis in order to discuss problems and possible solutions. This is the kind of professionalism both buyers and consultants strive to live by since they agree that the quality of the service is at its best when buyer and seller have confidence in each other.

Conclusion: Outlaw deals

One conclusion that can be drawn from the discussion above is that many deals between management consultants and public organizations tend to be illegal. However, the agency that has been given the authority to patrol the field of public procurement of management consulting services, the NOU, is powerless. The reason for this is that neither the law nor the agency is authorized by those who make these deals. Thus, it seems as if they treat LOU as a voluntary standard that may be followed in practice (or not). They follow it formally, but it is rare that they do it in practice. The practice is instead governed by institutionalized norms for professionalism in management consulting, which means close relations between the supplier and the client rather than tough competition where the service suppliers are treated as comparable.

In those cases where buyers struggle to bypass LOU, the process is characterized by informal inquiries and contracts, and suppliers are selected based on personal relations, trust, and habits. Conclusively, this implies that in areas where complex services are dealt with, i.e. where it is difficult to define clear needs, where services are difficult to compare, and where the effect of the service delivered is difficult to measure, close interaction seems to be the preferred method used by purchasers to reduce their uncertainty.

CHAPTER 11

Breaking the Personal Tie

On the formalization of the procurement of management consulting services

JONAS BÄCKLUND AND ANDREAS WERR

As illustrated by the previous chapter studying the purchase of management consultants in the public sector, where purchasing is subject to the public procurement act, there is an inherent tension between organizational efforts to ensure an efficient and effective purchasing process and the preferred practices of the managers and consultants wanting to come together to strike a deal. In this chapter, we will explore this tension further by turning from the public sector to the private sector. Here, no overarching laws or regulations limit the ways in which management consultants are dealt with, yet the same tension can be observed between corporate efforts to control individual managers' purchase of management consultants and the individual managers' and consultants' desires to act in an informal and trust-based way. As in the public sector (Chapter 10), a goal of corporate efforts is to break the personal ties between individual managers and consultants. But to what extent, for what reasons and in what ways are these efforts towards a "professionalization" of the use of management consultants driven in the private sector? These are the kind of issues that will be dealt with in this chapter.

The chapter is structured as follows: After a review of the current literature on purchasing management consulting services, we will turn to our empirical study. This is based on an interview survey of the 16 largest companies in Sweden and their handling of the purchase of management consultants, as well as 3 in-depth case studies of large organizations' efforts to control the use of management consultants. In the following, we will discuss the survey, identifying the main reasons for formalizing/not formalizing the procurement of management consultants, and the case studies, illustrating two purchasing strategies for management consulting services. The empirical patterns are discussed and conclusions are drawn in a final section of the chapter.

The interpersonal nature of management consulting services

As has been argued repeatedly in previous chapters of this book, management consulting is a highly interactive service in which interpersonal trust and "liking" play a central role. Gummesson (1977, p. 115) pictures the typical relation between consultant and client as a rather stable one and argues that consulting assignments are strongly person-oriented. Hiring consultants is thus described as very similar to recruiting an employee: "Experienced buyers purchase the services of individuals in whom they have confidence, not those of consulting companies." (Gummesson, 1977, p. 178; see also Edvardsson, 1990) Similar patterns confirming the importance of the interpersonal relationship are found in studies on how clients evaluate, choose and purchase management consultants. Dawes et al (1993) found that personal information sources – such as referrals, earlier experiences, etc, appear to be the most critical ones when searching for information in conjunction with complex purchase (ibid.). Among the three most important selection criteria, varying little across type of industry or assignment, is buyer knowledge about the specific consultant who will work on the project.[1]

The centrality of the interpersonal relationship is further strengthened by arguments linking the needs for management consultants to the individual manager rather than his/her company. From a more critical line of research on management consulting, it is often claimed that managers' personal needs (and insecurity) are key factors driving the demand for management consulting services (Clark, 1995; Huczynski, 1993; Jackall, 1988; Sturdy, 1997a). This further motivates an interpersonal approach, resisting regulation and structuration by laws or company policies.

---

[1] Differences were found for the relative experience of the buyers: users who make less frequent purchases rely more on referrals from satisfied clients and are influenced by an offer of assistance in the implementation phase (Dawes et al, 1992).

The professionalization of purchasing management consulting services

The purchase of management consultants has long been an exception from efforts of regulation and formalization. However, the evolvement of the purchasing function, its increasing sophistication and interest for services described in Chapter 3, has lead to a growing focus and literature on the specific challenges involved in purchasing management consultants (see e.g. Kubr, 1993; McGonagle and Vella, 2001; Zackrison and Freedman, 2000). The importance of central company polices is here often emphasized (although their content is typically given limited attention) as a central step in becoming a competent and professional buyer of consultants' services. Kubr (1993) mentions organizational policies for the use of consultants as an element of "becoming a competent user of consulting services." His main message is that every organization has to find the policies that suit it best since they are viewed as a formalization of successful practices (ibid.). Policies help, it is argued, because they force managers to decide: what consultants can do for the business, what they should do for the business, what problems they may cause and how they should be retained (McGonagle and Vella, 2001). A basic company policy covers questions such as: Who or what is responsible for preparing and keeping current the procedures that govern the retention and use of consultants? Are there overall limitations on the proper use of consultants? Is prior approval required to hire consultants? Etc. A common theme in the literature on how to become a professional buyer of services in general (see e.g. Chapter 3) and management consulting services more specifically (e.g. Kubr, 1993; McGonagle and Vella, 2001; Zackrison and Freedman, 2000) is a rather rational, sequential process starting with a definition of the buyer's needs, continuing with a selection of a suitable provider, contracting, negotiations and pricing, and ending with implementation and evaluation. Prerequisites for these kinds of processes are the buyer's ability to define his/her needs up-front, the comparability of different providers, and the suitability of involving a professional purchaser. In the following, we will look at how this general advice is turned into practice.

Managing the purchase of management consultants

Design of the study

The study of organizations' initiatives to improve their purchasing of management consultants targeted the top 20 largest Swedish multinational companies according to *Affärsvärlden's* (2001) listing. For each of these organizations, the CPO or designated purchaser for management consultants was approached for a telephone interview. Sixteen of the organizations participated in the study. On a few occasions, more than one person per company was interviewed. The interviews were carried out November-December 2002. With this study as a point of departure, a few firms that had taken steps to "professionalize" their procurement of management consulting services were identified and an in-depth case study conducted, including several visits to the companies and personal interviews with the person(s) responsible for the establishment and implementation of the procurement policy.

The companies' current interactions with management consultants

Our interviews with procurers from large multinational firms confirm research showing that management consulting services are typically procured in a relatively informal manner. Management consulting services are purchased and negotiated high up in the organizational hierarchy, by top managers who have a great deal of discretion with regard to what, whom, and how they procure these services. The procurement officers claimed that they and their department were only involved sporadically when management consultants were bought. As one procurer expressed it:

> *Management consulting services are probably the area in which the procurement department is the least involved.*

Accordingly, deviations from more "normal" routines for procurement are seldom questioned and the procurement department was rarely involved when consulting projects were initiated. In the vast majority of the companies, formal agreements, proper specifications, and negotiation of fees were unusual and formal follow-ups more or less non-existent. The same applied to the use of more formal guidelines for procurements (e.g. that the procurement department should be informed/take part, staying with preferred suppliers, etc.), which were typically not considered.

Instead, the quality of the procurement of these services, often amounting to large sums, appears to be dependent upon each manager's individual competence and interest in this area. Also, any formal responsibility to accumulate competence and experiences related to procurement of management consulting services and to the different suppliers was lacking. Intra-firm coordination with regard to the use of management consultants was thus perceived to be carried out sporadically at best.

A majority of firms did not have, at least in a formal sense, any written agreements or cooperations with management consulting firms going beyond specific assignments. This does not mean that there are no informal ties or long-term relationships with consultancies, but rather that they are not sanctioned by formal agreements. Several firms admitted having close ties to- and using the same supplier for a number of years. In these cases, management's personal ties were seen as the primary basis for these relationships. As expressed by one of the procurement officers:

We have preferred suppliers – they are preferred by the managers.

The managers themselves as the foundation for these relationships were noted also in other interviews:

When our CEO came to us, he brought with him an American consultancy specializing in our industry.

A shared perception among the procurement department was that "too much" was spent on management consulting, as exemplified by statements like: "we use far too many consultants," and "our costs have accelerated beyond what is acceptable." There was also consensus with regard to what group in the client company was responsible for this development – managers. In fact, several opinions were voiced with regard to this perceived managerial tendency to use management consultants. A first type of argument reflects the fact that the hiring of management consultants was not congruent with the company culture. A second, related argument reflects a view of managers as not supposed to be in need of help from consultants. One firm bluntly stated:

Here, we expect our managers to act like managers and not need help in doing this.

And one procurement officer noted:

We use far too many consultants, we really shouldn't be using any at all.

On several occasions, a direct link between the excessive use of management consultants and the (in)capability of the managers was noted. The following statement, where a procurer discusses possible explanations to the rising costs for management consulting services illustrates this view:

I think it has a little bit to do with the inadequacy of management, where managers use these [management consultants] as their life insurance.

Accordingly, data on the aggregate use of management consultants, which could be linked to individual managers and/or business units, were regarded as sensitive material by the procurement department. This kind of information had on at least one occasion been delivered by the procurement department in a company to its board of directors and there was speculation that this information was used to evaluate the current managers in the organization.

However, management consultants were also seen as a valuable means to improve the ongoing business and as important for the future competitiveness of the client's organization:

If we are going to stay competitive, we need to be dependent on good partners, as we are going to have to buy more and more services. Consequently, we need to be more careful when we make these choices and we must create better strategic arrangements than we have today.

The use of procurement policies for management consultants

Only very few (2 out of 16) firms had a particular strategy/policy for the procurement of management consulting services in place at the end of 2002. Two more firms were about to implement a policy for procurement of management consulting services, and one more was considering it. (Since then, several others have followed suit, though we lack a systematic follow-up of this.) Accordingly, a majority of firms did not have, nor plan to implement a specific strategy or policy for procurement of management consulting services in 2002. Instead, the decision to buy management consulting services fell under more general rules for procurement, i.e. to be made by those (managers) authorized to do so and with room in their budgets. In some cases, the procurement department offered their services in the process, and on other occasions, written instructions and guidelines, e.g. templates for written agreements, were made available to the managers.

This suggests that, despite the high costs involved and the complex nature of procuring management consulting services, the procurement of management consulting services is a process that appears to be taking place mainly in direct interaction between the end-user and the consultancies. In explaining the reasons for this, one procurement officer emphasized the importance and need for managers themselves to be actively involved in the evaluation and procurement of management consulting services:

Often, the professional elements in the procurement process are strong. This means that the competence is best judged by the buying manager rather than the procurement department, which represent different kinds of knowledge.

A different set of common arguments for this lack of formal regulation and central control among firms can best be described as "pragmatic", i.e. that a centralized policy for management's use of management consultants was not deemed realistic due to a lack of demand and internal support. A common argument is what is described as a "decentralized structure" where the different divisions were viewed as "independent". One procurer noted that:

We are decentralized with strong divisional managers and company cultures, which can sometimes be challenging from a procurement perspective.

Management consultants were also regarded a difficult area to regulate since there were often close personal ties at the management level with specific consulting firms. This view is exemplified by a procuring officer who notes that:

The higher up in the hierarchy, the more common it is that the managers themselves want to negotiate the agreement.

Another procurer offers a variation of this theme:

There is a tendency for management to see this as an unnecessary form of bureaucratization from the procurement side – they want to decide everything.

This form of "internal resistance" was partly based on a limited appreciation of the main goals for formalization – costs savings: "Cost savings as an argument is only valid for the board of directors – on lower levels of management this is not an argument." One explanation to this is that even if consultancies are expensive they constitute a small fraction of the total costs of a business area or segment and it is first when aggregated that they appear conspicuous.

Consequently, while some procurers had started working on specific policies and framework agreements, minimal perceived needs or a concern about their power position were limiting factors. In all cases, the procurement departments themselves initiated attempts to formalize the procurement of management consulting services (e.g. preceding the implementation of a policy). Several reasons for initiating and implementing a specific procurement policy were mentioned, in particular the aggregating costs for management consulting services. Against this background, the need to "professionalize" the procurement process was noted as an explicit goal by several firms. Management consultants were traditionally hired in a very informal manner, often without written agreements, directly by the managers leading to what was described as a "costly and less effective use of consultants."

We are surprised to find a lack among managers of carefully prepared plans concerning what firms to work with and how to work with them. Management lacks an understanding related to procuring these kinds of services.

Also, a perceived need to "align", i.e. to ensure that they didn't get "contradictory advice and strategies within the organization," was mentioned as an argument in favor of the implementation of a formal policy. Other perceived problems with a more traditional (i.e. informal) approach to procuring management consulting services included insufficient specification of assignments and implementation plans. Without proper specifications and written agreements, the argument was raised that they, as clients, ended up paying for senior consultants while newly graduated junior consultants would show up to do the work. A related type of argument raised was that, when different divisions and departments within a firm hired consultants, there was a perceived risk that the firm would end up paying twice for the same advice.

In the following, we will take a closer look at those companies that had implemented policies. This includes addressing questions such as how these policies were designed and the basic logic behind them.

Strategies for organizing the purchase of management consulting services

In the following, we will look more closely at three organizations – Alpha (multinational in the telecom industry), Beta (multinational in the automotive industry) and Gamma (mainly Swedish organization in the logistics industry) – that are on their way to implement policies for the purchase and use of management consultants. Their strategies could be said to have two separate components, the first focusing on the actual decision to hire consultants, and the second focusing on the selection of consultants. A common assumption among the purchasers was that, without their direct involvement in the interaction with consultants, consultants (and managers) would be left with the upper hand.

Controlling the use of consultants

In all of the organizations that had started to work with the purchase and use of management consultants, the procedures for authorizing consulting expenditures were under revision. Given the general perception among the purchasers, which was shared by top management, that too many consultants were used, the level of authorization was moved upwards in the organizational hierarchy to the bosses' boss or even to division management. Gamma (the logistics company) went the farthest in its efforts to centralize the use of management consultants by issuing a general stop for the use of consultants, exceptions to which could only be granted by a group of top level managers.

In Gamma's general efforts to lower its cost-base in order to reduce its losses, attention was directed also to the cost of management consultants, which, in relation to the corporation's size, were rather substantial. There was also a perception shared by most top managers, that Gamma used far too many management consultants. It was perceived that the organization had become lazy and the use of management consultants had become an accepted way to deal with problems that occurred and peaks in workloads. Also, the trade unions had for some time voiced strong critique against Gamma's broad use of consultants at the same time as the company laid off employees.

Against this background, in 2002, Gamma's top management issued a policy for the use of management consultants. This stipulated a general stop of the use of management consultants, exceptions to which could only be granted by a "consulting steering committee" consisting of four senior managers who met every second week to deal with applications for exception. Exceptions were to be requested in written form, clearly motivating why there were no internal resources, and how a transfer of competence would be managed in order to avoid further dependence on the consultants. Although the other organizations studied did not go quite as far in their efforts to control the use of consultants, the policies issued in all of the organizations had made it more difficult for the individual manager to hire management consultants. In Gamma in particular, these increased control measures were strongly criticized by managers, who felt the new procedures questioned their managerial competence and judgment.

Professionalizing the procurement process and structuring the supplier base

Besides formalizing and increasing hierarchical control over the decision to purchase management consultants, the efforts to professionalize the purchase and use of consultants also comprised the design of a "procurement process" as well as a structuring of the supplier base. In this context, two different strategies could be observed: one that may best be described as a "collaboration strategy", which focuses on the establishment of long-term relations with a limited number of suppliers, and a second that will be called a "competition strategy" and focuses on competitive bidding.

The collaboration strategy

The main characteristic of the collaboration strategy was the selection of a limited number of key suppliers. For theses suppliers, detailed and rather far-reaching framework contracts were negotiated, establishing a close, corporate relationship between buyer and supplier. Much effort was also put into the negotiation of standard prices, in order to keep them to a minimum. The central visibility of consulting assignments was also assured by demands on the suppliers to periodically report on their ongoing assignments within the corporation. The collaboration strategy may be illustrated by the work of Alpha (the telecom company).

Alpha began to review its purchase of management consultants in the late 1990s. At that time, management consultants had a rather permanent presence within Alpha and purchasing of these services took place in a decentralized and ad-hoc fashion. Most invoices from management consultants lacked purchase orders, creating administrative difficulties and indicating a general lack of control over consulting costs. Among top management, there was also a perception that the corporation could end up paying for the same project multiple times when consultants were used to solve similar problems in different places. At the same time, they also felt a need to build up close and longer-term relations to some consultants in order to ensure- and capitalize on these consultants' accumulated knowledge of the client organization. In one case (another company than Alpha), this was motivated by demographic changes. As many employees born in the 1940s were about to retire, consultants were seen as representing continuity and valuable experience. As one procurer argued, in a changeable environment with managers staying on their positions for shorter periods of times, a stable relation with management consultants may be "a way of bridging this latent knowledge gap."

In this situation, the corporate purchasing function took the initiative to "create some order" in the purchasing of management consultants. Based on the experiences gained from working with the sourcing of IT consultants, the aim was to reduce the supplier base to a small number of strategic partners. Competitive prices and standard business terms were negotiated in tough negotiations with these partners. The recession in the consulting industry at the time for the negotiations and the considerable size of Alpha created a favorable context for these negotiations.

Becoming a preferred supplier to Alpha meant more than just offering a special price list and business terms. It also meant providing quarterly reports of ongoing assignments within Alpha as well as annual quality reviews. The purchasing department also developed a training pack for managers on how to purchase and use consultants in order to increase the managers' competence within this area. Management consultants other than Alpha's partners were not to be purchased without clearly justifiable reasons for not using the preferred suppliers.

The initial reactions of managers to this system were rather negative as they felt that the new policy curtailed their independence and good relations to individual consultants. Not being able to contract the consultants they had traditionally used, because these were not among the preferred suppliers, was perceived as frustrating. Gradually however, attitudes towards the new purchasing policy for management consultants and the purchasing department became more positive as managers realized the help they could get from standard legal terms, standardized price lists, etc.

The competition strategy

Rather than controlling the cost and quality of management consulting through negotiation of general prices and terms and long-term agreements, the competition strategy focused on the individual assignment and the negotiations concerning that assignment. By stipulating that all larger consulting assignments should be bid on by at least three consultancies, competitive prices and designs for consulting assignments were to be achieved. Beta (the automotive company) may be used to illustrate the competition strategy.

Beta began its efforts to improve the use of management consultants in 2001. Driven by an overall desire to reduce costs, the total costs for management consultants came into focus and the purchasing department began designing a policy for how to buy consultants. Similarly to in the case of the collaboration strategy, an initial effort to identify a limited number of suppliers failed as different managers all had their favorite suppliers. Instead Beta chose to negotiate framework agreements with most of the larger available suppliers. These agreements also included negotiated standard prices for different categories of consultants as well as standard terms. However, less effort was put in negotiating these overall agreements than in Alpha. Rather, a procurement policy was issued, according to which offers from three consultancies should be solicited for each assignment. These offers were then compared with respect to content and price, and the most favorable one chosen. The purchasing department would also support the managers buying consulting services in further negotiations to further bring down the price.

This strategy put a lot of pressure on the managers using consultants to specify their needs in rather detailed manner early on, so that a proper request for proposal could be prepared. This was perceived as a rather time-consuming task, which, together with the time for soliciting and evaluating proposals, made the procurement process tedious. Many managers felt that they did not have the time necessary to do this. The two strategies – collaboration and competition – are summarized in Table 11:1.

	Collaboration	Competition
Authorization of consultant use	Centralization	Centralization
Basic logic	Reduce number of suppliers and negotiate low prices in framework agreements	Have competitive bidding for each assignment
Number of suppliers	Few	Many
Proximity to suppliers	High - supplier and client develop together	Low - distanced relationship with focus on each assignment
Stability in relationship	High	Low

Table 11:1 Two strategies for procuring management consulting services

Discussion and conclusions

Studies of the way in which management consulting services are bought and used by managers highlight the interpersonal and trust-based character of these processes. Managers' relations to management consultants are often long-term and personal rather than institutional, and described as something to value and develop (Clark, 1995; Edvardsson, 1990). Studies reported in this- and the previous chapter illustrate that managers are willing to go far in order to maintain this practice.

The challenges to this preferred practice of both managers and consultants have however been increasing not only in the public sector but also, as illustrated in this chapter, in the private sector. The study of large organizations' initiatives towards a more efficient purchasing of management consultants showed that there is a growing view in purchasing departments, supported by top management, that companies have become "victims" in the hands of high pressure consultants and managers pursuing their own personal career interests. Not only have consultants become a too familiar sight in the landscape of large organizations, it is argued, the way in which they are used and managed is far from efficient. The reliance on personal relations when hiring management consultants is argued to lead to more expensive deals than necessary, as there is a traditional reluctance to negotiate prices between managers and consultants, a suboptimal selection of consultants, as managers hire their contacts rather than the best experts, and suboptimal delivery, as the framework for the consulting assignments is left rather fuzzy and evaluations are avoided. In line with what is suggested in the purchasing literature, the purchasing departments therefore strive for a formalization of the consultant-client relationship. The trustful relationships between consultant and client are to be replaced, or at least complemented by, formal contracts, negotiated prices, competitive selection processes and rigorous searches for alternatives. The claim, that uncertainty concerning the quality of the service to be delivered by different suppliers may be reduced only through trust-based interaction is questioned by the purchasers.

Although somewhat more negotiable than the public procurement act, the two observed strategies (collaboration and competition) for a more formal handling of consultants both involved severe (intentional) disturbances of the interpersonal consultant-client relationship. In the "collaboration" strategy, the interpersonal relation between consultant and client was complemented by a distant and more market-like relation between the consulting organization and the purchasing department. According to the formal mandate of the purchasing department, it could both interfere with as well as terminate the relation with the consulting company. In the second strategy, "competition", personal relations were overridden by a demand to solicit competitive proposals. The logic behind these strategies, and the "competition" strategy in particular is similar to that of the public procurement act – although private sector translations of the idea allowed for a less rigid use when deemed appropriate, allowing e.g. for interpersonal meetings during the tender process.

Underlying the purchasing departments' efforts to professionalize the interaction with consultants is the implicit rejection of the special status of the management consulting service as requiring a close and trust-based relation between client manager and individual consultant in order to reduce the uncertainty involved in their purchase and delivery. Behind the motives for introducing specific policies for the purchase and use of management consultants, as well as for the use of framework agreements, an image of a consulting service rather similar to other types of services is emerging. Strongholds in the argumentations include the perceived need for clearly defining the assignment, evaluation and comparison, which presupposes rather standardized and commoditized services. Only one of the companies in our study emphasized the specific characteristics of the consulting service (i.e. uncertainty, immateriality, interactional) when justifying the personalized patterns of purchasing observed in current practice.

Thus, in the meeting between the managers' views and the purchasing initiatives, two different forms of "professionalism" that represent different views on what kinds of procurement procedures are in the best interest of the client organizations stand in opposition to each other. One is depersonalized and focuses on rules, policies and procedures aimed at identifying and comparing alternative suppliers and controlling and coordinating the use of consultants within large organizations, and the other is individualized, where the building of trust and interpersonal relations are central in choosing consultants and managing their work.

This reflects a tension between managers' (and consultants') view of the nature of consulting services and that implicit in the purchasing departments' efforts. An explanation of this discrepancy often put forward by managers and consultants stresses the purchasing department's ignorance of management consulting services. However, in the following we will explore a number of different explanations.

A first possible explanation is that managers and procurement officers indeed talk about different services. The diversity of management consulting services is large, ranging from highly creative problem-solving tasks that build on the expertise and experience of individual consultants, to rather standardized services purchased as extra resources (Greiner and Metzger, 1983; Kubr, 2002). These different kinds of services pose very different challenges to the buyer (Werr, 2004). The processes designed by the procurement departments might well handle the more standardized services, of which the clients possess considerable knowledge. However, in cases where the consultants are hired for more complex services in areas where the buyer lacks knowledge, judging their expertise in a formal procurement process becomes more difficult, thus demanding a higher reliance on interpersonal relations and trust (Clark, 1995). This calls for a more nuanced discussion within organizations, as well as in the procurement literature, about how to handle different kinds of management consulting services. The above also indicates that the different kinds of services need to be defined not according to the characteristics of the service, but rather according to the relation between the content of the service and the client's knowledge and expertise within the area of service.

A second possible explanation of the differences in views regarding the nature of management consulting services may be related to learning curve effects over time. It might be argued that the extensive use of consulting services in many organizations in past years has led to increased experience in many organizations. This increasing experience may have made consulting services susceptible to a more formal and distanced treatment in line with the procurement departments' suggested processes. As a department's knowledge and experience of the consultants' services increase, it becomes easier to formulate detailed assignments for the consultants and evaluate alternative suppliers with traditional procurement processes. This explanation highlights the client-manager's competence level in relation to the service bought from the consultant as an important variable for what kind of procurement processes may be used. Hence, the choice of strategy for purchasing management consulting services not only needs to take into account the variations of the service, but also that these variations are to some extent context-dependent. Depending on the competence level of a certain organization, a certain consulting service may be judged as fairly easy to specify and evaluate in one context, while in a different, less experienced organization, it may be viewed as very difficult to evaluate, calling for different strategies for purchasing in different situations (see also Chapter 6).

Thirdly, we may turn to political explanations in trying to understand the differences between the current practices of purchasing management consulting services and the efforts to professionalize the use of consultants. To begin with, we may view the purchasing department's intervention into the purchasing of management consultants as a strategic move aimed at securing and increasing its organizational position. As mentioned in Chapter 3, the purchasing organization is striving for a more strategic role in organizations. Becoming actively involved in the process of purchasing management consultants may be the ultimate way of expressing this importance, as it brings the procurement organization into contact with top management, to which it may thus demonstrate its worth and importance.

For the manager, the management consulting service is often described as one intimately linked to the manager's identity. Clark and Salaman (1996) argue that the main contribution of management consultants is not so much the solving of business problems, but the providing of a desirable identity to managers (see also Huczynski, 1993). Personal and organizational goals and purposes are thus blurred in the manager's use of management consultants (see also Watson, 1994) and it has sometimes been argued that the use of consultants for career or political purposes may dominate the use of consulting services for business purposes (Jackall, 1988; Macdonald, 2000). Against this background, the reluctance of managers towards the formalization of the procurement process, putting more emphasis on business value, problem formulation, evaluation, etc, becomes understandable. Consequently, we may view the different positions of the purchasing officials on the one hand, and managers and consultants on the other, as a situation of conflicting interest, where managers (and consultants) and purchasers benefit from different procedures.

Regardless of the reasons for the discrepancy between the procurement officers' approach to management consultants and the managers' preferred way of handling consultants, however, a more formalized way of handling management consultants may have strong consequences for the use of consultants and the consulting industry. The current focus on the cost of management consulting services (whether this is due to the current economical downturn or a long-lasting trend may be left unsaid) and the activities of the procurement departments in the studied organizations has already led to a tougher climate for the users of consulting services. In several of the cases, the use of management consultants was followed up at a business unit level. Given a rather common view of management consultants as "career- and competence insurance" and consulting costs as a corporate "lack of competence cost", this led to a situation where the use of management consultants became increasingly problematic for managers.

In a longer perspective, the emerging practice of purchasing management consultants reflected in the (rather extreme) enactment of a public procurement act and the more moderate applications of the same rationale in an increasing number of large private organizations may have a profound impact not only on demand but also on how the consulting industry operates. In the past, business, competence, career, and economic models in the industry have been built on the traditional, interpersonal way of doing business. Securing new business has been tightly linked to interpersonal networks, and skills in building and nurturing relationships to managers have been central and highly valued in consulting organizations, as well as linked to both promotion and compensation (see also Chapter 2). Given that these skills may lose their importance for generating business in consulting, new ways of securing business need to be developed, and necessary skills need to be identified and built into the reward structure of organizations. The emerging purchasing practices also significantly increase the cost of sales, putting pressure on the business models of consultants. In the wake of these developments, management consultants have been increasingly looking for new ways of motivating their services and their prices. One strategy that has received increasing attention has been that of "value-based pricing", which could be seen as a way of transcending both the interactive- and more professionalized approaches to making deals in management consulting. To what extent this may be a remedy to the emerging challenges of the consulting industry will be examined in the next chapter.

CHAPTER 12

Dealing with Values

SUSANNA ALEXIUS AND
STAFFAN FURUSTEN

Paying for the delivered value

Several chapters in this book (chapters 8, 9 and 10) have emphasized individualism as a convenient strategy for reducing uncertainties for buying organizations in choosing a reliable supplier of management advisory services (MAS). In the previous chapter, however, it was shown that collectivism, in terms of professional norms in management consulting, also had considerable impact on the construction of a buyer's expectation of what a trusted supplier could look like. This suggests that individualism and collectivism are not mutually exclusive strategies. It is more likely that deals involving MAS in general, and management consulting in particular, can be understood as the result of both individual- and collective mechanisms in different combinations.

Although, this is a most reasonable explanation of how deals come about, it is not the same as all involved parties being satisfied with the ways perceived uncertainties, such as what the service is really worth or what value the service brings to the organization, are dealt with. This is also what one experienced MAS buyer in a large Swedish corporation with global operations put into words when he said that "it would be great if we could pay only for the results, and thus the value the consultancy has brought to us." What he had in mind was a neutral way of setting the price on a delivered service, a price that could be vaccinated against both the individual- and collective mechanisms.

This would be very handy for the buyer since it would reduce the uncertainty related to what supplier to choose, as the consultant would take no payment if s/he did not deliver value.

The wishful thinking of this buyer corresponds well to a pricing model called Value-based Pricing (VBP) that has been used for quite some time in standardized service areas such as IT. It is not a widespread method in the area of management consulting, but it appears that the idea at least, of paying only in relation to a delivered value, is appealing to many management consultancy buyers, and VBP has been discussed as a pricing form of interest since the late 1990s.

To think of the value of a service in these terms can be seen as another strategy to reduce uncertainty and establish confidence in business relations, of a different type than individualism and collectivism, as discussed in Chapter 1, and in several other chapters in this book. In fact, it can be seen as a strategy that seeks to neutralize, and thus to deindividualize and decollectivize the price setting process, and thereby also objectivize the choice of consultancy.

In this chapter, we are going to follow one management consultancy's struggle to use a VBP method in their efforts to close deals with potential buyers. The purpose is to discuss what implications the pricing method has in the process where buyers of management consulting services choose a supplier to close a deal with.

The discussion will be structured as follows: First, we discuss the VBP method in contrast to other price setting methods. Second, we tell the story of how the consultancy struggles to use VBP in their business relations. And finally, we discuss what role the VBP contract may have when consultancy buyers make choices about suppliers.

Valuing and pricing management consulting

The price of a service is often the only "visible" characteristic available to suggest its "true" value (Groth, 1995). In the case of consulting services, to visualize the service in the form of a price per hour is the most common way to do this. In most cases, the pricing method used is an open running account. This means that buyers pay consultants a certain amount for each hour of project work. It is a straightforward method where the price is based on the real costs rendered for the consultancy. Buyers are able to compare the hourly fees of different consulting firms, and projects can be re-evaluated at an hourly basis.

A common alternative to open accounting is the fixed price deal. This means that a project has a known price tag, enabling buyers to then compare the price tags of different consulting firms. However, it happens that a fixed price offer can turn out to be far from fixed from the consultants' point of view, since the client may be tempted to broaden the project scope to get "more for less", or at least more for the same price. From the buyer's perspective, there is a risk that the consultant will not have delivered good enough services when the amount of project hours has reached the limit for the fixed price. A fixed price deal usually means a lower risk for the client. But since the client doesn't want to pay a great deal extra to get this lower risk, the consultant needs to have done it before, to have developed a method, to recycle things from past experience. The fixed price approach requires a certain repetitiveness if it is to be a reasonable deal from the consultant's point of view.

The idea of VBP is to let buyers pay in relation to the estimated actual value of the consultancy service, rather than paying for a certain number of hours or for the delivery of a specific product, such as an IT system.

Of these pricing methods, the vast majority of consultancies tend to use cost-based pricing methods, i.e. open accounting or fixed pricing (Noble and Gruca, 1999). One possible reason to why VBP not has won terrain is that management consultancy projects may be too complex, since the principles go against the consultant's advisory role and thus tend to threaten consultants' independence (Affärsvärlden, 24/3/2001).

In the late 1990s and early 2000s in particular, however, when there was a recession in the consultancy market and the hourly wages and fixed prices tended to drop, VBP was likely seen as a method to increase prices again (Swedish consultancy guide, www.konsult-guiden.se, 9/3/2004). This suspicion is strengthened in an early discussion about value-based pricing, where Edvinsson and Hallberg (1985) argue that VBP is a method for setting the highest possible price that the client is prepared to pay. Edvinsson and Hallberg suggest that prices set in this way are assumed to be higher than prices set through an open running account or fixed pricing. This implies that the whole idea behind the value-based method may be that the customer value of the service is higher than the consultant's actual production costs.

If this is true, the VBP method should be really attractive for consultancies. However, a less cynical view of consultancies and VBP describes it as a method by which buyers can acquire a long-term edge on their competitors as VBP offers consultants a bonus and thus makes it worthwhile for them to do their very best on these projects (Rosvall and Rosvall, 2000). It has been suggested that value-based pricing ought to work especially well for "qualified offers" such as management consultancy projects where the buyers tend to be looking for the best and fastest solution rather than just a good bargain (ibid).

To sum up, as an ideology VBP is great. It is easy to defend all the benefits that are supposed to come out of this pricing method. From the consultant's perspective, it is no doubt a brilliant idea to offer the client to pay for what they perceive the service to be worth. What buyer could resist that? However, although it is a very attractive idea, following the model and making fair calculations is far from uncomplicated – especially in a field of competence where the definition of the structure can be rather unclear (cf. Furusten, 2003).

We will now look at how consultants struggle to set this fabulous idea of VBP into practice. To do this, we focus on one consultancy's attempts to use the VBP method. The data analyzed consists of both interviews and documents. We have conducted three in-depth interviews with the VBP team leader at a consulting firm (CF), one interview with another CF consultant with experience of using the VBP approach, and one interview with one of CF's VBP clients. The interviews where all conducted during the fall of 2003, except for a follow-up interview with the team leader in February 2005. Various internal documents about the process to launch the VBP standard have also been analyzed.[1]

Value-based pricing in practice: Selling real improvements?

When the consulting firm (CF), offering management- and IT consulting, was founded in 1999, the founders agreed to use the following market slogan when presenting the new firm to the market: *"We help our customers gain real improvements fast."* VBP had been discussed from an early stage at the founders meetings. The founders knew of a small number of US consulting firms that had tried to put the VBP approach to use, though none of these attempts had yet been successful. The founders interpreted the careful US optimism as a sign of a potential future spread of VBP ideas to European markets.

---

1 Most importantly: a 58-page CF research team report on VBP, and a number of actual VBP contracts.

We'll take you to the top of the mountain!

An intense period of marketing began. CF consultants worked hard communicating the company mission to the environment. When pitching for new buyers and recruiting fellow consultants to the firm, CF consultants often used the educational story "We'll take you to the top of the mountain" to illustrate the firm's passion for real improvements and to convince others of the beauty of the VBP method. According to them, there are a few completely different approaches to delivering a service. One of the founders explains:

One kind of consultancy offers "ladders". They might be excellent ladders, lightweight and very flexible, etc. And ladders may be perceived as one possible means for getting to the top of the mountain. But the consultants selling "ladders" won't guarantee the client actually reaching the top of the mountain. The only guarantee they give is that the ladder won't break. If the client then decides to use the ladder in an inappropriate way... the ladder may well be too short or people might fall off...In any case, there is no assurance from the consultant.

Another classic consultancy offer says: "We have climbed mountains before"... These consultants emphasize their experience and offer buyers a lot of advice on which route they ought to take to the top. But they don't take responsibility for the actual journey, for buyers actually reaching the top...

And then, there is a third approach that says: "We're no experts on mountain climbing but we're full of strength and energy, we can help you carry your luggage on the way up."

These three offers differ from the fourth, which we represent. We say: "We'll get you to the top!" We won't decide now whether to use ladders or rope ladders, or whether to climb with bare hands and feet. But we'll maintain focus and get you to the top, and we're prepared to share the risks in such a way that our payment is linked to whether we get there or not.

The CF consultant used the "We'll take you to the top of the mountain" story to spur the interest of both buyers and possible new colleagues for the VBP method. Very few buyers and potential colleagues can be expected to want to buy or provide only "ladders", "climbing advice" or "baggage carrying". It can also be read into the story that the three traditional consultancy offers emphasize the best deal for the consultant, and that this happens when as much time and resources as possible are spent on a project. The value-based approach, on the other hand, suggests that the consultants get the highest turnover when they minimize the time and resources spent. Furthermore, the story reminds buyers that the risk is all on their side in an open running account or fixed price deal.

When pitching for new buyers, CF consultants were greeted with much enthusiasm as they presented the value-based concept at sales meetings and presentations. The CF also conducted a survey among senior managers at A-listed buyers that strengthened this view.[2] This made them think that value-based pricing was the natural way to conduct business.

Thus, CF consultants noticed that most people who heard their story came to like the idea of buying or selling the "all-inclusive trip to the top of the mountain." Few wanted to settle for less. But then again, perhaps the idea was too good to be true?

Turning a wonderful ideal into practice

During its first year on the market, CF expended a lot of effort trying to convince buyers and consultants to understand the meaning of the VBP method. In a report produced by an internal research team, two approaches to value-based pricing were suggested: subjective confidence and objective measurement.

The subjective confidence method

The subjective confidence method was first suggested by some of CF's buyers. The method prescribes that the consulting firm apply an open running account according to its usual price list. A number of project targets are defined beforehand and, when the project is complete, there is an evaluation based on the client's subjective *perceptions* of the project effects. If the client perceives that the consultants have managed to surpass his or her expectations, the client pays an extra, predefined bonus. If, on the other hand, the client is dissatisfied and feels that the project has failed considerably, the consultants must repay a predefined amount to the client.

---

2   The A-list is one of two lists at the Stockholm Stock Exchange. The other is the O-list.

The subjective confidence model resembles the pricing norm often used at restaurants. If a guest is highly satisfied, s/he will leave a tip for the waiter, but if the food and service is terrible, the guest may get a price reduction.

It is obvious that this approach requires a considerable level of confidence between the parties since the consultant leaves control of the final price setting to the client. The CF research team therefore suggests that a condition for using the subjective confidence method would be a personal relationship between the consultant and the buyer that is important enough to each that the price (on the personal cost scale) for letting the other down in business would be too high.

But does such an evaluation really stand a better chance of being "fair"? Some CF buyers believed so, but others strongly opposed this, suggesting it would be nearly impossible for an unsatisfied client to "tell the truth" and risk his personal relationship with the consultant. The CF research team was of the same opinion and therefore chose to concentrate mainly on the objective measurement method.

The objective measurement method

According to the objective measurement method, the consulting firm uses a running account but offers a discount on its prices. At a predefined date, the project effects are measured against the predefined targets. The targets, which are typically identified by the consultant during a pilot study, specify business factors that the client wishes to increase or decrease. The client may want an increase in stock turnover, customer satisfaction, delivery precision, market share, transaction value, etc, or a decrease in the number of mistakes made, the time spent completing various tasks, etc. If the targets are met and the effects exceed predefined expectations, the consultant receives an additional payment: the better the goal attainment, the more the consultant gets paid. The consultant gets no extra payment if the minimum target level has not been reached.

Confidence in persons or trust in numbers?

The objective measurement method was introduced as a means of selling value, but to make this possible, the price of the value has to be set before the value has been realized. The objective measurement method therefore requires predefined targets, a predefined evaluation date, and predefined payment- and discount levels. All of this has an "objective" tone to it. One might think of it as a method that strives to trade subjective confidence (in persons) for objective trust (in numbers).

Graphs and equations, like the ones described below (Figure 12:1), made up an important part of the objective measurement method presentation and can perhaps be seen as an important tool when trying to convince client management to choose the method.

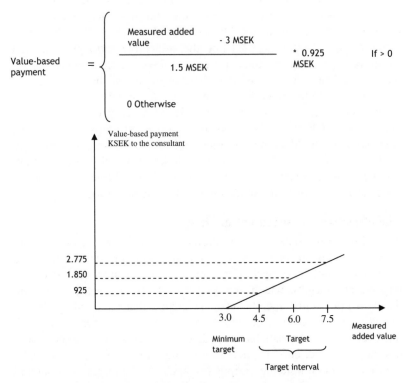

Figure 12:1 A model for defining value-based payment

Let us assume that the minimum value of the consulting project is estimated at 3 MSEK and that the maximum value-based payment is set at 4*925,000 SEK. Then, if results are poor and the added value reaches only the minimum value of 3 MSEK, the client pays nothing besides the discounted price/hour of the running account. If there is an estimated added value of 4.5 MSEK, the consultant gets 925,000 SEK extra, which corresponds to the discount received on the hourly prices. The target is set at 6.0 MSEK, where the value-based payment is 1.850 MSEK (2*925,000). At an estimated added value of 7.5 MSEK, the value-based payment is 2.775 MSEK (3*925.000) and at an estimated added value of 9 MSEK or more, the maximum of 4*925,000 is paid to the consultant, for the excellent results achieved.

At first glance, this may seem clear-cut and objective, but the obvious question is: Where do the numbers come from? These predefined targets and payment levels are usually suggested by the consultant during the final phase of the pre-study, whereupon the figures are negotiated until the parties reach an agreement. The truly difficult part is of course to agree on how, when and by whom the actual measuring is to be conducted. In CF, these matters were thoroughly defined in the VBP standard contract drawn up by the CF research team.

As an illustration, we can take the case of one of CF's buyers, a large insurance company in Sweden that wanted CF's help to reduce the yearly damage costs. When the client and CF consultants discussed a value-based deal, they predefined a target of a 6 MSEK reduction in yearly damage costs (see figure 12:1 above) and that there should be two times of measurement. For the period April-June 2002, measurements had to be done by 15/12/2002 at the latest, and for the latter period, April-June 2004, the last date set for measuring was 15/7/2004. Calculation of the resulting reduction in damage costs had to be done as soon as possible, after 30/6/2004, and by 15/7/2004 at the latest. All of these dates were clearly stated in the contract.

It was decided that the client and CF would arrange and perform the measuring and calculations together. The contract also very clearly stated that if the parties could not agree on the results of their "objective" measurements, then an independent auditing firm would be called in to settle the dispute and to get the numbers straight.

However, in one section of the report about the VBP pricing methods produced by the internal research team at CF, where the objective measurement method is compared to the subjective confidence method, it is emphasized that the aim must be to create not only a real value effect but, perhaps even more importantly, a perception of added value.

The subjective confidence method is a much less complicated method that can be understood and accepted rather quickly by client management. The various definitions of operative business ratios and measurement methods of the objective measurement approach may lead to debate and it may therefore be harder to convince client management to choose the method.

So, if the objective measurement method shows that the predefined target has been reached, but the client still does not perceive the project as a success, this may lead to a conflict and potentially endanger the relationship to this client. In a paragraph of decisive importance, the CF team writes that:

> *In the end, this means that our chances of actually getting a value-based payment for the objectively measured added value, depends on whether or not the client perceives the project to be a success, i.e. just as is the case in the subjective confidence method.*

> *Since the value-based pricing method is based on a win-win relationship, we suggest a model that encourages a relationship of mutual confidence between the consultant and client.*

And here again is the same ambivalence. First, the objective measuring is emphasized as a means of *gaining* the client's trust (through the numbers), then VBP is described as a pricing method which rather *requires* a strong existing mutual confidence between the consultant and the client.

Lessons learned after 5 years with VBP

CF has offered VBP deals since the year 2000. The VBP approach has been an important part of the firm's market slogan, and the VBP concept has been up for discussion in almost every offer submitted by CF consultants. In 20 percent of the contract talks, there have been serious negotiations about the setting up of a VBP deal. And in the end, 50 percent of these, or about 10 percent of all CF projects, have been VBP projects.

According to CF, the initial stages of predefining targets, times of measurement, etc, have typically not been difficult. What has been difficult is the discussion of how much the consultant will be paid in the end. This has come as a disappointment to CF consultants, who have had a hard time convincing buyers to discuss payment in relation to the added value. Another disappointment was the tendency toward an increasing demand for open running accounts, at the same time as the buying organizations' purchasing departments have promoted their positions (cf. Chapter 3 and 11). Obviously, buyers tend to prefer the hourly rates, and perhaps the fixed prices even more. The following is a common argument expressed by a client in an insurance company (the same as above), who was initially very positive to the VBP approach, although his firm later stopped this form of price setting.

> *The reason for not proceeding with the VBP agreement this time was that it's so hard to measure the effects of a consultancy service. Thus, if it were possible to measure the effects beyond any*

doubt I would have no problems with a VBP procedure since it gives the supplier an incentive to achieve what we want.

One lesson the CF has learned is that VBP does not fit all projects, as CF founders had first hoped. The VBP approach seems to be most suitable for projects where measurable targets can easily be identified, such as projects involving IT. VBP also requires a strong client-consultant relationship, especially between the individuals negotiating the deal. CF has noticed that VBP relies heavily on confidence:

It is extremely rare to close a VBP deal with a brand new client. It's more typical to have got to know one another previously in a number of traditional [running accounts or fixed price] deals.

Many CF consultants would like to sell VBP projects but so far only about 5 out of 25-30 senior sales consultants at CF have managed to draw up a VBP contract on their own. It is costly and time-consuming to teach the method to consultants and CF has invested a lot of time and effort into strengthening the buyer's ability to explain to their board of directors why the consultants ought to be paid more if they deliver more value. Usually, an expert from the CF research team is called in to help out during the more challenging VBP discussions with buyers.

Experiences of this kind have made the CF consultants think of VBP more as a powerful market message than a real opportunity to increase profitability. One of them explains:

We have written up the market value and lowered our expectations on the number of VBP projects to be performed.

If CF fails to set up a VBP contract for a deal, they can still profit from that client having noticed CF's interest and competence in delivering business effects and value – something everybody wants. When CF shows that they are prepared to take a risk on the client's project, this signals and builds confidence, which in turn helps to legitimize and differentiate CF from other firms in the business.

Measuring and comparing new-professional expertise

We have seen in Chapter 10 and 11 that public as well as private organizations are making serious attempts to rationalize the purchasing procedure and make the purchasers more professional (cf. Chapter 3). For public organizations a public procurement law (LOU) has been launched for this purpose, while private firms tend to develop internal procedures for purchasing services. In this chapter, we have set another strategy for making the business relation more rational in focus, the formal contract in which the client is only supposed to pay for the delivered value.

We have seen that the consultants in CF were very enthusiastic when they talked about the principles, but that it was quite obvious that the buyers were not as enthusiastic. This means that, although many agree that the idea of risk sharing is often worth striving for, it is not always easy to translate into practice.

Still, the VBP method was discussed in almost every business relation of the CF. This can be understood as VBP actually representing much more than a mere formula for price setting. It seems to be used, or at least advocated by the consultant, as one of many other cornerstones in the process of building confidence for oneself and the consultancy one represents in business relations with potential buyers. By referring to attributes such as delivered value, and that clients should only pay a price based on this value, the consultants deindividualize the business deal. They do not pay for who they are, what reputation they have, or whether or not they represent certain legitimacy platforms. The client should pay only for what he gets, and the VBP standard is a method for reducing uncertainties of how this value is measured.

Thus, the value-based contract had a strong focus on the project's presumed effects on the client organization, indicating that the parties had to agree beforehand on how the assumed effect would be "objectively measured". Uncertainty regarding whom to trust would then be regulated by reference to the value of these effects for the client organization. This suggests that VBP is hard to use for the consultant to establish confidence if it cannot be proven that there will be money to earn for the client organization. If confidence has already been established, however, this form of pricing has a greater potential to be put into use.

Due to its lack of an established and formalized core of knowledge, methods, prerequisites for membership in associations for professionals, codes of conducts and *rites de passage*, the field of management consulting does not meet the prerequisites for representing an abstract expert system (Furusten, 2003). In fact, it is not unusual that the representatives of the core must re-produce themselves as experts over and over again in almost every single business situation (ibid.). This lack of formal structures implies uncertainty and makes it difficult for buyers to judge and compare different consultants beforehand and, of course, to assess the value a possible delivered service might bring to the organization.

This chapter, as well as most of the others in this book, makes note of the fact that buyers and consultants tend to live in long-term business relations. As a consequence, the client often becomes involved in the actual production of the service (Gummesson, 1995; Normann, 1992; Grönroos, 1992). This is another dilemma in pinpointing the value produced by the consultant and how the client organization itself has contributed to this value.

Due to these circumstances, the value contributed by the consultant is difficult to judge. Thus, the abstract characteristics of the service paired with the simultaneous production and consumption of the service and dual client roles make it difficult for buyers to measure, test and compare the value of a service both before and after it has been delivered.

Closing deals without knowing, and setting a value on the unknown

The discussion above suggests that valuing the results of a consultancy service and comparing different alternatives on a neutral basis, which the VBP method attempts, is complicated. *First*, there have to be variables whose impact can be isolated and measured. *Second*, these measurements then have to enable comparison with measurements made on other alternatives, in order to learn whether or not the chosen alternative is or was worth the money. *Third*, it must be possible to measure and compare offers as well as the results of delivered services.

In the case of management consulting, it is very rare that these circumstances exist. Let us express the more likely situation by quoting one of the senior consultants in the CF:

> *If you're offering an IT business system that the client is familiar with, it might be him who knows the product and demands it. When it comes to management consulting, it's different. In almost 100 percent of the cases, it comes down to confidence based on a personal relationship. So buyers don't just call up a consulting business and ask them to send over a consultant. That's extremely rare. It's like "I want Peter because I know Peter and I've worked together with Peter before. I might accept Peter and others who Peter thinks will be right for the job."*

Thus, buyers may not feel as comfortable trusting a consulting firm or a consulting technique, or a management model provided by a consultancy. It is the consultant as a person they have or do not have confidence in. Such confidence, however, normally takes time to establish. For instance, it is quite common that it has its roots in personal networks that go a long way back in time (DiMaggio and Powell, 1983/1991; Rydmark, 2004). This suggests that when confidence has been established between a potential client and a consultant, the actual content of the service is of less importance. The same can be said about whether or not the consultant represents formal professionalism. It is the consultant as an individual that the client has confidence in, and if s/he says that his or her firm can deliver a particular service, the client may be more prone to trust others from the same firm and assign these people to do the job.

This implies (as argued especially in chapters 8, 9, and 10) that consultants and buyers oftentimes seek to solve the uncertainty of whom to trust through building personal ties and mutual personal confidence. This means that the knowledge required to make choices about who to close deals with is not the same type of knowledge needed to judge what management technique or method would be the best solution for the organization. It is instead a knowledge about- and of how to judge other persons. This suggests that confidence built on knowledge of particular individuals could be an attractive alternative to standards, certifications or authorizations, where generalized professionalism is confirmed by the abstract expert system that the consultant is able to prove that s/he represents. It also suggests that comparisons between different consultancies, consultants and their services are difficult, if what really matters is how well particular individuals cooperate with each other.

Using a standardized formula for price setting, such as VBP, therefore seems to be a great challenge when making deals, since it actually suggests a contradictory logic for the building of confidence – that the price represents the value consultants bring to the organization instead of what costs they incur while delivering their services. However, following the logic in the argumentation above, the value of a delivered service might lie not so much in what is produced and how well it was performed, but in the buyer's perception of how nice it has been to work with the consultant.

Conclusions: Beyond individualism and collectivism

The case of the CF shows that, in management consulting, it is very likely that unwritten, informal business agreements are preferred over written contracts that stipulate extensive regulation of details. Moreover, in cases where written contracts are used, it is not through the signing of the contract that confidence for the consultant is established. Confidence is more likely to be established in the process that precedes the formal signing. However, although this is the form of agreement most often used, it does not necessarily mean that everyone is happy with today's attempted solutions to deal with the uncertainty of whom to trust in business relations.

As can be noted in Chapter 10 and also in the interviews analyzed in this chapter, we hear consultants and buyers speak of a terribly costly and tiresome initial "qualifying" process during which the parties evaluate one another in order to decide whether or not they want to make a deal. Furthermore, this costly initial qualifying process is only a first step, following which comes a continuous process of evaluation and mutual adjustment throughout the project and beyond. Still, the question of what the signing of a VBP contract means for the building of confidence for the consultant remains to be answered.

In Chapter 1, Furusten and Werr argue that confidence between a buyer and a seller of consulting services is established either through individualism, in terms of close interaction where one person learns to know the other over time, or through moves towards collectivism of the service. However, VBP does not represent either of these methods. There does, for instance, not seem to be a belief that confidence can be established when the price is based on professionalism. In such cases, there would be no point for a buyer to pay a higher price, since the expert system the consultant represents would guarantee that the best service there is would be delivered anyway, due to professional ethics. If not, the consultant would risk being defined by the expert system as a "quack", and blacklisted from the group of pure professionals. Also, in the interaction case, the underlying logic is that consultants are expected to deliver the best possible service since they dare not risk their reputation on the market. The idea of VBP, however, is that neither the expert system nor relations put sufficient demands on consultants to do their best and deliver satisfying services. Neither professional ethics, nor personal relations and reputation are perceived as sufficient incentives for consultants to do their best.

This suggests that the only driving force for a consultant is money! If there were more money to earn if they did a good job, this would be the only thing that triggers them to do it! If they deliver good services that lead to good results according to the VBP equation, they will be well rewarded. If not, they will accept a lower fee for the work they deliver. The idea is, however, that they will do everything in their power to convince the client that they are worth the highest possible price.

So, what can we learn about the role of written contracts in general, and about VBP in particular, for confidence building in new-professional fields of expertise? To answer this question we borrow the words of another consultant at CF:

> *VBP cannot be used if you do not have a situation where confidence has already been achieved.*

What this consultant is suggesting, is that VBP is only a pricing formula for setting fair prices. However, it can be questioned if this is its major role. As intimated by the above quote, the VBP equation has little to do with confidence building. Instead, the suggestion is that once confidence is established, the consultant can charge as much as s/he likes, as long as this confidence is not challenged. Here, the identification of variables to measure and their quantification in equations can be seen as a powerful instrument for the consultant to claim that the buyer should pay more.

CHAPTER 13

The Three-Dimensional Construction of Management Advisory Services

STAFFAN FURUSTEN AND ANDREAS WERR

The chapters of this book have provided a number of illustrations of how deals between buyers and suppliers of management advisory services come about. In the introductory chapter, two generic strategies for establishing confidence between buyers and suppliers, and thus reducing uncertainty in the purchasing situation, were reviewed: individualism and collectivism. Individualism implied the reduction of uncertainty by building an individual trust-based relationship. Collectivism implied reliance on institutional structures, guaranteeing professional competence and conduct. As illustrated in the chapters of this book, these two strategies do not preclude each other – rather they come into play simultaneously in the establishment of single deals. In this and the following final chapter, we will take a closer look into such combinations of strategies.

As argued in Chapter 1, the purchasing of MAS involves a number of specific complexities linked to the character of the service and its knowledge base. The two main complexities discussed concerned the need for the service: Is the service really needed? Is it legitimate to purchase it from outside suppliers? And the choice of the supplier: Which supplier will provide most "value for money"? And how can we choose the best supplier? These complexities create considerable uncertainties for both buyers and suppliers to deal with. The buyer must deal with the uncertainty of not really knowing if they need a service and if so, what particular service they need, and why a certain provider should be trusted to deliver it. The seller, on the other hand, must deal with the uncertainty of not really knowing what service they should offer in order to be perceived as necessary and trustworthy. These situations have no simple, clear solutions. Rather, solutions are created locally and temporarily through ongoing negotiation of needs, solutions, expertise and trust.

The chapters of this book indicate that this kind of "uncertain" purchasing situation, to a large extent reliant on local negotiations, is an increasingly common one in modern organizations. However, it is a situation that has until now received limited attention from research. It is a situation that may be characterized as the "non-professional purchasing of non-professional expertise", as neither the observed purchasing procedures nor the kind of expertise purchased meet the standards of traditional professions and modernity. The purchasing procedures applied generally fall short of central values such as rationality, predictability, accountability and progress, and the expertise purchased lacks the institutional legitimation of traditional professions. Still, deals come about and organizations establish purchasing procedures, which they themselves regard as professional and which tend to be rather widely institutionalized in many areas, creating what we in chapters 1 and 2 called "new professionalism".

The existing literature on professional purchasing of management advisory services repeatedly points out that the modern standards for professional purchasing, focusing on rationality, predictability and accountability, do not seem to be used in practice. Thus, it is not surprising that the cases reported in this book show similar patterns – that business actors do not fully trust some business parties because they represent a claimed professional collective. Rather, a buyer wants to get to know and interact with the other party before venturing to do business with them. The purchasing literature, however, often sees this as a problem or dysfunctionality. In its ambition to identify and provide images of best purchasing practice for different situations, rational and objective systems of purchasing are depicted, leaving little room for the kind of practices observed above (cf. Chapter 3). Our ambition in this book has not been to define what is best (or worst) practice in the purchasing of MAS. Rather, we have been intrigued by the (often rather different) practices for purchasing MAS that have become established and thus sought to *understand why the purchasing practice of different types of MAS takes certain forms*. In pursuing this question, we also fill an empirical void, as the purchasing literature has devoted limited attention to the advisory services based on a "new-professional" knowledge base focused on here.

The (limited) current literature to be found, e.g. in the management consulting field, has been either directed at what the situation would look like if things had been different (e.g. if a professional knowledge base had existed), or at criticizing the whole idea of organizations hiring external suppliers of management advisory services. Our purpose in these last two chapters is to move beyond existing approaches to the purchase of MAS as new-professional services and, based on the empirical chapters of the book, seek possible new patterns and combinations of theoretical explanations. In the current chapter, we will explore three dimensions central to the understanding of deals involving MAS and how these dimensions interact in the construction of the need for- and the professional supplier of MAS. In the final chapter, we will then elaborate on the concept of "arenas for expertise construction" in an effort to further deepen our understanding of the dynamics forming the local dealing with MAS.

Three organizing dimensions for the construction of needs and trust

As discussed briefly in Chapter 1 and in more detail in Chapter 2, the traditional organizing processes discussed in the literature, such as professionalization, structuration through market mechanisms, interaction in networks, or exploitation of the vulnerable buyer are, on their own, insufficient vehicles for understanding what is going on in the making of deals concerning MAS. Rather, all these processes may be at work in negotiation of a single MAS assignment.

In order to understand how different organizing processes affect the specification of needs and the establishment of trust for a particular MAS supplier in local business negotiations between two business parties, we believe that it is necessary to recognize and understand mechanisms and activities in three parallel dimensions – the individual, the organizational and the institutional dimension (Figure 13:1). An activity, mechanism or process such as purchasing cannot be understood without relating it to activities, mechanisms and processes that take place in the other, parallel dimensions. This way of viewing organizational activities is emphasized by March (1981a) in his discussion of organizational change. March argues that if we want to understand processes of change, we cannot only focus on matters such as what a particular individual is doing, or what is happening in a particular organization or in the institutional environment. Rather, the different dimensions must be seen as parallel dimensions that together form particular actions taken by particular actors. It can thus be argued that no activity in organizations can be understood fully if it is not related to what is happening in other dimensions in which this activity is also embedded. This means that activities such as leadership, production and purchasing cannot be understood if we isolate our observations, for example, to only what particular actors do when they purchase. Instead, we have to see this particular activity as embedded in two business parties' organizational structures, and the institutional environment(s) in which these structures are embedded.

We will, in the remainder of this chapter, elaborate on the three dimensions that create the context and rules for dealing with confidence. We will deal with the question of how needs for MAS and trust for individual MAS suppliers are established in an interplay between forces related to the three different dimensions.

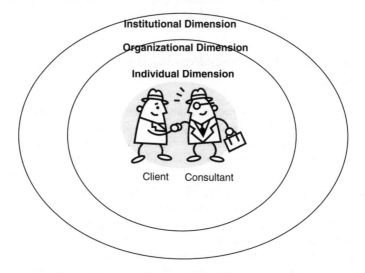

Figure 13:1 Three dimensions of dealing with confidence

Constructing need and trust in the individual dimension

The interpersonal relation between the individual buyer and supplier of MAS is, as illustrated by the different chapters of this book, central to understanding both the need for MAS and the choice of a certain supplier of the service. In several of the chapters, rather than being a result of a need, a trustful relationship was found to be a prerequisite for the emergence of the need. In Chapter 8, for example, it was concluded that deep and sustained interaction between advisor and buyer is a prerequisite for the purchase of additional advisory services from auditors.

This indicates that the need for an external advisor, rather than being external to the relation (as generally assumed in the purchasing literature, where a need is viewed as a trigger to establishing a relationship, (e.g. Axelsson and Wynstra, 2002), may also be the result of such a relation. This is well illustrated by the ongoing "pitching" activities of financial consultants (Chapter 5). Although the services of financial consultants can be viewed as based on a rather well-defined expert knowledge in financial analysis not accessible to the buyer or others in the buying organization, the perceived need for the services offered was to a large extent based on a trustful interpersonal relationship. Long-term, trustful relationships were striven for by the consultants as an important prerequisite for striking a deal. Without this relationship, potential clients would not even bother to listen to their proposals.

The importance of interpersonal trust and interaction for the construction of the need for services and trust for particular suppliers would seem to be a generic characteristic of the individual dimension. This is further illustrated by the high rate of repeat business, e.g. in the management consulting industry, and by the consultants' strong focus on add-on sales (chapters 9, 10 and 11), indicating that once a relationship is established a need for external services enabled by this relation may emerge more easily. This suggests that a close relationship to potential purchasers is important for service suppliers that want to close deals with potential buyers. "Being around" has elsewhere been identified as an important sales strategy for management consultants. Not only does a closer relationship create needs for additional services, but it also channels the needs that arise towards already established relationships (Furusten, 2003).

These observations support arguments in the literature that address the relation between buyers and sellers of management and IT consulting in particular, showing that consultants are active in creating a demand for their services in local action (e.g. Czarniawska-Joerges, 1988; Berglund and Werr, 2000; Bloomfield and Vurdubakis, 1994; Furusten, 2003). This literature often takes a rather critical standpoint towards MAS suppliers and depicts the buyer as a rather helpless victim of the consultants' persuasive efforts. Although clients may be such victims in some cases, the large variations in the use of advisors illustrated in this book give reason to establish a more nuanced picture of the consultant buyer and his ability to resist the sales rhetorics of advisors. The client's observed reliance on trustful relationships in purchasing MAS need not be a sign of client weakness. Given the characteristics of most advisory services, and especially the problem of clearly defining them (we will come back to this later) the observed strategy may be the best available (cf. Clark, 1995). The claim, that a reliance on relationships automatically creates a vulnerable client may thus be challenged. A focus on a trustful relationship did not stop buyers from being rather sceptical towards consultants and demanding of the results delivered (Chapter 9). The focus on the interpersonal relationship also poses problems for consulting organizations, when clients demand individual consultants. We saw this in Chapter 10, where public buyers of management consulting services wanted to make deals with certain consultants and therefore tried to handle the law on public procurement in such a way so that, in the end, they could choose the consultants they had decided to hire from the outset. In this case, the law was just a long side track to rationalize the choice already made, causing numerous other consultants trying to compete for the contract a lot of extra work. The buyers knew from the outset that they would get a good service from a particular consultant they trusted, putting the consultants who wanted to compete for that contract in a vulnerable position.

That interpersonal trust and confidence between manager and advisor were identified as the preferred mechanisms for judging the professionalism of certain advisors by those consuming their services is evident from observations in most of the chapters of this book. In Chapter 9 for example, the criteria top managers used to choose from different management consultants were analyzed. The study compared the importance of criteria related to the product offered, such as the quality of the presentation of a bid, the price, the quality of the bid, the applied methodologies, etc, with more personal and trust-based characteristics of the single consultant, such as his/her competence, experience, reputation, etc. This comparison indicated a strong dominance of the trust-based aspects when it came to selecting management consultants. The single most important selection criterion was the consultant's competence, or at least how the buyers perceived this. What this competence consisted of was rather broadly defined, with subject matter knowledge being but one dimension. At least as important was the consultant's social competence and ability to fit with the client and into the client organization. Consequently, having the opportunity to judge potential consultants' competence in the form of a personal judgment gained through interaction was a central desire of the buyers studied in Chapter 10. The focus on the individual dimension in establishing trust for a certain supplier also held true for services based on traditional professions, such as auditing services (Chapter 8) and law services (Chapter 4).

The above indicates that the preferred mode of operation of MAS buyers is to turn to suppliers with whom they (or trusted members of the buyer's network, which we will come to in the next section) have had good experiences. Once trust has been established, the ties between advisor and buyer become rather strong. As illustrated in Chapter 10, buyers invested considerable energy- and even broke the law to circumvent formal rules and regulations (in this case, the law on public procurement), in order to hire their preferred and trusted management consultants. This heavy focus on interpersonal confidence in the establishment of trust for the supplier and in ensuring professional conduct throughout the interaction, indicates a scepticism of the formal contract as a way of establishing and regulating deals concerning MAS. This is clearly illustrated in Chapter 12, where the shortcomings of the formal contract in regulating the consultant-client relationship are illustrated and discussed. Here, the formal contract is viewed more as a result of a trustful relationship than an antecedent to- or substitute for it. The above reasoning is summarized in Figure 13:2.

Figure 13:2 Constructing needs and trust in the interpersonal dimension through interpersonal trust

Constructing needs and trust in the organizational dimension

Although we view the final closing of a deal as the outcome of negotiations between two physical actors, when they sign a contract (or in other ways agree on a service to be delivered), these negotiations do not take place in a vacuum. The closing of a particular deal is embedded in the organizational structures of both the selling and the buying organization. The kind of needs that can be constructed in the individual dimension are limited by organizational processes that define the division of work between internal and external resources, and organizational norms concerning the acceptability of- and need for external advisors. Similarly, the establishment of trust is embedded in an organizational context, with networks of individuals as well as organizational reputation playing an important role (cf. chapters 9, 10 and 11). However, as indicated in several chapters, there is in practice a tension between the buyer's preference for interpersonal trust as a way of choosing supplier, and organizational efforts to replace such personal ties with organizational procedures.

Different organizations use MAS in rather different ways. Some organizations buy large amounts of advisory services from external suppliers, while others prefer to produce these services internally, or perceive no need for them at all. Such differences are shown in the case of interactive media services (Chapter 7), additional advice from auditors (Chapter 8) and management consultants (Chapter 6). These variations are systemic in nature, which makes them difficult to explain by differences in the individual dimension. Instead we suggest the organizational dimension as an important mediator of the use of MAS. One mediating factor identified in several of the studies reported in this book is the organization's perception of its own level of knowledge in different areas as well as its judgment as to whether a certain kind of knowledge constitutes core knowledge or is of peripheral importance to the business.

In Chapter 6, Werr argues that a self-identified lack of "self-confidence" in the organization led to a large acceptance for the use of management consultants. As there was a general feeling in the organization that the internal level of knowledge on management issues was far from the available level of knowledge, the use of management consultants as "experts" was widely accepted and applied among managers. A need was rather easily constructed in the individual dimension, as the organizational norms presupposed the superior knowledge of external experts. This organization's approach was compared to a second organization that valued its internal competence considerably higher. In this second organization, the use of external advisors was less accepted, managers' extensive use of external advisors was frowned upon and viewed as an indicator of "managerial incompetence", and the money spent on external advisors was considerably more limited. A similar pattern could be observed in relation to the purchase of advisory services from auditors in Chapter 8, which also showed large differences between different organizations. Among the common denominators of those organizations that were large consumers of additional advisory services was their use of these services to gain "legitimacy and security", indicating a weak confidence in and acceptance for the internal expertise.

Besides the organization's confidence in its internal expertise, the judgment of the centrality of this expertise in terms of being core or non-core, was identified as an additional mediator of the perceived need for external advisors. In the case of interactive media solutions (Chapter 7), the organization's perception of this expertise as being outside its core competencies was an important driver towards the use of external advisors.

Related to the organization's confidence in its internal expertise as a mediator of the use of external advisors was the organization's way of making decisions and the related political processes. In the study of two organizations' differing uses of management consultants (Chapter 6), it could be observed that management consultants had strong political roles in decision-making processes, such as legitimating certain stakeholders' views, or establishing "neutral" grounds for decision-making in a highly political context. It is thus suggested that management consultants may be seen as a parallel management structure. As such, the need for MAS must be understood in relation to structures and processes of the local management system. In this context, a richer image of the need for MAS emerges, focusing not only on the role of advisors as objective experts but also on their involvement in political power play, uncertainty reduction, and legitimation. Different ways of making and implementing decisions thus create rather different needs and levels of acceptance for MAS.

Needs for external advisors were however not only mediated by the organization's judgment of its own competence or the internal decision-making structures, but also by the possibilities available in established networks of relations. As illustrated by the use of advisory services from auditors in Chapter 8, a successfully established auditing relationship was a strong driver for the purchase of additional services from this provider. An organization's network can thus be a trigger for the use of advisory services by pointing at new kinds of services to be purchased, by making the services more accessible (through already existing networks), or even by more or less explicitly demanding their use as a way of expressing a development towards becoming a modern, flexible and efficient organization. The expansion of large MAS providers' service lines (e.g. Accenture, IBM) in recent years may be seen as an illustration of efforts made from suppliers to capitalize on their existing relationships.

Having dealt with the construction of needs for MAS in the organizational dimension, we will now turn to the construction of trust in a certain supplier in this dimension. The studies in this book indicate strong organizational pressures towards a replacement of forces in the individual dimension by mechanisms in an organizational dimension.

The establishment of the "professional" supplier of advisory services and the establishment of the "professional buyer" of these services has gained increasing attention among policy makers in both private and public organizations. The rather informal and trust-based way of choosing "professional" advisors described in the previous section has been regarded as unsatisfactory in ensuring a "good" use of advisory services. Instead, more "rational" procedures have been sought. In Chapter 10, the public procurement act is described and discussed as the archetypical illustration of an impersonal way of establishing professional suppliers. The main aims behind the act, as formulated in the EU directives, is to ensure competitive, non-discriminatory markets in which public money is rationally allocated and the best product/service chosen. In realizing these aims, an open, competitive, impersonal procurement process is prescribed, in which a manager's/organization's needs are to be publicly announced, and competing tenders received and objectively evaluated in relation to predefined criteria. Interaction between individual managers and consultants during the process is strongly restricted. The existence or building of interpersonal relations is in this context regarded as problematic, creating a risk for favoritism. Instead, organizational relations are to replace the individual, trust-based relations through mechanisms such as framework contracts (see also Chapter 11).

MAS supplier organizations also struggle with their dependence on individual advisors and their networks, and therefore often strive to substitute these by organizational mechanisms. Examples of such mechanisms include the promotion of specific products or services and strong brands that provide representatives of these brands with a strong reputation. Glückler and Armbrüster (2003) argue that besides the important relationship-based trust established in the individual dimension, uncertainty in purchasing management consulting services may be reduced by public and networked reputation, which plays out largely in the organizational dimension. Both of these mechanisms rely on organizational- rather than individual characteristics and networks in establishing who is a trustworthy supplier of a certain service.

While these mechanisms highlighted the management of uncertainty concerning the value of the service and the quality of its supplier by reliance on different substitute indicators – such as previous interaction (in the individual dimension) or reputation (in the organizational dimension), some suppliers advocate a rather different strategy aimed at reducing the uncertainty in dealing with MAS by introducing mechanisms of risk sharing (see Chapter 12). By introducing a pricing mechanism that makes the cost of consulting dependent on the value created, it was claimed by consultants that the client's and the consultant's interests could be aligned, thus reducing uncertainty and risk in selecting consultants. Only "professional" consultants would be willing to offer these kinds of services, as they would not be paid if they were not professional enough to deliver what they had promised – as the argument put forward by the consultants went.

While convincing in its rhetoric, the study on value-based pricing (VBP) reported in Chapter 12 shows that the above arguments were not as well received by clients. VBP – at least in the case studied – did not work as a substitute to close and trust-based relationships. Instead, establishing VBP contracts *per se* contained so much uncertainty, that a trustful relationship was found to be a prerequisite for agreeing on VBP agreements, thus partly reducing their attractiveness.

To summarize, both the need for management advisory services and the trust for a specific supplier of these services needs to be understood in its organizational context. In this dimension a number of aspects and mechanisms were identified: including an organization's network relations, self-confidence, decision-making culture, reputation, and formal purchasing procedures (see Figure 13:3).

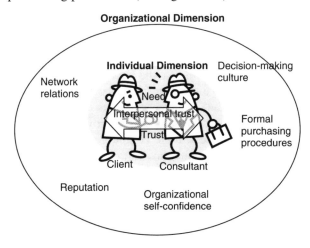

Figure 13:3 Aspects mediating the construction of need and trust in the organizational dimension

Constructing need and trust in the institutional dimension

When managers face specific situations, they are likely to refer to patterns in the institutional dimension in order to come to grips with the kind of situation they are in and what they, as managers, are supposed to do in such situations (cf. March, 1981b; Sevón, 1996).

The institutional dimension is permeated by images of what a modern organization looks like, how it is supposed to act, and how managers are supposed to manage it. Such ideas may be argued to be formative for the problems and the possible remedies for these problems perceived by managers (see e.g. Huczynski, 1993). Organizations that, according to managers' interpretations, deviate from these institutionalized images automatically have problems, and the institutional dimension provides them with solutions as to how they can make changes in order to meet the institutionalized standards (Brunsson and Olsen, 1998). Thus, if managers in local organizations feel that they deviate from a standard, they are likely to feel that they have problems, and that they thereby have a need for a solution to fix it – a solution that often involves management advisory services. Another way of expressing the relation between managers in local organizations and ideas and trends in the institutional dimension is to say that the supply of MAS, through its close relation to the (re)production of management standards, contributes not only to the solving of management problems but also to the construction of these problems and thereby the need for services that deal with these problems (see e.g. Czarniawska-Joerges, 1988).

The general argument about the need for MAS being anchored in general institutional structures is illustrated by several of the empirical examples in this volume. One is the increasing importance many organizations experience today for advisory services in corporate finance. As described in Chapter 5, it is common today that organizations feel an unquestionable need for advisors that can provide them with such services. New, more complex models provided in the institutional dimension for capital acquisition, the increasing focus on shareholder value in society, and models of value creation through mergers and acquisitions, have together created an increasingly sophisticated financial industry that represents a prospering field of management advisory services. To not hire experts from well-known investment analysts is more or less out of question today for large organizations, for example, when they are about to engage in mergers and acquisition activities or when looking for new capital. Thus, the appropriate way to handle issues such as presenting economic value to the capital market is to hire an independent expert who can be expected to analyze the situation according to the latest and most sophisticated models and do this in an objective, unbiased way. While the use of experts such as traditional management consultants has increasingly become the object of scrutiny (see e.g. chapters 10 and 11), the use of financial advice has remained largely unquestioned and exempt from efforts to "professionalize" its purchase in most organizations. The services provided by the financial advisors included both aspects of specific financial competence, but also of symbolic assets ingrained in the image and brands of the large (and very expensive) financial advisors. Given the perceived complexities in judging something like a specific investment opportunity, the reputation of the advisor behind the deal becomes a proxy of the quality of the opportunity, thus creating an important role for the advisor that goes beyond providing mere expert knowledge in a new area.

This indicates that the emergence of new fields of knowledge, as in the case of finance services or the expertization of "older" fields of knowledge such as management consulting, is an important driver of the need for MAS. In addition to this, the need for MAS is also influenced by general institutional ideas concerning the division of work between organizations. As argued in Chapter 7, dealing with the purchasing of interactive media solutions, the perception that this expertise was outside the purchasing organization's "core competencies" was the single most important reason for turning to outside expertise on interactive media solutions rather than developing this expertise internally. While this was discussed as an organizational factor in the previous section, such choices are not made independently of what is regarded "good management practice". These observations support the argument from Chapter 1 that current trends towards specialization, expertization, globalization, etc, associated with modernity provide a strong force in creating a need for external services (see also Badaracco, 1991; Ackroyd and Lawrenson, 1996)

While the emergence of new areas of expertise, the elaboration of existing areas of expertise, or the reevaluation of the legitimate domain of a single organization's activities are important forces in creating a need for MAS, our studies have also shown that organizations have considerable discretion in relating to these forces. Their needs are not mechanically (at least not explicitly) related to popular management concepts (Chapter 9), and efforts to "professionalize" the purchasing of MAS not explicitly- and directly linked to a desire to comply with norms of expertization and marketization. The organizations studied in the different chapters react rather differently to challenges such as the emerging market for "interactive media solutions" (Chapter 7), where some organizations turned to outside suppliers, some developed internal competence, and many turned to mixed solutions where services were provided partly by in-house expertise, and partly by external parties. Individual managers in organizations thus made (implicit or explicit) choices concerning how to react to institutional pressures, choices that were open for negotiation and rethinking, implying constant renegotiation of the need for external services. These responses may eventually reflect back on the triggers, making their influence transitory. In the domain of management consulting, for example, as many organizations become more sceptical of the models and concepts delivered by consultants, buying organizations hired people with a background in consulting and thereby accumulated the specific expertise of management consultants. This may be one of the reasons for the decline of the consulting market in the early years of this millennium, and the increasing price and other pressures on management consultants (see e.g. Schmidt and Vogt, 2004).

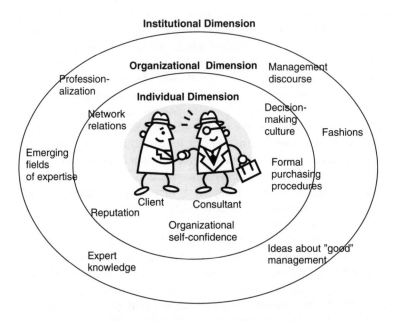

Figure 13:4 The institutional embeddedness of need and trust for Management Advisory services

The creation of trust in the institutional dimension is to a large extent related to the creation of the need for MAS in this dimension. As argued, the character of the knowledge base of a specific kind of MAS is to a large extent established in the institutional dimension. It is in this dimension that the specificity and expert nature of financial services is created, and the legitimacy of management knowledge as reflected in management consultants' concepts and models is currently losing its expert nature. Depending on the kind of knowledge base a MAS has and how this is established in the institutional dimension, the building of trust for a certain service provider may take different forms. With a firm knowledge base, like the one for auditing services which is actually protected by law, trust may be built more on professionalism, whereas in services, the knowledge base of which is less firmly established, as in the case of management consulting, individualist mechanisms, including the reliance on network relations, tend to become a more important way of building trust.

Consequently, forces in the institutional dimension such as the ones identified above (see Figure 13:4) trigger actions in organizations – actions that may or may not involve the hiring of MAS. These forces in the institutional dimension thus contribute to the construction of needs and trust for MAS, although these constructions can take different paths in different situations.

Three-dimensional constructions of need and trust for MAS

Our ambition in this first of the two final chapters has been to draw together some of the lessons learned in regard to the construction of need and trust in the purchase of MAS. Based on the studies reported throughout the book, three parallel dimensions that provide the context for the local construction of MAS were identified – the local, the organizational and the institutional (see Figure 13:4). In the local dimension, a trustful relationship was found to be important. In the organizational dimension, organizational self-confidence, specific decision-making structures, network relations, reputation and formal purchasing procedures were identified as important variables. And in a globalized institutional dimension, the emergence of new fields of "expertise" the professionalization of existing fields, as well as changes in overall management ideas, fashions and discourses were noted. This illustrates the simultaneous presence of both individual mechanisms (interpersonal trust in the local dimension) and more collective structures (institutionalized expertise) in dealing with the uncertainties concerning MAS. While the above is not intended as a complete list, of neither contextual dimensions nor contextual variables, we hope it will provide a first tentative step into the development of a more contextual understanding in need of further refinement of the use of MAS.

With this focus on the local construction of MAS and the context in which this construction takes place, we aim to add a dimension to the currently dominant understanding of the purchase of business services (e.g. Chapter 3). Current approaches to the purchase of business services have addressed service, buyer and market characteristics in trying to explain both the extent and process of purchase. While we do not deny the importance of these aspects, we have argued above that these characteristics are difficult to define *ex ante*. Neither the service, the buyer, nor the market can exist independently of each other or the context in which they are embedded. Rather than being an input to the purchasing situation, explaining the purchase or non-purchase of a certain service, or the establishment of trust for a specific supplier, we suggest the characteristics of the service, the market and the buyer to be local outcomes of negotiations between buyers and suppliers in the embedded purchasing process. In the following, last chapter of this book we will look more closely at these negotiations and their outcomes.

CHAPTER 14

Arena Mechanisms

STAFFAN FURUSTEN AND ANDREAS WERR

In the previous chapter, we argued that deals between buyers and sellers of management advisory services could be explained as outcomes of three-dimensional constructions of needs for particular services and trust for particular service suppliers. Thus, pressures in the three parallel dimensions – the institutional-, organizational- and local dimension – construct particular characteristics of the service, the market and the buyer. Put another way, the understanding of why a particular deal is made in a certain way with a certain content cannot be isolated to negotiations between two business parties. Instead, this has to be understood as outcomes of interacting mechanisms in the noted dimensions. The aim of this final chapter is to specify what these mechanisms consist of and to say something of what we can learn from this book about how MAS provided by external suppliers are brought into organizations.

In Chapter 1, we briefly argued that deals concerning the delivery of management advisory services are closed on what we call "arenas for expertise construction". We will now elaborate on the mechanisms that constitute the arenas and regulate the activities there.

We see arenas as a kind of space where needs for MAS and trust for MAS suppliers are constructed, through which deals between buyers and sellers are closed. We will argue that the activities on these arenas are regulated by pressures and mechanisms that force buyers into a customer, a client or a victim role. The question this chapter seeks to answer is how the arena concept and the games played there are related to more traditional understandings of how organizations satisfy their need of various MAS, e.g. through internal hierarchies or markets.

First, we discuss the meaning of the arena concept as used here. This is followed by a discussion of games we claim are played in the arena and the mechanisms that regulate them. Finally, we discuss how the arguments pursued in this chapter affect our understandings of markets where organizations that deal with MAS provided by external "new-professional" experts are in focus.

An arena for need and trust construction

The concept "arena" has been chosen here to capture a non-physical space between organizations where we suggest that buyers and suppliers of MAS meet to establish confidence for services buyers perceive they are in need of, and for suppliers that they want to close deals with. This can to some extent be understood as us primarily focusing on the backstage activities that take place before the actors go on stage and close deals, that is, what happens before they go on stage and perform service delivery and economic transactions. Our argument is that, when it comes to MAS, it is not as simple as some organizations having needs and others services, and these organizations meeting in markets to make business agreements. That exchanges between buyers and sellers are not as straightforward and anonymous as claimed in theoretical depictions of the market (e.g. Williamsson, 1975), has been well established in the network approach to markets that studies the internationalization of firms (e.g. Johanson, 1994) and industrial marketing (e.g. Håkansson, 1982). These studies show that organizations live in long-term relations and adapt logistics, production, development, maintenance, etc, to each other over time. Cooperation, it is argued, is not something that comes automatically. It takes years of negotiations, social accomplishments, habits and agreements for this cooperation to evolve. Representatives of the network approach claim that all of these things take place on markets. The studies reported in this book strengthen the observation that these activities do in fact take place. It becomes clear from the discussions in the previous chapter that organizations cannot just be snapped together or hooked on like a trailer hitch. Organizations need to adjust to each other in order to construct interfaces where needs for MAS and trust for suppliers evolve. We do suggest, however, that these processes do not take place on the market. In markets, deals are closed and transactions made. Our argument is that, by the time a deal can be closed, the processes of organizations adjusting to one another have already taken place. We suggest that these processes play out in arenas for trust and need construction.

To some extent, the arena can be understood as the sum of all mutual adjustments and negotiations that take place as networks evolve, but we also suggest that all of this is embedded in the institutional dimension. The arena is not as broad and generic as an organizational field, however, which DiMaggio and Powell (1991, p. 64-65) define as "organizations that, in the aggregate constitute a recognized area of institutional life: key suppliers, resource and product consumers, regulatory agencies, and other organizations which produce similar services or products." Organizational fields emerge through processes of interaction among organizations, interorganizational structures of domination and patterns of coalition, the information load with which organizations in a field must contend, and a mutual awareness of the participants in a set of organizations. "Organizational fields" is a very broad concept that draws attention to general conditions for actors that do not necessarily interact with each other, although together they can be said to be parts of a common enterprise. As pointed out by many, Powell and DiMaggio (1991) included, one weakness of taking this macro perspective is that we miss mechanisms in organizations and in local interaction between individuals.

Using the "arena" concept proposed here, mechanisms from both the network and the organizational field approaches will be brought together. The arena concept should be seen as a narrower concept than "organizational field", and a wider concept than "network". We are talking in part about a physical network consisting of business- and social relations between individuals and organizations, and in part of more or less specified rules and norms that exist somewhere in between selling- and buying organizations. Thus, the arenas we are talking about do not exist as places that can be visited. They are to be viewed more as socially constructed virtual spaces with no specific location.

Rules on arenas for need and trust construction

In the previous chapter, we discussed the three-dimensional construction of need for MAS and trust for MAS suppliers. Mechanisms in these dimensions combine to drive buyers to have certain needs, suppliers to offer certain services, and buyers to put their trust in certain suppliers. We will argue below that these mechanisms can be reduced to the rules of three generic games played in the arena. These rules are not textualized and it is rare that they are made explicit. Still, they drive actors, that in one way or another can be seen as involved in a game, to act in certain ways in their relations to MAS suppliers (if they are a buyer) or to MAS buyers (if they are a supplier). Thus, the actors engaged in a process to close a deal are likely to feel pressure to follow the rules of the game they believe they are part of.

Three ideal-type games - customerization, clientization and victimization

The observations in this book imply that locally perceived needs for particular MAS and trust for particular suppliers of MAS are constantly (re)negotiated in arenas for need and trust construction. We suggest that one important aspect of these negotiations is the establishment of the power relation between the buyer and the supplier. Who is in control of the assignment? Whose interpretation of need and expertise wields the largest influence? While both parties strive to maximize their own influence, both are also interested in maintaining a trustful relationship as a basis for future work together, thus counteracting explicit confrontations.

When this has been discussed in the literature on management advisory services particularly in management consulting, a rather ambivalent image of buyer-seller power relations evolves. Images of the buyer range from that of the customer in complete control of the relationship (McGonagle and Vella, 2001) to that of the victim in the hands of the manipulative management consultant (Kieser, 1998). The literature is quite categorical here, arguing that the buyer is positioned in either one role or the other. In this book, however, it has been pointed out that, in practice, systematic attempts are made to specifically make the buyer act in the role of "customer" (e.g. Chapter 10 and 11). Elaborating on the arena metaphor, this means that the images of the buyer propagated in the literature can be seen as games that both buyers and sellers try to play.

In the following, we discuss the characteristics (rules) of three ideal-type games in the arena, based on our reading of the literature on MAS, and on management consulting in particular: *customerization*, *clientization* and *victimization*. In each game, the buyer of MAS takes a different position in relation to the seller (*customer, client, victim*).

Customerization

In its ideal form, the customerization game builds on marketized professionalism. It is a materialization of the modern assumptions of specialization, expertization and the division of work. The professional system is believed to be accountable for the performance of the professionals, and the professionals are expected to meet the prerequisites for being included in the profession. The conditions for this game are, thus, that the rules for professionalism are clear, and that the interfaces between the buyer and the supplier of MAS are also clear. The supplier has something that the buyer lacks. In its ideal form, this "something" is well-defined expert knowledge. All authorized representatives of the professional system are guaranteed, to have this expertise. The buyer is thus empowered as a customer to pick anyone who is authorized by the profession, enabling comparisons, price negotiations, etc. The supplier, on the other hand, has the power of his legitimate expert knowledge. The professional system, with its professional norms, ensures that the risk of exploitation by the expert is limited.

Clientization

In the clientization game, the interface between a buyer and a seller of MAS is much less clearly defined than in the customerization game. The suppliers in this game represent new-professional systems, which implies that there is no single actor who guarantees the quality of the services delivered by professionals. Instead, suppliers must employ different ways of claiming that they represent something more than themselves, that they represent a profession. In this vein, suppliers may organize themselves in alliances, partnerships or international groups in which only a limited number of actors are members (Furusten, 2003). This lack of a well-defined professional system means that more effort from both supplier and buyer must go into negotiation of why the buyer is in need of a particular service and why a particular supplier should be trusted to deliver that service. Important input to these negotiations includes the suppliers' efforts to establish themselves as professionals by showing membership in an international group or a national association of a specific type of service providers, by being licensed to work with certain methods, or having a certificate that implies coherence to certain standards. A main condition for the clientization game is that buyers be perceived as having a problem that they need help with. However, exactly what they need help with, what service they need, and what service provider they should trust, is negotiable and, is essence, what the clientization game is all about.

Victimization

In the victimization game, the MAS buyer takes the position of a victim of the seller's persuasive powers. A central prerequisite for the victimization game is a very weak professional structure, making the establishment of needs and trust mainly an interpersonal accomplishment. Suppliers can inform buyers of their earlier assignments, the backgrounds of employees in their firm, their connections to academia, etc, but it is hard for potential buyers to verify this information and to assess what relevance it may have for the success and quality of the service. The only way for a buyer to judge such information is to consider recommendations from friends, listen to rumors in the business, and to get to know the service provider in person. These conditions very much place the power in the business relation with the seller, since the buyer has little opportunity to control the quality of the service or compare services offered by different service providers. In this game, the need for the service is to a large extent viewed as having been created by the supplier. Service providers may approach anguished managers with offerings such as new management concepts that point out new problems to be solved by the service provider.

The games in practice

Although the three games referred to here can be seen as ideals that buyers and sellers try to live up to (especially the good ones, customerization and clientization), this does not necessarily mean that they adhere to the rules of one game or the other. In fact, as described in the chapters of this book, the ways in which deals concerning MAS emerge can vary considerably, representing variants and combinations of the ideal-type games described above. In some cases, e.g. the purchase of auditing services, a game similar to the customerization game was played, with buyers comparing different offers, negotiating prices, etc. (Chapter 8). In other cases, e.g. the purchase of management consultants described in Chapter 6 a victimization-like game was played, with advisors in control and buyers feeling that they were victims in the hands of their advisors. Depending on the conditions of the situation, along the individual, organizational and institutional dimensions outlined in the previous chapter, different combinations of the above ideal-type games were triggered.

In the case of *financial services* (Chapter 5), extensive local negotiations, including clientization of the deal, were necessary in order to define the character of the service. Thus, deals were to a large extent made on the basis of trust-based relations. Still, when the roles of the buyer and the supplier were constructed, it seemed to leave the supplier in a rather strong position, with the client in a more dependent role, as if the deal was closed according to the victimization game. For instance, no examples were found of buyers exploiting their "buying power" in order to negotiate the (often very high) prices of financial advisors. This mix of ideal-type games was to a large extent triggered by the generally accepted, unique knowledge base of the supplier, containing complicated scientific methods and tools of financial analysis as well as unique experience in applying these tools. The high stakes involved in the service area were also important in this context. The perceived high stakes and the buyers' limited knowledge of the subject matter made them potential victims of the advisors' persuasive powers. Although clients often turned down the pitches of their advisors, as if they had the position as a customer, in those cases when a deal was accepted, the advisors had an unquestioned role in their realization. The game played in purchasing financial services could thus be described primarily in terms of a combination of clientization/ victimization, but with some elements of the customerization game.

In the case of *management consulting* services, the variations of games played was larger than in the case of financial services. In Chapter 5, for example, it was illustrated that managers in different companies seemed to have very different images of the kind of game they were playing with their suppliers. In one organization, managers took more of a customer role, playing a customerization game, while managers in the other organization perceived themselves more as victims of their management consultants, playing a victimization game.

Compared to other MAS, the tension between the different ways of establishing professional suppliers – individual/trust-based vs. collectivism/ professionalization – is most pronounced in management consulting services. Building on observations made in Chapter 10, it can be argued that there is considerable pressure in the institutional dimension, in the form of legislation, driving the players towards the customerization game. Similar pressures were observed in the organizational dimension, with purchasing departments striving for stronger positions and more formalized purchasing processes (chapters 3 and 11).

This pressure towards the customerization game can be contrasted to the observation that buying managers themselves seem to prefer to play the clientization game, as they experience the rules for the customerization game as rather ambiguous and hard to follow. For example, they perceived difficulties in defining their need for services in detail beforehand. The esoteric knowledge base of management consultants was observed to be a driver of this preference. This not only made the supplier part of need definition, but often gave him/her the upper hand in defining and solving the buyer's problems. This, in combination with the buyers' often perceived inferior knowledge, was what even drove some buyers into a victimization game.

Also in the case of *additional accounting services* (Chapter 8), the combining of game elements in specific deal construction processes is obvious. This is more surprising here than in management consulting and financial services, since auditing is often considered a traditional profession (cf. Ackroyd, 1996). Due to the clear structures for professionalism in auditing, it could be expected that deals would follow the customerization game. This seems to be true in the case of the statutory audit, where structured purchasing processes are carried out to compare different suppliers, and price competition in the industry is tough, indicating that buyers exploit their power as customer. A strong contributing factor to this method of dealing with auditing services was that they were well-defined (the content of the statutory audit is defined by law) and based on a protected knowledge base. In Chapter 8, however, it was also observed that as soon as additional services were bought the game played shifted from customerization towards clientization. The roles of the buyer and the seller were no longer as clear-cut as they were in deals concerning statutory auditing. The service also became less well-defined and understood, and the interactive character of value creation increased, thus moving the buyer further away from the customerization game in the direction of the clientization and victimization game (cf. Grey, 1998).

Also in the case of *interactive media services* (Chapter 7), the games played in the arenas for need and trust construction varied considerably. Although these services can be argued to be more tangible than the other MAS due to their clear technical construction, trust-based deal making, indicating a clientization game, dominated. Moreover, buyers also felt rather dependent on the suppliers, especially those buyers that produced part of the services themselves and used external suppliers as sub-contractors. This indicates that "co-production" as a characteristic of the service production steers the outcome of role negotiations towards a trust-based/interactive relationship and thus the clientization or even victimization game.

This discussion on the games played in the establishment of deals for different MAS indicates that deals are constructed according to the rules of several different ideal-type games (see Figure 14:1). Buying financial consulting was primarily a clientization game, and buying auditing services a customerization game. The purchase of additional advisory service and management consulting spanned all of the games, while buying interactive media involved a mixture of customerization and clientization. The arrows in the table suggest the direction of the different games, meaning that there are no specific end-points.

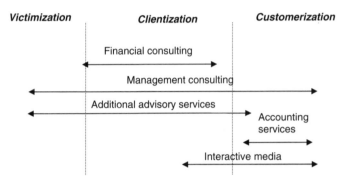

Figure 14:1 The range of games played in dealing with different services

None of the ideal-type games of customerization, clientization and victimization thus really captures how deals involving MAS come about. Rather than following the rules of one of the games, the nature of dealing with MAS seems to be this flexible mixing of different game elements for the sole purpose of gaining confidence. This indicates the existence of a fourth game, relating to the flexible application of the other games, which seems to be what most actors play in the arena in practice. We will call this the "confidence game". In practice, it seems as though the most important aspect in a business relation between a buyer and a seller of any kind of MAS is the establishment of confidence. Once confidence is established, irrespective of the game played to establish it, it is very likely that a deal will be closed. The confidence game, however, is different from the ideal type games as it lacks well-defined rules. Rather, the rules of this game consist of local combinations of the other games that make sense in local situations.

The confidence game, individualism and collectivism

One clear pattern in the book is that strong pressures in the institutional dimension of arenas for need and trust construction drive the players towards the customerization game as the one preferred in theory. In practice, however, we have above argued that the confidence game seems to be preferred. The rules of this game are not as well-defined as the ideal-type games, and likely to vary between situations. This means that the purchasing situation is uncertain, that it is hard to predict the rules by which the improvisations in the confidence game will be played. Still, the confidence game seems to be effective in bringing about deals. In an ambition to specify the mechanisms at work in the arena for need and trust construction, this paragraph relates the confidence game to the two basic mechanisms for creating trust between buyers and suppliers – individualism and collectivism – discussed in Chapter 1. These different mechanisms are relied upon to different degrees in the different games, with the confidence game making the most of both mechanisms.

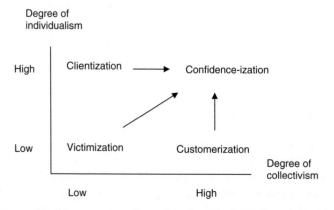

Figure 14:2 Four ideal type games versus individualism and collectivism

The customerization game relies mainly on the mechanism of collectivism. The service in question must to be standardized enough and dictated by institutionalized norms so that buyers can compare offers from different suppliers. Customerized services should thereby score low in individualism since no personal trust should be required. The clientization game, on the other hand, shows the opposite. Here, individualism is an important aspect since buyers often need to be reassured and need help to define what their needs really are. Trust for the individual supplier is crucial, while the legitimacy of the supplier in a collective of professionals is of less importance. Victimization is the worst game from a buyer's perspective since there are few collective structures to rely on and the seller has the upper hand in the individual dimension as well, meaning that the buyer has little possibility to control the construction of needs and trust. And finally, the confidence game can be described as the ideal, potentially relying on both individual trust in local business relations and collectivism, perhaps in the form of a strong professional association that authorizes its members.

Thus, in practice, the ideal situation would be "confidence-ization", where there are both collective structures that ensure competence and space in the arena for the development of individual trust between local buyers and sellers. This game is fair to describe as an improvised game, with the rules from the ideal-type games as points of departure. As the famous jazz bassist Charlie Mingus put it: "You can't improvise on nothin', there has to be somethin'" (Barret and Peplowski, 1998). Thus, the rules of the confidence game are local combinations of the rules of the customerization, clientization and victimization games. The rules of these games thereby become the *somethin'* that improvisations in the confidence game are based upon. What this game is all about is establishing confidence between a seller and a buyer. In doing this, combinations of individualism and collectivism are common practice.

The lack of well-defined rules for the "confidence-ization" game does not mean, however, that the combining of the ideal type games, the improvisations, is arbitrary. The above discussions of the games played when dealing with financial consulting, management consulting, accounting services and interactive media services, reveal a number of forces in the different dimensions of the arena that pressure actors into getting involved in different versions of the confidence game. Our conclusion is that there are four types of pressure on the arena that are especially important in this regard: (1) the nature of the knowledge base of the services offered, (2) the buyer's understanding of the service area, (3) the nature of the service, and (4) the professionalization pressures on purchasing.

The nature of management advisors' *knowledge base* has in this book repeatedly been argued to be an important explanation to the kind of purchasing behavior observed when dealing with MAS. In particular, the elusive, often esoteric knowledge of many management advisors, lacking the backing of formal professional systems, has been pointed out as a pressure towards the clientization or even victimization game observed in areas such as management consulting. In the cases where there existed a more well-defined and legitimized knowledge, such as the statutory audit, we observed more customization games.

A second factor seen as influential in determining the mix of games observed in arenas when closing specific deals was the *nature of the service*. The more well-defined the service was, the more it was apt to be dealt with in a customerization game. Services like the statutory audit, the content of which were well-defined and even supported by laws, could involve significant portions of the customerization game. Less well-defined services, like some instances of management consulting services, on the other hand, needed the interaction involved in the clientization or even victimization games to acquire their shape. Our discussion above also indicates that the stakes involved in delivering a service were of importance. Large stakes, such as in the case of financial advice, created significant uncertainty among buyers pushing relations towards clientization, A third aspect of the service observed as important was the level of co-production involved. A high level of co-production, such as in some cases of interactive media services and management consulting, seemed to drive the relation away from customerization towards clientization.

The third factor influencing the mix of games in the confidence game was *the buyer's knowledge* of the specific service area. The greater this knowledge, and the more elaborate the buyer's understanding of the service to be bought, the more the confidence game involved the rules of the customerization game. Knowledgeable buyers had the ability to define clear services, to judge alternative suppliers, and to evaluate the results of the service. If the buyers lacked this knowledge, strong pressures pushed deals in the direction of the victimization game as illustrated in Chapter 6.

Finally, the efforts towards the *professionalization of purchasing* represented another driver, acting mainly in the direction of the customerization game. Although it has been argued that many MAS buyers will never be able to fully specify their needs, efforts towards more professional purchasing push them in the direction of becoming more explicit in construction of both their needs and trust for the supplier, and thus to act more as customers. However, as argued in chapters 10 and 11, pressures stemming from the buyers' perceived inability to do this in a majority of cases, based on their lack of knowledge, the service's unclear knowledge base, and the nature of the services, represented strong counter forces.

Arenas, markets and organizations

Our investigation into MAS deals has directed our attention towards activities that take place before deals are formally closed, activities carried out in arenas aimed at constructing needs for MAS and trust for specific suppliers of MAS. This implies that arena mechanisms are of a backstage character. Market mechanisms on the other hand – such as demand, supply, equilibrium and competition – are of a more front-stage nature but offer little input to our understanding of how MAS deals come about. The focus on intense, interactive activities that forego the signing of deals questions central assumptions of the modernistic purchasing approach, e.g. concerning the existence of clear needs and preferences. The reason for this is that these assumptions are based on the belief that deals involving MAS are governed by market mechanisms. Such understandings of deal construction fail to recognize the purchasing practice we have observed in this book – the confidence game. Thus, in arenas, buyers may not know, at least initially, what kind of needs for external providers of MAS they have. There are of course situations where buyers are confident in what they want, and there are also situations where they are confident in whom they want. A buyer may want a particular person or a particular firm as a business partner even though, initially, he/she does not have a well-defined need for the particular service that that person can deliver. Rather, this need is created in the arena and further refined in the delivery process. Consequently, there are likely situations where confidence for a supplier, rather than a specific need, triggers the closing of a deal. The need for the service is rather the result of this deal, not its origin.

According to the ideal type games in the arena, this way of dealing with MAS carries the risk of turning the buyer into a victim. However, this only occurs if we are locked into a modernistic belief of markets where the value of MAS is defined by how well it meets a particular need, in turn defined by the organization before the service was delivered. As it may be questioned whether buyers know what they need, there is no guarantee that organizations that get what they demand also get the services they need. We can thus not neglect the possibility that the real victims are the buyers that get what they clearly demanded but did not need, since they may have been the victims of external pressures such as hard-selling advisors or new management concepts that invent new problems. This scenario naturally depends on the type of service we have in mind. The more technical and standardized a service is, the easier it is to measure the results and also estimate beforehand whether it is something the organization should buy, make itself, or does not need at all.

Dealing with confidence in arenas for need and trust construction is thus different from purchasing in markets. Technically, we are looking at a market situation, since business agreements are made between formal organizations and services are traded for money. However, the concept of "market" does not fit here with the patterns observed in MAS dealings. The market analogy would have been appropriate if the game played in practice, not only rhetorically, had been customerization. The buying organization would then act like a proper rational customer with clear preferences and needs, comparing different alternatives and making the best choices. These choices would also be something the buying organization fully controls, not choices made under the influence from sellers, organizational structures, or institutional pressures and mechanisms.

That these assumptions do not fit MAS has however been illustrated over and over in the book. It is very rare for buyers of MAS to be in full control of the definition of their needs and choices of suppliers. The confidence game implies that buyers are not alone in the construction of needs and trust. Rather, interaction and trust are essential in the construction process.

We have already noted that the importance of interaction and trust in bringing about deals is also a core argument in network theories. In fact, it is argued there to be one of the core mechanisms forcing organizations to live in long-term relations to each other. However, the "network" understanding of confidence sets the local dimension in focus, where individuals struggle to establish confidence in their relations to their counterparts (e.g. Johanson and Hägg, 1982). In network analyses, individual confidence relations are argued to become, over time, components in the network structure, which means that they advance, so to speak, from the individual dimension to the organizational dimension. Still, the network analogy implies that there are clear interfaces between organizational processes, and thus that there are processes in different organizations that can be adjusted to each other in more or less binding and tight relations.

In the MAS case, however, our argument is that it is rare that interfaces between the buyers' and the sellers' processes exist by nature. They have to be constructed. And this is what is happening when needs for MAS and trust for MAS suppliers are constructed.

As argued in the introduction to this chapter, the arena concept focuses on something wider than the network and narrower than the organizational field. It brings together pressures and mechanisms in the institutional dimension, interorganizational structures in the organizational dimension, and individual trust in the local dimension. It also draws attention to a dimension in business relations overlooked in the network approach, namely that organizations meet and make agreements and close deals in a form of no-man's-land that exists between organizations. This non-physical space serves as the stage for a lot of negotiating aimed at making the suppliers compatible with the buyers. In the case of MAS, it is very rare that there is a perfect match between a buyer's needs for a service and the services offered by a seller. There is thus no obvious place for buyers and sellers to meet, as the "market" presupposes clear needs and offers. For MAS, there are no marketplace stands where the seller shows his or her wares and where the buyer can go to browse and compare quality and prices with other sellers at the market. In the case of MAS, the degree of productification is most often low, meaning that it is as hard for a seller to be clear about what he/she offers, as it is for a buyer to search for and compare services that match his/her needs.

Clarity about what is to be bought and from whom thus needs to be established prior to the purchase. This is what is taking place in arenas for need and trust construction under the influence of forces and mechanisms from the individual, the organizational- and the institutional dimension. Thus, the buyer and the seller primarily act out their roles in the arena while uncertainties in the knowledge base of the service, the nature of the service, the buyers' knowledge of the service area, and the professionalization pressures on purchasing are dealt with. These uncertainties have been reduced to a manageable level (for the business parties) when a confident interface – consisting of a defined need and trust for a particular supplier – has been constructed. Before this interface has been established, the confidence game suggests that no deal can be closed. Our argument is that it is the mechanisms in the arenas that construct these interfaces, not market mechanisms such as demand, supply, competition and equilibrium. This means that the closing of a deal can be seen as agreement on an interface where the seller is invited to enter the buyer's organization. The closing of a deal can thus be seen as the construction of interfaces where the seller's and buyer's organizations can dock to each other.

Conclusions

We may conclude from the above that the relation a service supplier has with a buyer is formally a market relation. Thus, organizations technically buy services provided by other organizations. Consequently, it cannot be denied that market mechanisms drive the construction of the deal. However, it is not a market relation where purchasing is carried out in competition between equivalent suppliers. Our argument is that the market relation is really the result of the games played in arenas for need and trust construction. Thus, for a market relation to work, clear interfaces between the buying and the supplying organizations are needed. These interfaces do not automatically appear when MAS are about to be purchased. A common pattern is rather that buyers do not really know what they want, and sellers do not really know what service to offer in order to create business. This book has illustrated how buyers and sellers first meet at arenas for need and trust construction, where covarying mechanisms in three dimensions (the institutional, the organizational, and the local dimensions) are combined such that they create interfaces that enable business negotiations. The arena is thus a place where uncertain actors receive guidance. It is a place where needs and confidence in certain suppliers is established. Depending on the guidance received, the uncertain buyer may end up with different needs and trust for different suppliers. The practical implication of this for purchasers is that it is very important to bear these insights in mind when considering whether or not to hire a MAS supplier. Whose need is it that a supplier will satisfy, and for what reasons is confidence given to a certain supplier? Although they are not always in control of the reasons for why they hire a supplier, these are dilemmas that organizations that purchase MAS constantly have to deal with.

References

Abbott, Andrew; *The System of Professions: An Essay on the Division of Expert Labor*. Chicago: University of Chicago Press, 1988.

Abrahamson, Eric; Management Fashion. *Academy of Management Review*, 21(1), pp. 254-285, 1996.

Ackroyd, Stephen; Organization Contra Organizations: Professions and Organizational Change in the United Kingdom. *Organization Studies*, 17 (4), 599-621, 1996

Ackroyd, Stephen and David Lawrenson; Knowledge-work and organisational transformation: analysing contemporary change in the social use of expertise, in Robert Fincham (ed.), *New Relationships in the Organized Professions*. Aldershot: Avebury, 1996.

Adam, Barbara; *Timewatch. The Social Analysis of Time*, Cambridge: Polity, 1995.

Adstream; *Adstream is chosen supplier of content solution by the Swedish Children's Ombudsman (BO)*. www.adstream.se, *4/8/2004*.

Affärsvärlden, 24/3/2003.

Affärsvärlden; Sverige 500 - Affärsvärldens årliga granskning av dom svenska storbolagen. 7/6/2001

AICPA; *Report of the special committee on assurance services*. New York: American Institute of Certified Public Accountants, 1997.

Albert, Stuart and David A. Whetten; Organizational Identity, *Research in Organizational Behavior,* 7, Greenwich, CT: JAI Press, pp. 263-295, 1985.

Alchian, Armen A. and Harold Demsetz; Production, Information Costs, and the Economic Organization, in Oliver E. Williamson and Scott E. Masten (eds.), *Economics of Transaction Costs*. Cheltenham: Elgar Critical Writings Reader, 1999.

Alter, Catherine, and Jerald T. Hage; *Organizations Working Together*. London: Sage, 1993.

Alvesson, Mats; *Knowledge Work and Knowledge-Intensive Firms*. Oxford: Oxford University Press, 2004.

Anderson, James C and James A. Narus; *Business Market Management*. London: Prentice Hall, 2004.

Archer, Margaret S; *Realist Social Theory: The morphogenetic approach*. Cambridge: Cambridge University Press, 1995.

Armbrüster, Thomas and Christoph Barchewitz; Marketing Instruments of Management Consulting Firms — An Empirical Study. *Academy of Management Best Paper Proceedings*, 2004.

Aspers, Patrik; *Markets in Fashion. A Phenomenological Approach.* Stockholm: City University Press, 2001.

Augustsson, Fredrik; *Division of Labour Within and Between Firms. Towards a new model to describe the organisation of work.* Paper presented at the European Sociological Association Conference, Helsinki, 2001.

Augustsson, Fredrik; *Behind the Scenes of Creating Interactive Media. Inter-firm collaboration and production networks in the Swedish field of interactive media production.* Paper presented at the Nordic Sociological Conference, Reykjavik, 2002a.

Augustsson, Fredrik; *Designing the Digital and Producing Aesthetics: The Organisation of Production Within and Between Swedish Interactive Media Firms.* MITIOR Working Paper presented at Lancaster and Strathclyde University. Stockholm: National Institute for Working Life, 2002b.

Augustsson, Fredrik; Webbsidor som visuella uttryck, in Patrik Aspers, Paul Fuerher and Arni Sverrison (eds.), *Bild och samhälle. Visuell analys som vetenskaplig metod.* Lund: Studentlitteratur, pp. 139-159, 2004.

Augustsson, Fredrik and Åke Sandberg; IT i omvandlingen av arbetsorganisationer, in Carsten von Otter (ed.), *Ute och inne i svenskt arbetsliv. Forskare analyserar och spekulerar om trender i framtidens arbete.* Stockholm: National Institute for Working Life, pp. 175-201, 2003a.

Augustsson, Fredrik and Åke Sandberg; Teknik, organisation och ledning - vad nytt inom interaktiva medier? in Åke Sandberg (ed.), *Ledning för Alla? Om perspektivbrytningar i arbetsliv och företagsledning.* Stockholm: SNS förlag, pp. 433-462, 2003b.

Augustsson, Fredrik and Åke Sandberg; *Interactive Media in Swedish Organisations. In-house Production and Purchase of Internet and Multimedia Solutions in Swedish Firms and Government Agencies.* Stockholm: National Institute for Working Life, 2004a.

Augustsson, Fredrik and Åke Sandberg; Time for Competence? Competence development among interactive media workers, in Christina Garsten and Kerstin Jacobsson (eds.), *Learning to be Employable: New Agendas on Work, Responsibility and Learning in a Globalizing World.* Hampshire: Palgrave Macmillan, pp. 210-230, 2004b.

Axelsson, Björn and Finn Wynstra; *Buying Business Services.* Chichester: Wiley, 2002.

Badaracco, Joseph L.; *The Knowledge Link.* Boston, MA: Harvard Business School Press, 1991.

Balmer, John M. T.; Corporate Identity and the Advantage of Corporate Marketin*g, Journal of Marketing Management*, 15 (1-3), pp. 963-997, 1998.

Barney, Jay B.; Looking inside for competitive advantage, *Academy of Management Executive*, 9, pp. 49-61, 1995.

Barret, Frank, and Ken Peplowski; Minimal Structures Within a Song: An Analysis of 'All of Me', *Organization Science,* 9(5), pp. 558-56, 1998.

Bauman, Zygmunt; *Life in Fragments.* Oxford: Blackwell, 1995.

Beattie, Vivien, Stella Fearnley and Richard Brandt; *Behind closed doors: What company audit is really about.* Hampshire: Palgrave, 2001.

Beck, Ulrich; *Risk Society.* London: Sage, 1992.

Becker, Gary S. and Kevin M. Murphy; The Division of Labor, Coordination Costs, and Knowledge, *The Quarterly Journal of Economics,* CVII, pp. 1137-1160, 1992.

Berger, Peter and Thomas Luckmann; *The Social Construction of Reality.* London: Penguin Books, 1966.

Berglund, Johan and Andreas Werr; The Invincible Character of Management Consulting Rhetoric: How One Blends Incommensurates While Keeping Them Apart, *Organization*, 7(4), pp. 633-656, 2000.

Berry, Leonard L; Services Marketing is Different. *Business Magazine*, 30, May-June, pp. 24-29, 1980.

Berry, Leonard L; Delivering Excellent Service in Retailing, *Retailing Issues Letter*, No. 4, Arthur Andersen and Co. Center for Retailing Studies: Texas A&M University Press, pp. 1-3, 1988.

Bessant, John and Howard Rush; Building bridges for innovation: The role of consultants in technology transfer, *Research Policy*, 24, pp. 97-114, 1995.

Bijker, Wiebe E. and John Law (eds.); *Shaping Technology/ Building Society.* Cambridge, MA: MIT Press, 1992.

Bitner, Mary Jo; The Impact of Physical Surroundings on Customers and Employees. *Journal of Marketing*, (56) 2, pp. 57-71, 1992.

Block, Peter; *Flawless Consulting.* San Francisco: Jossey-Bass Pfeifer, 2000.

Bloomfield, Brian P. and Ardha Best; Management consultants: systems development, power and the translation of problems, *The Sociological Review*, 40(3), pp. 533-560, 1992.

Bloomfield, Brian P. and Theo Vurdubakis; Re-presenting technology: IT consultancy reports as textual reality constructions, *Sociology*, 28(2), pp. 455-477, 1994.

Brassington, Frances and Stephen Pettitt; *Principles of Marketing*. London: Prentice Hall, 2000.

Braverman, Harry; *Labor and Monopoly Capital. The Degradation of Work in the Twentieth Century*. New York: Monthly Review Press, 1974.

Brunsson, Nils and Johan P. Olsen (eds.); *The Reforming Organization*, Oslo: Fagbokforlaget, 1998.

Brunsson, Nils and Kerstin Sahlin Andersson; Constructing Organizations: The Example of Public Sector Reform, *Organization Studies*, 21(4), pp. 721-746, 2000.

Bryntse, Karin; *Kontraktsstyrning i teori och praktik*. Lund: Lund Business Press, 2000.

Burrage, Michael and Rolf Torstendahl (eds); *Professions in theory and history. Rethinking the study of the professions*. London: Sage, 1990.

Burrell, Gibson; Hard Times for the Salitariat, in Harry Scarbrough (ed.); *The Management of Expertise*. London: McMillan, pp. 48-65, 1996.

Bäcklund, Jonas and Andreas Werr; *The discursive construction of the manager as a legitimate client of consulting services*. Paper presented at the Academy of Management Meeting, Seattle, 2003.

Callon, Michel, Cécile Méadel and Vololona Rabeharisoa; The Economy of Qualities, *Economy and Society*, 31(2), pp. 194-217, 2002.

CEO Europe, May, 1998.

Chow, Chee W. and Steven. J. Rice; Qualified audit reports and auditor switching, *Accounting Review*, 57(2), pp. 326-335, 1982.

Clark, Timothy; *Managing Consultants. Consultancy and the Management of Impressions*. Buckingham: Open University Press, 1995.

Clark, Timothy and Graeme Salaman; Telling Tales: Management Consultancy as the Art of Story Telling, in David Grant and Cliff Oswick (eds.), *Metaphor and Organizations*. London: Sage, pp. 167-184, 1996.

Clark, Timothy, and Graeme Salaman; The Management Guru as Organizational Witchdoctor, *Organization* 3(1), pp. 85-107, 1996.

Clark, Timothy, and Graeme Salaman; Telling Tales: Management Gurus' Narratives and the Construction of Managerial Identity, *Journal of Management Studies*, 35(2), pp. 137-161, 1998.

Coase, Ronald H; The Nature of the Firm, *Economica*, 4, pp. 386-405, 1937.

Cole, Robert; *The Death and Life of the American Quality Movement.* New York: Oxford University Press, 1995.

Cooper, Robin and Robert S. Kaplan; *The Design of Cost Management Systems.* Englewood Cliffs, NJ: Prentice-Hall, 1991.

Corman, Joel, Robert Lussier and Lori Pennel; *Small Business Management: A Planning Approach.* Cincinnati, OH: Atomic Dog Publishing, 2005.

Craswell, Allen T., Jere R. Francis and Stephen L. Taylor; Auditor brand name reputation and industry specialization, *Journal of Accounting and Economics*, 20, pp. 297-322, 1995.

Czarniawska-Joerges, Barbara; *To coin a phrase: On organizational talk, organizational control and management consulting.* Stockholm: The Economic Research Institute, 1988.

D'Aunno, Thomas, Melissa Succi and Jeffrey Alexander; The Role of Institutional and Market Forces in Divergent Organizational Change. *Administrative Science Quarterly*, 45, pp. 679-703, 2000.

Das, T. K and Bing-Sheng Teng; Trust, Control and Risk in Strategic Alliances: An Integrated Framework, *Organization Studies,* 22(2), pp. 251-283, 2001.

Dauphinais, G. William and Colin Price; *Straight From the CEO. The World's Top Business Leaders Reveal Ideas that Every Manager Can Use.* New York: Simon and Schuster, 1998.

Davidow, William H; *Total Customer Service: The Ultimate Weapon*, New York: Harper and Row, 1989.

Dawes, Philip L., Grahame R. Dowling and Paul G. Patterson; Criteria used to select management consultants, *Industrial Marketing Management*, 21, pp. 187-193, 1992.

Dawes, Philip L., Grahame R. Dowling and Paul G. Patterson; Determinants of pre-purchase information search effort for management cosnulting services, *Journal for Business to Business Marketing*, 1(1), pp. 31-60, 1993.

Deal, Terrence. E. and Allan A. Kennedy; *Corporate Cultures.* Reading, MA: Addison-Wesley, 1982.

DiMaggio, Paul and Walter Powell; The Iron Cage Revisited: Institutional Isomorphism and Collective Rationality, in Walter Powell and Paul DiMaggio (eds.), *The New Institutionalism in Organizational Analysis.* Chicago: The University of Chicago Press, pp. 63-82, 1983/1991.

DiMaggio, Paul and Walter Powell; Introduction, in Walter Powell and Paul DiMaggio (eds.), *The New Institutionalism in Organizational Analysis*, Chicago: The University of Chicago Press, pp. 1-40, 1991.

Djelic, Marie-Laure, 1998, *Exporting the American Model*, Oxford: Oxford University Press, 1998.

Dobler, Donald W. and David N. Burt; *Purchasing and Materials Management: Text and Cases*. New York: McGraw-Hill, 1996.

Dopuch, Nicholas, Ronald R. King and Rachel Schwartz; Independence in appearance and in fact: An experimental investigation, *Contemporary Accounting Research*, 20(1), pp. 79-114, 2003.

Dowling, Grahame R.; *Corporate Reputations. Identity, Image and Performance*. Oxford: Oxford University Press, 2001.

Eccles, Robert and Dwight Crane; *Doing Deals – Investment Banks at Work*. Boston, MA: Harvard Business School Press, 1988.

Edvardsson, Bo; Purchasing management consultancy, in Leif Lindmark (ed.), *Kunskap som kritisk resurs*. Umeå: Handelshögskolan i Umeå, Umeå Universitet, 1990.

Edvinsson, Leif and Pär Hallberg; *Marknadtjänster – paketering, kvalitet, prissättning*. Stockholm: Kugel Tryckeri AB, 1985.

Edvinsson, Leif and Michael S. Malone; *Intellectual Capital. Realizing Your Company's True Value by Finding Its Hidden Brainpower*. New York: Harper Collins, 1997.

Elliott, Robert K.; Assurance service opportunities: Implications for academia, *Accounting Horizons*, 11(4), pp. 61-74, 1997.

Engwall, Lars, Staffan Furusten and Eva Wallerstedt; The Changing Relationship between Management Consulting and Academia: Evidence from Sweden, in Matthias Kipping and Lars Engwall (eds.), *Management Consulting. Emergence and Dynamics of a Knowledge Industry*. Oxford: Oxford University Press, pp. 36-51, 2002.

Ernst, Berit and Alfred Kieser; In Search of Explanations for the Consulting Explosion, in Kerstin Sahlin-Andersson and Lars Engwall, (eds.), *The Expansion of Management Knowledge. Carriers, Flows and Sources*. Stanford, CA: Stanford Business Books, pp. 47-73, 2002.

EU Commission Green Paper; Public Procurement in the EU; *Exploring the way forward*, 1996.

Fearon, Harold and W.A. Bales; *Purchasing of non-traditional goods and services*. Center for advanced purchasing studies (CAPS), Tempe, AZ, 1995.

Fisher, Lawrence; *Industrial Marketing: An Analytical Approach to Planning and Execution*, 2nd Ed. London: Business Books, 1970.

Fincham, Robin; The consultant-client relationship: Critical perspectives on the management of organizational change, *Journal of Management Studies*, 36(3), pp. 331-351, 1999.

Fincham, Robin and Timothy Clark; Introduction: The Emergence of Critical Perspectives on Consulting, in Timothy Clark and Robin Fincham (eds.), *Critical Consulting*. Oxford: Blackwell Business, pp. 1-18, 2002.

Fligstein, Neil and Iona Mara-Drita; How to Make a Market: Reflections on the Attempt to Create a Single Market in the European Union, *American Journal of Sociology*, 102(1), pp. 1-33, 1996.

Fombrun, Charles J. and Mark Shanley; What's in a Name? Reputation Building and Corporate Strategy, *Academy of Management Journal*, 33(2), pp. 233-258, 1990.

Furusten, Staffan; *Popular Management Books - How they are made and what they mean for organizations*. London: Routledge, 1999.

Furusten, Staffan; The Knowledge Base of Standards, in Nils Brunsson, Bengt Jacobsson et al; *A World of Standards*. Oxford: Oxford University Press, pp.71-84, 2000.

Furusten, Staffan; *God managementkonsultation – reglerad expertis eller improviserat artisteri?* Lund: Studentlitteratur, 2003.

Furusten, Staffan and Nils Brunsson; *The Organization of Management Consulting*, paper presented at the EGOS Colloquium, Sub-theme The Impact of Managerial Knowledge on the Convergence of European Management Practices, Helsinki, 2-6 July, 2000.

Gadde, Lars-Erik and Håkan Håkansson; *Professional Purchasing*. London: Routledge, 1993.

Gadde, Lars-Erik and Håkan Håkansson; *Supply Network Strategies*. Chichester: Wiley, 2001.

Gammelsæter, Hallgeir; Managers and Consultants as Embedded Actors: Evidence from Norway, in Matthias Kipping and Lars Engwall (eds.), *Management Consulting: Emergence and Dynamics of a Knowledge Industry*. Oxford: Oxford University Press, pp. 222-237, 2002.

Garsten, Christina; Betwixt and Between: Temporary Employees as Liminal Subjects in Flexible Organizations, *Organization Studies*, 20(4), pp. 601-617, 1999a.

Garsten, Christina; Loose Links and Tight Attachments: Modes of Employment and Meaning-making in a Changing Labor Market, in Robert Goodman (ed.), *Modern Organisations and Emerging Conundrums*. Lanham, Maryland: New Lexington Press, 1999b.

Garsten, Christina; Colleague, competitor, or client: Social boundaries in flexible work arrangements, in Neil Paulsen and Tor Hernes (eds.), *Managing Boundaries in Organizations: Multiple Perspectives*. Basingstoke: Palgrave Macmillan, 2003.

Garsten, Christina and Chris Grey; Trust, control and post-bureaucracy, *Organization Studies*, 22(2), 2001.

Gergen, Kenneth J.; *The Saturated Self. Dilemmas of Identity in Contemporary Life*. New York: Basic Books, 1991.

Giddens, Anthony; *The Consequences of Modernity*. Stanford: Stanford University Press, 1990.

Gioia, Dennis A; Symbols, Scripts, and Sensemaking: Creating Meaning in the Organizational Experience, in Henry P Sims Jr. and Dennis A. Gioia (eds.), *The Thinking Organization*. San Francisco: Jossey-Bass, pp. 49-74, 1986.

Glückler, Johannes and Thomas Armbrüster; Bridging uncertainty in management consulting: The mechanisms of trust and networked reputation, *Organization Studies*, 24(2), pp. 269, 2003.

Granovetter, Mark; Economic Action and Social Stucture: The Problem of Embeddedness, *American Journal of Sociology*, 91(3), pp. 481-510, 1985.

Greenwood, Royston, C. R. Hinings and D. J. Cooper; An Institutional Theory of Change: Contextual and Interpretive Dynamics in the Accounting Industry, in Walter W. Powell, and D. Jones (eds.), *Bending the Bars of the Iron Cage: Institutional Dynamics and Processes*. University of Chicago Press, Chicago, 2005.

Greiner, Larry E. and Robert O. Metzger; *Consulting to Management*. Englewood Cliffs, N.J.: Prentice Hall, 1983.

Grey, Chris; On being a professional in a 'Big Six' firm, *Accounting, Organization and Society*, 23(5/6), pp. 569-587, 1998.

Groth, John; Important factors in the sale and pricing of services, *Management Decision*, 33(7), pp. 29-34, 1995.

Grönroos, Christian; *Service Management and Marketing - Managing the Moments of Truth in Service Competition*. Massachusetts/Toronto: Lexington Books, 1990.

Grönroos, Christian; *Service management; ledning, strategi, marknadsföring i servicekonkurrens*. Göteborg: ISL Förlag, 1992.

Gummesson, Evert; *Marknadsföring och inköp av konsulttjänster*. Unpublished PhD Thesis, Stockholm: Stockholm University,1977.

Gummesson, Evert; *Relationsmarknadsföring: Från 4P till 30R*. Malmö: Liber-Hermods, 1995.

Hacking, Ian; *The Social Construction of What?* Cambridge, MA: Harvard University Press, 1999.

Hammer, Michael and James Champy ; *Reengineering the Corporation*. London: Brealy, 1993.

Hannerz, Ulf; Cosmopolitans and Locals in World Culture, in Mike Featherstone (ed.), *Global Culture: Nationalism, Globalization and Modernity*. London: Sage, 1990.

Hassett, Brian; *The Temp Survival Guide*. Secaucus, NJ: Citadel Press, 1997.

Heckscher Charles and Anne Donnellon (eds.); *The Post-Bureaucratic Organization*. Thousand Oaks, CA: Sage, 1994.

Heelas, Paul, Scott Lash and Paul Morris (eds.); *Detraditionalization*. Oxford: Blackwell, 1996.

Heinritz, Stuart, Paul V. Farrell and Clifton L. Smith; *Purchasing: Principles and Applications*. Englewood Cliffs, NJ: Prentice-Hall, 1986.

Helgesson, Claes-Fredrik, Hans Kjellberg and Anders Liljenberg (eds.); *Den där marknaden*. Lund: Studenlitteratur, 2004.

Hill, Terry; *Production-Operations Management*. London: Prentice Hall, 1991.

Hilmer, Frederick. G. and Lex Donaldson; *Management Redeemed. Debunking the Fads that Undermine Corporate Performance*. East Rosewill NSW: Free Press Australia, 1996.

Hislop, Donald; The client role in consultancy relations during the appropriation of technological innovations, *Research Policy*, 31, pp. 657-671, 2002.

Hochschild, Arlie Russel; *The Managed Heart*. Berkeley, CA: University of California Press, 1983.

Huczynski, Andrzej; *Management Gurus. What Makes Them and How to Become One*. London: Routledge, 1993.

Håkansson, Håkan (ed); *International Marketing and Purchasing of Industrial Goods*, New York: John Wiley, 1982.

Håkansson, Håkan; Technological Collaboration in Industrial Networks, *European Management Journal*, 8 (September), pp. 371-379, 1990.

Håkansson, Håkan, Economics of Technological Relationships, in Ove Granstrand, (ed.), *Economics of Technology*, Amsterdam: Elsevier, 1994.

Håkansson, Håkan and Björn Wootz. *Företags inköpsbeteende,* Lund: Studentlitteratur, 1975

Jackall, Robert; *Moral Mazes - The World of Corporate Managers*. New York: Oxford University Press, 1988.

Jeppesen, Kim Klarskov; Reinventing auditing, redefining consulting and independence, *European Accounting Review*, 7(3), pp. 517-539, 1998.

Johanson, Jan, and associates; *Internationalization, Relationships and Networks*, Acta Universitatis Upsaliensis. Studia Oeconomiae Negotiorum 36, Stockholm: Almqvist and Wiksell International, 1994.

References

Johanson, Jan and Ingemund Hägg (eds.); *Företag i Nätverk - ny syn på konkurrenskraft* (Enterprise in Network), Stockholm: SNS, 1982.

Jonsson, Seth; *Den strategiska försörjningsprocessen med focus på uppbyggnaden av företagets leverantörsbas*. Licentiate thesis, Linköping: Linköping University, 1998.

Kaplan, Robert S. and David P. Norton; *The Balanced Scorecard*. Boston, MA: Harvard Business School Press, 1996.

Katzenbach, Jon R. and Douglas K. Smith; *The Wisdom of Teams. Creating High-Performance Organization*. Boston, MA: Harvard Business School Press, 1993.

Kieser, Alfred; Why Organization Theory Needs Historical Analyses – And How This Should Be Performed, *Organization Science*, 45, 1994, pp. 608-620, 1994.

Kieser, Alfred; Business Process Reengineering. Neue Kleider für den Kaiser? *Zeitschrift für Organisation*, 65(3), pp. 179-185, 1996.

Kieser, Alfred; Unternehmensberater - Händler in Problemen, Praktiken und Sinn, in Horst Glaser, Ernst F. Schröder and Axel von Werder (eds.), *Organisation im Wandel der Märkte*. Wiesbaden: Dr. Th. Gabler Verlag, pp. 191-226, 1998.

Kieser, Alfred; On Communication Barriers between Management Science, Consultancies and Business Companies, in Timothy Clark and Robin Fincham, (eds.), *Critical Consulting. New Perspectives on the Management Advice Industry*. Oxford: Blackwell, pp. 206-227, 2002a.

Kieser, Alfred; Managers as Marionettes? Using Fashion Theories to Explain the Success of Consultancies, in Matthias Kipping and Lars Engwall (eds.), *Management Consulting: Emergence and Dynamics of a Knowledge Industry*. Oxford: Oxford University Press, pp. 167-183, 2002b.

Kipping, Matthias and Thomas Armbrüster; *Management Consultants and Management Knowledge - A literature review*, University of Reading, 1998.

Kipping, Matthias; Trapped in Their Wave: The Evolution of Management Consultancies, in Timothy Clark and Robin Fincham (eds.), *Critical Consulting*. Oxford: Blackwell Business, pp. 21-27, 2002.

Knorr-Cetina, Karin; Primitive Classification and Postmodernity: Towards a Sociological Notion of Fiction, *Theory, Culture and Society*, 11, pp. 1-22, 1994.

Knorr-Cetina, Karin; *Epistemic Cultures: How the Sciences Make Knowledge*. Cambridge, MA: Harvard University Press, 1999.

Knorr-Cetina, Karin and Urs Breuggers; The Market as an Object of Attachment: Exploring Postsocial Relations in Financial Markets, *Canadian Journal of Sociology*, 25(2), pp. 141-168, 2000.

Kogut, Bruce, Weijian Shan and Gordon Walker; The Make-or-Buy Cooperate Decision in the Context of an Industry Network, in Nitin Nohria and Robert G. Eccles (eds.), *Networks and Organizations. Structure, Form, and Action*. Boston, MA: Harvard Business School Press, pp. 348-365, 1992.

Konsultguiden; Stockholm: Affärsvärlden förlag, 1998.

Konsultguiden, www.konsultguiden.se, 9/3/2004.

Kopytoff, Igor; The Cultural Biography of Things: Commoditization as Process, in Arjun Appadurai (ed.) *The Social Life of Things - Commodities in Cultural Perspective*. Cambridge, MA: Cambridge University Press, 1986.

KPMG; *Investment in Sweden*. Stockholm: KPMG Bohlins, 1997.

Kraljic, Peter; Purchasing must become supply management, *Harvard Business Review*, (Sept-Oct), pp. 109-117, 1983.

Kubr, Milan; *Management Consulting - A guide to the profession*. Geneva: ILO, 1982.

Kubr, Milan; *How to Select and Use Consultants: A Client's Guide (Management Development Series)*. Geneva: ILO, 1993.

Kubr, Milan; *Management Consulting - A guide to the profession*. (3rd revised edition). Geneva: ILO, 1996.

Kubr, Milan; *Management Consulting - a guide to the profession*. (4th edition ed.). Geneva: ILO, 2002.

Kurtz, David L. and Kenneth E. Clow; *Services Marketing*. New York: John Wiley and Sons, 1993.

Larson, Margareta Sarafatti; *The Rise of Professionalism*. Berkeley, CA: University of California Press, 1977.

Latour, Bruno; *Aramis, or the love of technology*. Cambridge, MA: Harvard University Press, 1996.

Law, John and Michael Callon; The Life and Death of an Aircraft: A Network Analysis of Technical Change, in Wiebe E. Bijker and John Law (eds.), *Shaping Technology/ Building Society. Studies in Sociotechnical Change*. Cambridge, MA: MIT Press, pp. 21-52, 1992.

Law, John and John Hassard (eds.); *Actor Network Theory and After*. Oxford: Blackwell, 1999.

Lee, Peggy M; What's in a Name.com?: The Effects of '.Com' Name Changes on Stock Prices and Trading Activity, *Strategic Management Journal*, 22(8), pp. 793-804, 2001.

Lindahl, David P. and William B. Beyers; The Creation of Competitive Advantage by Producer Service Establishments, *Economic Geography,* 75(1), pp. 1-20, 1999.

Lindvall, Jan; The Creation of Management Practice: A Literature Review, *CEMP Report No. 1,* September, 1998.

LOU; *Upphandling av konsulttjänster enligt 6 kap.* LOU ("Procurement consulting services according to Chapter 6 of the Public Procurement Act"), Page 2 (in Swedish). National Board of Public Procurement (NOU) website, www.nou.se. 2002.

Lovelock, Christopher; Distinctive Aspects of Service Marketing, in C. Lovelock (ed.), *Services Marketing.* Englewood Cliffs, NJ: Prentice-Hall, pp. 1-9, 1984.

Løwendahl, Bente R., Øivind Revang and Siw M. Fosstenlökken; Knowledge and value creation in professional service firms: A framework for analysis, *Human Relations,* 54(7), pp. 911-931, 2001.

Macdonald, Stuart; *From Babes and Sucklings: Management Consultants and Novice Clients,* paper presented at the EIASM Workshop on the Management Advice Industry, Brussels, 2000.

Mackenzie, Donald and Judy Wajcman (eds.); *The Social Shaping of Technology.* Buckingham: Open University Press, 1999.

Maister, David; *Managing the Professional Service Firm.* New York: Free Press, 1993.

Manovich, Lev; *The Language of New Media.* Cambridge, MA: MIT Press, 2001.

March, James G.; Fotnootes to Organizational Change, *Administrative Science Quarterly,* Vol. 26, pp.563-577, 1981a.

March, James G.; Decisions in Organizations and Theories of Choice, in Andrew Van de Ven and William F, Joyce (eds.), *Perspectives of Organizational Design and Behaviour.* New York: Wiley, 1981b.

March, James G. and Johan P. Olsen; *Ambiguity and Choice in Organizations.* Bergen: Universitetsforlaget, 1976.

McGonagle, John J. and Carolyn Vella; *How to Find and Use a Consultant in Your Company: A Managers' and Executives' Guide.* Chichester: Wiley, 2001.

Meyer, John; Rationalized Environments, in Walter Scott and John W. Meyer (eds.), *Institutional environments and organizations.* Thousand Oaks, CA: Sage, pp. 28-54, 1994.

Meyer, John and Ronald Jepperson; The "Actors" of Modern Society: Cultural Rationalization and the Ongoing Expression of Social Agency, *Sociological Theory,* 18(1), pp. 100-120, 2000.

Micklethwait, John and Adrian Wooldridge; *The Witch Doctors. What the management gurus are saying, why it matters and how to make sense of it.* London: Heinemann, 1996.

Morrow, Michael; *Activity-based Management.* New York: Woodhead-Faulkner, 1992.

Mähring, Magnus; *IT Project Governance.* Stockholm: Stockholm School of Economics, 2002.

Needles, Belverd E. Jr.; Taxonomy of auditing standards, in Frederick D. S. Choi (ed.), *International accounting and finance handbook.* New York: John Wiley and Sons, 2000.

Newell, Sue, Maxine Robertson, Harry Scarbrough and Jacky Swan; *Managing knowledge work.* Basingstoke, Hampshire: Houndsmills, 2002.

Noble, Peter and Thomas Gruca; Industrial Pricing: Theory and Managerial Practice, *Marketing Science,* 18 (3), pp. 435-454, 1999.

Nonaka, Ikujiro and Reinmoeller, Patrick; Dynamic Business Systems for Knowledge Creation and Utilization, in Charles Despres and Daniele Chauvel (eds.), *Knowledge Horizons.* Boston, MA: 2000.

Normann, Richard; *Service Management; ledning och strategi i tjänsteproduktionen.* Malmö: Liber Ekonomi, 1992.

Normann, Richard; *Service Management – Strategy and Leadership in the Service Business.* Chichester: John Wiley and Sons Ltd., 2000.

North, Douglass C; *Structure and Change in Economic History.* New York: W.W. Norton and Co, 1981.

NOU; *Kort om LOU och NOU* ("A brief description of LOU and NOU"). National Board of Public Procurement (NOU) website, www.nou.se, 2001.

O'Shea, James and Charles Madigan; *Dangerous Company. The Consulting Powerhouses and the Businesses They Save and Ruin.* London: Nicholas Brealey, 1997.

Oudshoorn, Nelly, Els Rommes and Marcelle Stienstra; Configuring the User as Everybody: Gender and Design Cultures in Information and Communication Technologies, *Science, Technology and Human Values,* 29(1), pp. 30-63, 2004.

Pavlik, John V.; *New Media Technology. Cultural and Commercial Perspectives.* Boston, MA: Allyn and Bacon, 1998.

Penrose, Edith Tilton; *The Theory of the Growth of the Firm.* New York: Wiley, 1959.

Petterson, Anna and Viktoria Leigard; *Samling vid pumpen. Mediernas bevakning av IT-bubblan.* Stockholm: Stiftelsen Institutet för Mediestudier, 2002.

Pfeffer, Jeffrey; *Power in Organizations.* Cambridge, MA: Ballinger Publishing Company, 1981.

Pfeffer, Jeffrey and James N. Baron; Taking the workers back out: recent trends on the structuring of employment, *Research in Organizational Behavior,* Vol 10, pp. 257-303, 1988.

Pine, Joseph and James Gilmore; *The Experience Economy*. Boston, MA: Harvard University Press, 1998.

Planander, Agneta; *Strategic Alliances and Trust Processes - A Study of Strategic Collaborations Between High-Technology Companies.* Lund: Lund Business Press, 2002.

Powell, Walter W. and Paul J. DiMaggio; *The New Institutionalism in Organizational Analysis.* Chicago, IL: Chicago University Press, 1991.

Prahalad, C.K. and Gary Hamel; The Core Competence of the Corporation, *Harvard Business Review,* (May/June), pp. 79-91, 1990.

Reed, Michael I.; Expert Power and Control in Late Modernity: An Empirical Review and Theoretical Synthesis, *Organization Studies,* 17(4), pp. 573-597, 1996.

Rhenman, Erik; *Organization Theory for Long-Range Planning.* London: Wiley, 1973.

Robertson, Maxine, Harry Scarbrough and Jacky Swan; Knowledge Creation in Professional Service Firms: Institutional Effects, *Organization Studies* 24(6), pp. 831-857, 2003.

Rose, Nikolas; Authority and the Genealogy of Subjectivity, in Paul Heelas, Scott Lash and Paul Morris (eds.), *Detraditionalization.* Oxford: Blackwell, 1996.

Rosvall, Kristian and Lage Rosvall; *Prissättning efter kundvärde.* Stockholm: Industrilitteratur, 2000.

Rydmark, Susanna; Hur man undviker regler – fallet managementkonsulterna, in Göran Ahrne and Nils Brunsson (eds.), *Regelexplosionen.* Stockholm: EFI, 2004.

Räisinen, Christine and Anneli Linde; Technologizing Discourse to Standardize Projects in Multi-Project Organizations: Hegemony by Consensus, *Organization,* 11(1), pp. 101-121, 2004.

Salaman, Graeme; Understanding Advice: Towards a Sociology of Management Consultancy, in Timothy Clark and Robin Fincham (eds.), *Critical Consulting - New Perspectives on the Management Advice Industry.* Oxford: Blackwell, pp. 347-360, 2002.

SAMC, *Managementkonsulter - en tillväxtbransch för kunskapsspridning och strukturomvandling,* www.samc.se, 2002.

Sandberg, Åke and Fredrik Augustsson; *Interactive Media in Sweden 2001. The Second Interactive Media, Internet and Multimedia Industry Survey. Work Life in Transition 2002:2.* Stockholm: National Institute for Working Life, 2002.

Sanders, WM. Gerard and Steven Boivie; Sorting Things Out: Valuation of New Firms in Uncertain Markets, *Strategic Management Journal,* 25(2), pp. 167-186, 2004.

Saxenian, AnnaLee; *Regional Advantage: Culture and Competition in Silicon Valley and Route 128*. Cambridge, MA: Harvard University Press, 1994.

Saxton, Todd; The impact of third parties on strategic decision making. Roles, timing and organizational outcomes, *Journal of Organizational Change Management*, 8(3), pp. 47-62, 1995.

Sayer, Andrew and Richard Walker; *The New Social Economy. Reworking the Division of Labor*. Cambridge, MA: Blackwell, 1992.

Scarbrough, Harry; Introduction, in Harry Scarbrough, (ed.), *The Management of Expertise*. London: McMillan, pp 1-20, 1996.

SCB; *Företagens användning av datorer och Internet 2002*. Stockholm: Statistics Sweden, 2003.

Schein, Edgar H.; *Process Consultation - Its Role in Organization Development*. Reading: Addison Wesley, 1988.

Schmidt, Sascha and Patrick Vogt; *Disaggregation of the Value Chain: Emergence of new business models in strategy consulting*, paper presented at the 2nd International Conference of Management Consulting, Lausanne, 2004

Schonberger, Richard J.; *World Class Manufacturing. The Next Decade*. New York: The Free Press, 1996.

Scott, Richard and John Meyer (eds); *Institutional Environments and Organizations - Structural Complexity and Individualism*. London: Sage, 1994.

Senge, Peter M.; *The Fifth Discipline. The Art and Practice of Learning Organization*. London: Century Press, 1992.

Sevón, Guje; Organizational Imitation and Identity Transformation, in Barbara Czarniawska and Guje Sevón (eds.), *Translating Organizational Change*. Berlin: de Gruyter, 1996.

Shostack, G. Lynn; Breaking Free from Product Marketing, *The Journal of Marketing*, 41(april), pp. 73-80, 1977.

Shostack, G. Lynn; How to Design a Service, in James H. Donnelly and William R. George (eds.); *Marketing of Services*, Proceedings series. Chicago: American Marketing Association, pp. 221-229, 1981.

Shostack, G. Lynn; Understanding Services Through Blueprinting, in T. Schwartz and S. Brown (eds.), *Services Marketing and Management*. Greenwich, CT: JAI Press, pp. 75-90, 1992.

Shapiro, Eileen C.; *Fad Surfing in the Boardroom: Managing the Age of Instant Answers*. Reading, MA: Addison-Wesley, 1996.

Sigma; *Internet med fokus på handel*. Alingsås: Sigma ehandel AB, 2000.

Sipilä, Jorma; *Asianajopalvelujen markkinointi*. Helsinki: Suomen Asianajaliiton julkaisuja 1, 2000.

Skjølsvik, Tale; *Aligning Roles, Clients and Strategies for Supperior Client Value Creation in Management Consulting*, paper presented at the Academy of Management Meeting, New Orleans, Lousiana, 2004.

Smith, Adam; *An Inquiry Into the Nature and Causes of the Wealth of Nations*. Chicago: Encyclopaedia Britannica Inc, 1952.

Stalk, George and Thomas M. Hout; *Competing Against Time: How Time-Based Competition is Reshaping Global Markets*. New York: Free Press, 1990.

Stewart, G. Bennett; *The Quest for Value. The EVA Management Guide*. New York: Harper, 1998.

Strang, David and John Meyer; Institutional Conditions for Diffusion, in Richard Scott and John Meyer (eds), *Institutional Environments and Organizations*. London: Sage, pp. 100-112, 1994.

Sturdy, Andrew; The Consultancy Process - An Insecure Business, *Journal of Management Studies*, 34(3), pp. 389-413, 1997a.

Sturdy, Andrew; The Dialectics of Consultancy, *Critical Perspectives on Accounting*, 8, pp. 511-535, 1997b.

Svenska Dagbladet Näringsliv, 17/1/2003.

Uzzi, Brian; Embeddedness and Price Formation in the Corporate Law Market, *American Sociological Review*, 69(June), pp. 319-344, 2004.

Van Weele, Arjan; *Purchasing and Supply Chain Management: Analysis, Planning and Practice*. London: Business Press, 2001.

Velthuis, Olav; Symbolic Meaning of Prices: Constructing the Value of Contemporary Art in Amsterdam and New York Galleries, *Theory and Society*, 32(2), pp.181-215, 2003.

Vähänäkki, Maija; *Pakottavien normien soveltamisesta Suomen kansainvälisessä yksityisoikeudessa*. Helsinki: Helsingin yliopisto, 1991.

Watson, Tony J.; Management 'Flavours of the Month': Their role in Managers' Lives, *The International Journal of Human Resource Management*, 5(4), pp. 893-909, 1994.

Werr, Andreas; *The Language of Change*, Stockholm: Stockholm School of Economics/EFI, 1999.

Werr, Andreas; *Managing the use of management consultants - towards a contingency approach*, paper presented at the 2nd International Conference on Management Consulting, June 23-25, Lausanne, 2004.

Werr, Andreas and Alexander Styhre; Management Consultants - Friend or Foe? Understanding the Ambiguous Client-Consultant

Relationship, *International Studies of Organization and Management*, 32(4), pp. 43-63, 2003.

Werr, Andreas and Håkan Linnarsson; Management Consulting for Client Learning? Clients' perceptions on learning in management consulting, in Anthony F. Buono (ed.), *Knowledge and Value Development in Management Consulting*. Greenwich: Information Age Publishing, pp. 3-31, 2002.

White, Harrison C; *Identity and Control*. Princeton: Princeton University Press, 1992.

White, Harrison C; *Markets from Networks. Socioeconomic Models of Production*. Princeton, NJ: Princeton University Press, 2002.

Williamson, Oliver E.; *Markets and Hierarchies. Analysis and antitrust implications*. New York: The Free Press, 1975.

Williamson, Oliver E.; *The Economic Institutions of Capitalism: Firms, Markets, Relational Contracting*. New York: The Free Press, 1985.

Willim, Robert; *Framtid.nu. Flyt och friktion i ett snabbt företag*. Stockholm/Stehag: Brutus Östlings Bokförlag Symposium, 2002.

Wiklund, Johan and Dean Shepherd; Knowledge-Based Resources, Entrepreneurial Orientation, and the Performance of Small and Medium-Sized Businesses, *Strategic Management Journal,* 24(13), pp. 1307-1314, 2003.

Winroth, Karin; Management på advokatbyråer – att göra byrån till ett företag, *Nordiske Organisasjonsstudier*, (3)2, pp. 25-53, 2000.

Winroth, Karin; *The Organizing of Expert Firms*. GRI Report 2002:4, Gothenburg Research Institute, 2002.

Winroth, Karin; Från antikropp till aktie - hur en produkt konstrueras genom text och grafer (From an Antibody to a Share - Constructing a Product by Text and Graphs), in Claes-Fredrik Helgesson, Hans Kjellberg, and Anders Liljenberg (eds.) *Den där marknaden – om utbyten, normer och bilder*. Lund: Studenlitteratur, 2004.

Womack, James P., Daniel T. Jones and Daniel Roos; *The Machine That Changed the World*. New York: Rawson Associates, 1990.

Wynstra, Finn, *Purchasing Involvmentt in Product Development*, Eindhoven: Eindhoven University of Technology, 1998.

Zackrison, Richard E. and Arthur M. Freedman; *An executive guide to employing consultants*. Aldershot: Gower, 2000.

Zeithaml, Valerie; How Consumers' Evaluation Processes Differ Between Goods and Services, in James Donnelly and William George (eds.), *Marketing of Services*. Chicago, IL: American Marketing Association, pp. 186-190, 1981.

Notes on Contributors

Antti Ainamo is in 2005 and 2006 researching global project strategies of firms at the Scandinavian Consortium for Organizational Research (SCANCOR), Stanford University. His publications include "Coevolution of New Organization Forms in the Fashion Industry" (with Marie-Laure Djelic, *Organization Science*, 1999), *Handbook of Product and Service Development in Communication and Information Technology* (edited with Timo Korhonen, Kluwer, 2003), and "Coevolution of Individual and Firm-Specific Competences" (*Scandinavian Economic History Review*, 2005).

Susanna Alexius is a doctoral student of Business Administration at the Stockholm School of Economics and Score (the Stockholm Center for Organizational Research). She is currently writing on her licentiate thesis with the working title "Rule resistance – why do formal rules for management consulting fail?" Susanna's main interest lies in organizational theory and institutional theory relating to rules and regulations, with an empirical focus on knowledge-intensive fields.

Fredrik Augustsson is a doctoral student in sociology at the National Institute for Working Life (NIWL) and former visiting lecturer at Lancaster University Management School, UK. His dissertation deals with the formation and organization of interactive media production. His research interests include work, organization and technology. He has authored and co-authored several reports and book chapters, including "Time for Competence" in Garsten and Jacobsson's *Learning to be Employable* (Palgrave, 2004) and "Interactive Media in Swedish Organizations" (*NIWL*, 2004) together with Åke Sandberg.

Björn Axelsson is a tenured professor at Stockholm School of Economics (SSE) and first holder of the Silf Professor of Purchasing and Supply Management chair at the school. He has previously served as professor of marketing at SSE and also at Jönköping International Business School. Björn started his career at Uppsala University where he was responsible for the executive MBA program for more than a decade. His published works include several books on purchasing issues, one of which is *Buying Business Services* (Wiley, 2002) co-authored with Finn Wynstra. The latest is *Developing Sourcing Capabilities* (Wiley, 2005), with Finn Wynstra and Frank Rozemeier.

His research centers around business-to-business operations in a markets-as-networks view, which is seen in another of his works, *Industrial Networks – A New View of Reality* (Routledge, 1992), with Geoff Easton.

Jonas Bäcklund holds a PhD in Business Administration from Uppsala University. During his doctoral studies, Jonas served as a visiting scholar both at Score and the Wharton School, University of Pennsylvania. His research interests include development of the management consulting industry and leading firms within it, communicative strategies of consultants and consulting firms, and procurement of consulting services. Jonas Bäcklund is Head of Credit Research at Handelsbanken Capital Markets.

Lars Engwall has been Professor of Business Administration at Uppsala University since 1981 and has also held visiting positions in Belgium, France and the United States. His research has been oriented to structural analyses of industries and organizations, and the creation and diffusion of management knowledge. Lars has published over one hundred papers and a number of books in the area of management. His most recent editing works are *Management Consulting: The Emergence and Dynamics of a Knowledge Industry* (Oxford University Press, 2002, with Matthias Kipping) and *The Expansion of Management Knowledge. Carriers, Flows and Sources* (Stanford Business Books, 2002, with Kerstin Sahlin-Andersson).

Carin B. Eriksson is an associate professor at the Department of Business Studies at Uppsala University. Her research interests are focused on organizational change and leadership. Recent publications include articles about emotions in organizations, such as "The Effects of Change Programs on Employees' Emotions," *Personnel Review* (Vol. 33, No. 1, 2004, pp. 110-126) and organizational identity. Carin is managing director at the Institute of Personnel and Management Development.

Staffan Furusten is an associate professor in Business Administration at Stockholm School of Economics and Score (Stockholm Center for Organizational Research). His research focuses on the production and diffusion of popular management knowledge, and on the standardization of organizational forms, the construction of markets, and regulation and professionalization of new forms of expertise. In addition to a number of articles and book chapters in these areas, Staffan has written *Popular Management Books – How they are made and what they mean for organizations* (Routledge, 1999) and *Managementkonsultation – reglerad expertis eller improviserad konst* ("Management Consultation – Regulated expertise or improvised art") (Studentlitteratur, 2003).

Christina Garsten is associate professor, senior lecturer and chair of the Department of Social Anthropology (Stockholm University) and research director at Score (Stockholm University and Stockholm School of Economics). Her research interests include the anthropology of organizations and markets, with a current focus on emerging forms of regulation and accountability in the labor market and transnational trade. She has published a number of articles on organizational culture, flexibilization of employment, and corporate social responsibility. Her recent books include *Market Matters* (co-edited with Monica Lindh de Montoya, Palgrave, 2004), *Learning to be Employable* (co-edited with Kerstin Jacobsson, Palgrave, 2004), and *New Technologies at Work* (co-edited with Helena Wulff, Berg, 2003).

Niclas Hellman holds a PhD in Business Administration and is assistant professor at the Department of Accounting and Managerial Finance at Stockholm School of Economics. His research focuses on behavioral aspects of accounting, auditing and corporate control issues. Recent publications include *Investor Behaviour – An Empirical Study of How Large Swedish Institutional Investors Make Equity Investment Decisions* (EFI, 2000) and "Can we expect institutional investors to improve corporate governance?" (*Scandinavian Journal of Management*, forthcoming 2005).

Kristina "Nina" Lindberg is a doctoral student in Purchasing Management at the Center for Marketing, Distribution and Industry Dynamics at Stockholm School of Economics. Her research interest concerns the purchase of business services and more specifically the interaction between buyers and suppliers of knowledge-intensive business services.

Karin Svedberg Nilsson holds a PhD in Business Administration and is a research fellow at the Stockholm School of Economics and Score (Stockholm Center for Organizational Research). Among her research interests are issues of governance and accountability, including a current project on how firms handle demands for corporate social responsibility in procurement. Another interest is the interrelationship between knowledge and regulation. Karin has previously published on privatization and market reform.

Andreas Werr is an associate professor at the Stockholm School of Economics, where he also earned his PhD with a dissertation focusing on the functions of methodologies in the work of management consultants. His current research interests focus on the rhetoric of management consulting, the procurement, use and consequences of management consultants in client organizations, and the management of consulting companies, specifically the management of knowledge and knowledge processes. Andreas' work has been reported in several award-winning conference papers and published in journals such as the *Journal of Organizational Change Management, Organization, Organization Studies* and *International Studies of Management and Organization*.

Karin Winroth holds a PhD in Business Administration and is lecturer and research fellow at Södertörn University College. Her research focuses on leadership and organizing in professional service firms, such as law firms and investment banks. Her publications include discussions about construction of identity, organizing knowledge-intensive practice, and collegial leadership. Her latest publications focus on the social construction of products and how markets are to be understood from a constructivist perspective.